Reporting Baseball's
Sensational Season of 1890

Reporting Baseball's Sensational Season of 1890

The Brotherhood War and the Rise of Modern Sports Journalism

SCOTT D. PETERSON

McFarland & Company, Inc., Publishers
Jefferson, North Carolina

LIBRARY OF CONGRESS CATALOGUING-IN-PUBLICATION DATA

Peterson, Scott D.
 Reporting baseball's sensational season of 1890 : the brotherhood war and the rise of modern sports journalism / Scott D. Peterson.
     p. cm.
 Includes bibliographical references and index.

 ISBN 978-0-7864-7368-7 (softcover : acid free paper) ∞
 ISBN 978-1-4766-1903-3 (ebook)

 1. Baseball—United States—History—19th century.
 2. Sports journalism. 3. Mass media and sports—United States. I. Title.
 GV863.A1P48 2015
 796.357097309034—dc23   2015000180

BRITISH LIBRARY CATALOGUING DATA ARE AVAILABLE

© 2015 Scott D. Peterson. All rights reserved

No part of this book may be reproduced or transmitted in any form or by any means, electronic or mechanical, including photocopying or recording, or by any information storage and retrieval system, without permission in writing from the publisher.

On the cover: Cartoon of John Montgomery Ward from *The Daily Graphic: An Illustrated Evening Newspaper*, November 17, 1888 (Rucker Archive).

Printed in the United States of America

McFarland & Company, Inc., Publishers
 Box 611, Jefferson, North Carolina 28640
   www.mcfarlandpub.com

For Kris,
who brought us back

Table of Contents

Acknowledgments	ix
Preface	1
Introduction	3
Prelude: The Player, the Magnate and the Journalist in December	15
1. Pre-Season: Taking Sides and Establishing Credibility	27
2. Early Season: Identifying the Issues and Defining the Conflict	58
3. Mid-Season: Going to Extremes and Staying the Course	92
4. Late Season: Returning to Form and Feeling the Grind	128
5. Post-Season: Reporting on the Scene and Watching from the Sidelines	162
Conclusion	192
Appendix A: Full Texts of Significant Columns from the 1890 Season	199
Appendix B: Individuals, Teams and Leagues	249
Chapter Notes	256
Works Cited	262
Index	267

Acknowledgments

In one form or another, this project has been with me for almost ten years, giving me a number of people to thank for their assistance in its genesis, research, and writing phases. I will mention as many as I can recall at this point; should I fail to include anyone, the omission is one of a tired brain and not an ungrateful heart.

In 2005, Jean Ardell's book *Breaking into Baseball* introduced me to Ella Black and put the 1890 season on my radar. A few years later, Jean, John Thorn, Lee Lowenfish, Trey and Geri Strecker, and several other members of the NINE conference crew became colleagues who supported and encouraged the project when I presented various papers related to the topic. I would also like to thank David Sachsman and my new colleagues from the Symposium on the 19th Century Press, the Civil War, and Free Expression for their feedback and encouragement. While I did not inflict any presentations on them that were directly related to this project, I am also indebted to Michael Oriard, Eric Solomon, Susan Bandy, and the rest of my colleagues and friends from the Sport Literature Association for their ongoing support and encouragement. I would also like to thank several colleagues and mentors from the University of Maine who were helpful at the earliest stages of the process: David Kress, Michael Socolow, and Nathan Godfried, as well as Alexander Irvine at the University of Southern Maine and Timothy Morris of the University of Texas at Arlington. All of the above helped me see the potential of the project and encouraged me to "stay with it" over the years.

I would also like to thank a number of people and groups who assisted me with the research required to undertake this project. The Fogler Library reference and interlibrary loan staffs at the University of Maine were always ready and willing to help me find, access, and print miles and miles of microfilm and arrange for me to borrow texts that

Acknowledgments

hadn't been dusted off for many a year. By the same token, the reference and interlibrary loan staffs at Wright State University's Dunbar Library have been equally invaluable over the last year while I was completing the book. I would also like to thank the staff at the A. Bartlett Giamatti Center at the Baseball Hall of Fame for their assistance. Finally, I would like to thank Bob Odenkirk by name for his help in the search for Ella Black; even though we didn't find her, it was nice to know that I wasn't looking in the wrong places or had missed her in the right ones.

Anyone who has written a book knows those Dante's *Inferno* moments that arrive early in the process and take on a special intensity near the end. The friends and colleagues who assist with the drafting, editing, and proofing make it possible for authors finally to emerge from the woods or the dream relatively unscathed. Toward that end, I would like to thank Amber Roessner and Melissa Spirek, who read and provided valuable feedback on early drafts. The insightful feedback from two anonymous external reviewers for McFarland helped shape the book's final revision and I would like to thank them for their assistance. J. Martin and Paul Ringel offered several helpful comments on a late draft and Michele Schiavone proved once more that she is a proofreader extraordinaire by finding the typos and rough spots I missed.

While it may be a truism, I would not have been able to complete this project without the ongoing support of my family. My mom and dad listened attentively as I read from the final draft during a return trip from the East. My sons, Nate and Nick, and daughters, Emma and VK, were all understanding when I was unavailable for various functions and homework assistance while I was working on "the book." My spouse, Kristin Sobolik, deserves the greatest thanks of all for her unflagging support and patience during the countless times that I needed to transition between the nineteenth and twenty-first centuries.

Preface

The year 1890 was significant in a number of ways. Situated at the crossroads of the genteel, Victorian Gilded Age and the modern, reform-minded Progressive Era, the events of that year demonstrate how sports culture developed alongside American society. Geographically, the United States added Idaho and Wyoming as the 43rd and 44th states, and the territory of Oklahoma was created. To assist in the country's growth through immigration, Ellis Island was designated and opened. American business was restricted and protected by the passage of the Sherman Anti-Trust and McKinley Tariff Acts, while ongoing labor issues between the capitalist and working classes were marked by the formation of the United Mine Workers of America and the strike of the New York Central Railroad by the Knights of Labor. A young Pittsburgh journalist writing under the pen name of Nellie Bly completed her much-advertised trip around the world, illustrating changes underway in the Fourth Estate. In sports, the year saw the first Ohio State football game, the first gridiron matchup between Army and Navy, and the 16th running of the Kentucky Derby. Eighteen ninety was also the year of baseball's Brotherhood War, which contained many of the same political, economic, and social issues that characterized the cultural clashes and growing pains of the late nineteenth century.

That year, after being pushed to the wall by a series of more and more restrictive labor practices, a group of skilled artisans who played baseball for a living formed a league of their own, found moneyed men to back it, and in some cases risked their life savings to have a say in the direction and operation of their profession. The aptly named Players' League was made up of men who remained loyal to the Brotherhood players' union and was opposed by the National League, which saw it as an outlaw organization that needed to be crushed. Although the parallels are not exact, the move by the 1890 players was as radical and as potentially "game-changing" as the efforts of college football players today to unionize. Just as the shape of college sports might become fundamentally different if athletes win the right to negotiate as employees, the face of professional baseball would have been remarkably altered if the reserve clause had been broken in 1890 instead of 85 years later in 1975.

Oddly enough, very little has been written about this episode in American sports history, which, as many now recognize after a generation of scholarly attention to sports, serves as a microcosm of American culture and society in general. The present study seeks to fill that niche and argue for the significance of that season while quoting someone other than Walt Whitman, Mark Twain, Thomas Wolfe, or Jacques Barzun. At the risk of leading my readers on a forced march, I wanted to take them through the 1890 season week by week so that they might experience it more deeply than they would have if I'd asked them to take my word for it with a few examples and a few waves of my hand. In short, I wanted to produce a study that would answer Gorn and Oriard's 1995 call for sports historians and rhetoricians to make more use of the interdisciplinary approaches of cultural studies to examine the intersections of history, cultural meaning, and power structures. To answer that call, the methodology of this study included what Stuart Hall termed a "long soak" in the sports journalism found in *Sporting Life*, the *Boston Globe*, and other venues. In addition, I selected three journalists to represent the owners, the players, and the marginalized middle found in the class and labor struggle of the culturally significant 1890 baseball season. The work of the three writers also illustrated the development of sportswriting within the larger changes underway in the profession of journalism during the last decades of the nineteenth century. Eighteen ninety marked the end of an age and the beginning of an era, both of which helped shape our contemporary landscape; the Gilded Age and Progressive Era have since passed into antiquity, but the roots of baseball writing as we know it today were visible in sports journalism of that year, as this book seeks to illustrate.

Introduction

The 1890 season marked the cusp of our modern age in three key areas: the celebrity status of baseball players and the popularity of the game, the rise of professional spectator sports as a viable and important economic force, and the development of sports journalism. Until recently, the Brotherhood War has received little in-depth scholarly treatment.

According to Ronald Story, baseball's increased popularity in the 1880s derived from a generation of American men who came of age after playing the game in their youth during the 1870s. By 1890, the transitions underway in American society and culture, as well as the economic upheavals of the late nineteenth century, might have encouraged many of those same men to turn to baseball as a touchstone of simpler times. Local businesses began to give way to corporate ownership, leading to the loss of local control, along with the "illusion of authority" that many small town leaders held to in an effort to protect the autonomy of their communities. Large numbers of Americans migrated to cities, where they had to adjust to living conditions that contrasted with their rural upbringings. By the end of the nineteenth century, the consumer culture that was developing with the rise of corporate capitalism compounded these economic and social transitions and led to the development of a professional middle class that emerged in America as a result of the Second Industrial Revolution—along with labor conflicts between the capitalists of the upper class and the wage-earning lower class. Taken together, these changes point to how America was at a "critical juncture" by the 1890s.[1]

Baseball's development paralleled these larger changes. Even though the Knickerbocker Club of New York City has been credited for codifying the rules of baseball in 1845, the roots of the game stretched back into the eighteenth century activities of rounders and town ball. Remaining an urban sport throughout most of its development as observed by

Introduction

Adelman, the organized game started as an amateur activity for urban artisans, branched into a source of occupational identity for firemen and other civil servants, and eventually became a professional game by 1871 with the advent of the National Association (NA). By the 1880s, the game as we know it today was largely in place, and from that time until the middle of the twentieth century, baseball was an integral part of the transitional narratives that made up American history. Economically, the game developed into a commercial enterprise while the country was in the process of changing from a rural, agrarian nation to an urban, industrial one. While individual teams were often family-owned and -operated into the twentieth century, the transition from the player-directed NA to the capitalist-operated National League (NL) was called a "startling coup d'état" by Henry Chadwick and has been identified as an "owner hegemony" by William Anderson, a twenty-first century journalism scholar. The salaries paid to baseball players put them on a par with the professional middle class that was being created by the Second Industrial Revolution; however, the owners did what they could to suppress salaries when players began "jumping" to other teams and leagues for more lucrative contracts, implementing in turn the National Agreement, reserve clause, and Brush Classification System. All of these measures, as noted above, created unrest among the players.[2]

Culturally, the game of baseball was at odds with a number of elements of American society in the late nineteenth century. After the game shifted in less than one generation from an amateur, player-directed club activity to a hierarchical spectator sport run by sporting goods magnates and other venture capitalists, an upper-class bias kept the "better class of patrons" away due to the professional element, the rowdyism on the field, the immigrant backgrounds of many of the players, and the gambling element in the stands. The aspects of the game that had appealed so much to the American men who made the game popular saw the shift toward corporate capitalism remove the deep-seated physical and psychological elements that drew them to the game in the first place: comradeship, recognition, and order. Many of those same qualities served as the basis for arguments made against the Players' League (PL) players by journalists who supported the NL, but ultimately, the conflict was one of labor and class, given the large number of immigrants on major league rosters and the low-culture perception of the players despite their middle-class salaries.[3]

Introduction

The Brotherhood War of 1890 encouraged sportswriters on both sides of the issue to take the players, the game, the business of baseball, and their own journalism more seriously because so much was at stake. Baseball players were identified as "celebrities" as early as 1870, as the cover of the June 25 edition of the *New York Clipper* attested. From that point forward, baseball writers began to watch for individual exploits on the field to use as raw material for creating heroes in print; however, those efforts were often countered by the rowdy and unruly behavior of players seeking to bend the rules, as noted by Oriard. Within the community of sporting enthusiasts, the increasing celebrity of players like John Montgomery Ward helped foster the sense that playing baseball was just another way to make a living and less of an embarrassing oddity or curiosity. Adding to the newfound gravity of the 1890 season, Ward and the members of the Brotherhood who left the NL were risking their careers and their reputations by forming their own league. The labor conflict also put the business of the game into a more serious spotlight at a time when owners and employees were at odds in workplaces all across America. Despite the growing popularity of the game in the 1880s, the negative press resulting from the conflict threatened to erode the support of upper-class patrons who were starting to make their way to the ballparks even as journalists of all stripes were seeking to establish their profession. Combined, these elements made the 1890 season a crucible that contributed to the development of American culture, business, and media.[4]

John Ward's later life demonstrated both the slow development of celebrity status for baseball players in the late nineteenth and early twentieth centuries and how the Brotherhood War was downplayed into the next century. Contrary to Albert Spalding's predictions made during a meeting with Ward in December of 1890 (see Prelude), Ward played only four more seasons and did not go into "the business"; instead, the Pennsylvania native practiced law and took up golf. In 1909, the law-trained former player withdrew his name as a candidate for NL president after eight deadlocked and politically charged votes. While the sporting media was beginning to shape the celebrity images of Ty Cobb, Christy Mathewson, and other star players actively, Albert Spalding appeared to undersell the influence of his former adversary in his 1911 memoir, referring to the labor leader as "the famous old time player," damning his book on the game with the faint praise of being an "admirable little

Introduction

work," and including a photo that showed the player-manager in street clothes. Several years after unsuccessful ownership and business connections with the Boston Braves and the Brooklyn Tip-Tops of the Federal League, Ward got the opportunity to speak for himself at the NL Jubilee celebration in 1925. Addressing one of the game's contemporary issues, the former player attested to seeing no evidence of gambling in his 17 years of baseball. Ward indicated that he wanted to keep the memory of the PL alive when he launched into a speech defending the Brotherhood and arguing how the owners had been on the wrong side in the labor conflict of 1890. Ward's efforts were largely unsuccessful, however. Until recently, few wanted to discuss the season in detail. For example, Connie Mack invested and lost his life savings of $500 as a 27-year-old catcher for the PL's Buffalo Bisons. When it came time to speak of the 1890 season as one of his 66 years in baseball, Mack gave the PL just a single line in his autobiography.[5]

Beyond shaping Ward's image, Spalding's memoir attested to the Brotherhood War's role in the development of the game's business side. While the magnate wrote that he was willing to believe that the players had acted with "the utmost sincerity of motive" when they abandoned the NL, he blamed the Brotherhood for breeding the disatisfacation among the "ball playing fraternity" and provided posterity with lists of the players who had defected and those who had remained loyal to the NL. Identifying himself as the chairman of the NL's "war committee," the player-turned-capitalist described the complexities of the 1890 season: "We had been playing two games all through, Base Ball and bluff." According to the NL leader, that game of "bluff" damaged the business of baseball and delayed its "natural development" by five to ten years. Without noting the contributing actions of the NL, Spalding blamed the conflict for the death of the American Association (AA) in 1892, named it as the source of "utmost bitterness" between the players and club owners, cited it as the source of financial loss to both the promoters of the NL and the backers of the PL, and claimed the public had become disgusted with "the whole Base Ball business" and the "unscrupulous mischief-makers" who had started the conflict due to their greed and self-aggrandizement. The magnate argued that the PL "was a mistake from every standpoint," yet he did allow that the Brotherhood conflict had: (1) "settled forever the theory that professional baseball players can at the same time direct both the business and the playing ends of the game"; and (2) "established

Introduction

the absolute honest integrity of professional Base Ball." The first point alluded to how the capitalist model of the NL had supplanted the cooperative model of the NA in 1876; it was also one of the three consistent messages found by William Anderson in his comparison of coverage for the 1890 and 1970 labor issues. The other two recurring themes by the owners were that the players were overpaid to play a game and that baseball would be destroyed if the owners gave into the players' demands. Spalding's second point attested to the fact that the game still had a public image problem in the early twentieth century.[6]

Indirectly and unintentionally, Spalding's memoir demonstrated the growing importance of sports journalism and the role it played in the Brotherhood conflict. The magnate credited Ward by name with starting the "simply fraternal" players' union in 1885, but failed to identify the labor leader as the mastermind of the PL in the chapter devoted to the war. For the most damning accusations of how Ward and the Brotherhood leaders had "duped" the players, Spalding quoted Henry Chadwick, the editor of *Spalding's Guide* in 1890. If they had read the Mills Commission's report in 1907, contemporary fans might have recalled Chadwick's support of his rounders theory as the source of American baseball, which was denounced in favor of the Doubleday Cooperstown hoax; few fans at that time, however, would have remembered how Chadwick had been the *Sporting Life*'s (*SL*) Brooklyn correspondent in 1890 and how he'd been a partisan for the NL's capitalist cause. With the publication of Spalding's book in 1911, it was clear that Chadwick, baseball's first prominent journalist, was still working for the sporting goods mogul, even though the former had been dead for three years.[7]

Despite having seats close to the action in 1890, the editors of major sporting weeklies later demonstrated the importance of the Brotherhood conflict to the development of the game and the relative lack of discussion of that season once it was completed. *SL* editor Francis Richter dispatched the entire Brotherhood War and the PL in under two pages in his 1915 book. The Philadelphia sportswriter's overview listed the causes, the primary players, the winners, and the losers. While the *SL* had covered all three major leagues during the conflict, Richter's sympathies for the labor cause of the PL nonetheless contributed to the divided press in Spalding's mind that "led to an excessive amount of public recrimination." Because the PL came close to Richter's own "millennial plan" for a baseball future that included revenue-sharing cooperation between

Introduction

the NL and the AA and changes to the reserve rule to create the same kind of player movement brought about by the defection of the NL's players, the editor might be forgiven for supporting the Brotherhood cause. In a similar fashion, Alfred Spink, who was Richter's competitor as the editor of *The Sporting News*, covered the PL and the Brotherhood in less than two pages in his 1910 book, *The National Game*.[8]

After Spalding, Richter, and Spink, baseball historians touched lightly on the Brotherhood War until recent years. Robert Smith's 1947 history, *Baseball*, described Ward's appearance, the frugal nature of the owners, and the events that took place in October of 1890, but left out the bulk of the season in the three pages allotted to the topic. In 1960, Harold Seymour and the then uncredited Dorothy Seymour Mills devoted a chapter of *The Early Years* to discussing the events leading up to the conflict and part of another chapter to explaining its aftermath, but skipped over the season itself. As late as 2007, Richard Davies followed suit, covering the 1890 season in a brisk one-and-a-half pages, but he might be forgiven because his topic was much broader in *Sports in American Life*.

More recently, historians have paid greater attention to the 1890 season, but only a few have looked at it closely. Lee Lowenfish's 2010 update of his 1991 history of baseball's labor wars, *The Imperfect Diamond*, and Robert Gelzheiser's *Labor and Capital in 19th Century Baseball* both treated Ward's Brotherhood of Players, the legal battles before the season started, the high points of the season, and the post-season wrangling. Daniel Pearson's *Baseball in 1889* covered the undercurrents of struggle between the owners and the players in an extensive look at the season leading up to the Brotherhood War. Ed Koszarek's and Ethan Lewis' histories of the PL provided outlines of the league's history and a wealth of reference material, but Charles Alexander's *Turbulent Seasons* has presented the closest examination of the 1890 and 1891 seasons to date.

Following the lead of Alexander and Lewis to use the sports journalism of the period, *Reporting Baseball's Sensational Season of 1890* seeks to be a companion piece to these recent histories of the PL while delving deeper into the fabric of the week-to-week developments to show how the events of the Brotherhood War helped galvanize sports journalism. Prior to 1890, journalists had only sporadic opportunities to cover events that would move sports and sports journalism toward mainstream acceptance within a society and culture that tended to relegate such pursuits to "Curiosity Shop" status. The America's Cup challenges that started in 1851 and a prize fight in 1860 between American and British champions generated news coverage that reflected and shaped nationalistic responses, but neither of these events was as sustained or as far-reaching as the "baseball war" of 1890. Working from a hypothesis similar to that used by Hall et al. in *Paper Voices*, the present analysis starts with the simple, yet powerful premise that a significant subject leads to significant journalism. Following W. Joseph Campbell's argument for the merits of year studies, a focus on the 1890 season will seek to "capture or freeze-frame key moments amid the trajectory of long-term change, and then consider those moments in detail."[9]

Why the Sporting Life?

In 1914, *SL* editor Francis Richter credited journalism with making significant contributions to the popularity of the game: "It is impossible to overestimate the enormous influence of the press in the evolution of the game, in its superior organization, in the integrity of its promoters and governors, and in the absolute honesty of its players." While identifying the press, the owners, and the players as the architects of the sport, as well as alluding to the gambling issue addressed by Ward and Spalding contemporaneously, Richter recognized sports journalism's ability to reflect and shape sporting culture in particular and American culture in general.

When Francis Richter started publishing *Sporting Life* in 1883, a separate section in newspaper for sports news was more than a decade away. When daily newspapers covered sports at all, the box scores and minimal write-ups shared space with theater notices, shipping news, and sometimes classified ads. In 1867, Henry Chadwick brought out *The Ball Players' Chronicle*, a weekly devoted to the game, but did not find enough of an audience to keep it in print despite casting a wider net with a more general title for the second volume: *The American Chronicle of Sports and Pastimes: A Family Journal Devoted to the Advancement of Physical Education*. *Harper's Weekly*, *Frank Leslie's Illustrated Newspaper*, and other weeklies published for middle- and upper-class audiences covered sports sporadically after the Civil War and rarely mentioned professional sports. By 1890, the generation of young men who grew up

Introduction

with sports as a more prominent part of American culture provided the audience to support sporting weeklies.[10]

Thus, *SL* was more than a weekly news supplement; it was all things sports for a growing audience of enthusiasts who were still held at arm's length as "fanatics" by a mainstream society that was not yet ready to embrace sporting culture. Richter's weekly covered a range of sports from archery and aquatics through bicycling, billiards, cricket, croquet, and homing pigeons to the ring, the stage, the trigger, and tennis. Correspondents from the four corners of the country wrote in with the local sporting news, much of which focused on baseball. During the 1890 baseball season, readers of *SL* came away each week with box scores and standings of the NL, PL, and AA, along with at least one full report from Boston, New York, Philadelphia, Chicago, and other major league cities. Despite the bias toward the Northeast and the Midwest, the overall coverage of the paper was truly national due to the news and reports from the minor leagues that were spread coast to coast: the Atlantic League, New York State League, Illinois-Iowa League, the Texas League, the Western League, and the Northwest League. Thus, *SL* became a national paper in effect and contributed to the creation of a national consciousness, making it a key element in a sport version of Benedict Anderson's "imagined political community" because it helped bind together baseball fans from Maine to California and Minnesota to Galveston. If the combined weekly circulation of as much as 140,000 of the *SL* (40,000 per week according to Richter) and *The Sporting News* (started in St. Louis in 1886 by the Spink brothers with a 60,000 circulation by 1889 according to Seymour and Mills, to 100,000 in Reidenbaugh) were added to the "pass around" numbers from the copies that were found in barber shops, saloons, and pool halls, the two sporting weeklies would have nearly reached the mass communication of a million people reading similar information at roughly the same time, thus contributing to the unification of a "nation" using Anderson's definition.[11]

In 1890, *SL* and the rest of the sporting press both reflected the interests of the growing audience of baseball fans and shaped public opinion due to the political nature of the Brotherhood conflict. Just at the time identified by John Thorn as the period when sportswriting was becoming viable as a source of full-time employment, Henry Chadwick, Ella Black, T. H. Murnane, and other sports journalists from the seven battleground cities became "war correspondents" reporting the news

Introduction

from the various fronts of the conflict. Parallel to Hazel Dicken-Garcia's assertion of how the Civil War helped instill the habit for seeking "news," galvanizing American journalism in the process, sports journalism moved from the "curiosity shop" topic for sports "fanatics" to the subject of serious discourse as the players—as the instruments of labor—seized the means of production and threatened to take control of baseball away from Spalding and the other capitalist owners. In contrast to Richter's characteristically self-congratulatory remarks from his 1914 book about the efforts of the players, the owners, and the press, the publisher's weekly *SL* 1890 editorials and active support of the PL served as an extension of his earlier involvement with the Union Association (UA) in 1884, the National Base Ball Reporters Association in 1887, and the advancement of his "millennial plan" to help protect the minor leagues, as outlined by Roessner.[12]

Richter's efforts in *SL* were consistent with the development of American journalism in general, not just baseball journalism. Parallel once more to the task of mainstream journalists described by Dicken-Garcia, the sporting weekly editor and his correspondents struggled with characteristic elements of nineteenth century journalism: sensationalism, gossip, and bias against the trivial. Amid the "fake" stories fueled by "Madame Rumor" and the upper-class disdain for any publication that gave undeserved press attention to a trivial child's game played professionally by grown men who were the sons of immigrants, Richter's efforts also contributed to the developing journalistic models of delivering information and operating as a business. At the same time *SL* was providing its readers with box scores, news items from around the country, and developments in a number of sports, the weekly sought to double its readership and profit by publishing correspondents from both sides of the conflict, even if it meant conducting business with the controversial tone avoided by mainstream papers. Following Dicken-Garcia's argument of how American journalism "came of age" in the crucible of the Civil War, sports journalism in general, and baseball journalism in particular, became significant for perhaps the first time during the Brotherhood War. Afterwards, as evidenced by Richter's 1914 remarks, the stance of sports journalism editors would move away from independence toward the symbiotic relationship with the owners identified by William Anderson. In other words, the 1890 season marked baseball journalism's exit from the mainstream indifference of "Curiosity

Shop" to the cultural importance of "News Room" before the descent back into the mainstream disdain it found in the "Toy Department" of the early twentieth century.¹³

Why "Sensational Season"?

The importance of the Brotherhood War and the role played by *SL* point toward the significance of the work of the sports journalists who covered the season week by week. This study will use the reports of three key writers as texts that serve as the basis for analysis and interpretation of the historical moments of 1890. Following the methods outlined by Hall in *Paper Voices*, the work of these writers will be seen as historical artifacts that provide insight into the process of writing baseball into American culture that took place in the late nineteenth and early twentieth centuries.¹⁴

Using the sport journalism of 1890 as a historical text, the analysis will peel back Bahktin's "stratigraphies of meaning" to, as Hall puts it, "uncover the unnoticed social framework of reference which shaped the manifest content." Following Hall's hypothesis that the definition of "news" is a constantly evolving process, the analysis will examine both what was said and how it was said to uncover the meanings that reflect the social and cultural elements of the events. Thus, the following chapters will seek to provide the reader with numerous examples of the writers' significant messages—what Hall calls "special rhetorics"—that provide keys to the deeper cultural messages being constructed. Finally, the object of the sustained analysis of those special rhetorics—or significant messages—over the course of the season will be to find patterns of how those meanings were constructed within the bigger picture of the social, economic, and cultural developments of the late nineteenth century. Thus, the reader will be immersed in the week-to-week events of the 1890 season through the examples of the phrasings and styles of the individual writers. Beyond providing ample evidence for the analysis, the presentation of extensive quotations is intended to illustrate how much—and in many cases how little—sportswriting has changed in 125 years.¹⁵

To carry out this deep immersion into the baseball culture of 1890—and American culture as a whole through metonymic extension—the

Introduction

following methods make up this book. Chapter 1 introduces the three writers who will serve as the basis for the study through their pre-season work and explains their representative roles within the developments underway in American journalism: Henry Chadwick as the Editorialist, Ella Black as the Modern Woman Journalist, and T.H. Murnane as the Reporter. In addition to introducing the writers and their roles, the analysis of Chapter 1 will identify their significant messages at the beginning of the season. Despite his claims of independence from his employer (Spalding), Chadwick was as much a partisan NL supporter as *Boston Globe* writer Murnane promoted the PL as a former player. Seeking to speak for female journalists who had been marginalized to the garden and fashion sections of newspapers, Black worked from the middle of the conflict—despite her expressed support for the Brotherhood's labor cause that may have encouraged Richter to hire her as an exception to his restrictive policies regarding women and baseball.[16]

To take the reader into the fabric of the season's events, Chapters 2–5 discuss how the week-by-week coverage by the three writers shaped the image of the players and the game, critiqued the business elements of baseball, and responded to the changes underway in sports journalism in particular and American journalism in general. By showing how the significant messages of the three writers evolved over the course of the season, the present work seeks to extend Alexander's, Koszarek's, and Lewis's treatment of the 1890 season and fill a niche by examining the practice, development, and rhetorical strategies of baseball writing, all of which have received little scholarly attention to date. The book thus uses the journalism of the period to find the culturally driven meanings behind and beyond the statistics. Chapter 2 establishes the baseline for the work of Chadwick, Black, and Murnane at the beginning of the season. Chapter 3 examines how each writer sought to validate his/her individual agendas in the middle of the season. Chapter 4 studies the final voices of the writers in response to the end of the season and the aftermath of the Brotherhood War. Through an examination of the post-season work of the three writers, Chapter 5 demonstrates their individual development while telling the story of the Brotherhood War's resolution, and noting their contributions to the development of baseball journalism. The week-by-week structure of these chapters thus mimics the arrival of the *SL* each week, allowing the present readers to watch the "sensational season" unfold in front of them.

Introduction

Providing the reader with eight representative reports from April to November, Appendix A illustrates the arguments advanced in Chapters 1–5 and is intended to serve as an additional opportunity to experience the 1890 season. Further, the appendix is designed to replicate the process of conducting a qualitative cultural analysis of the full texts of representative reports by Chadwick, Black, and Murnane using the methods outlined by Stuart Hall in his introduction to *Paper Voices*. The eight reports were selected from key points in the regular season and post-season to provide the reader with another close look at the effects of the Brotherhood War. Extensive notes are provided to take the reader deeper into the fabric of the season and show how the journalists worked to write the game of baseball into American culture. Appendix B is a handy list of the individuals, teams and leagues mentioned in the text.

Through the significant messages of the reports that appeared in *SL*, Henry Chadwick, Ella Black, and T.H. Murnane all proved that they were aware that something significant was happening in front of them. Their treatment of the players and the game, the business of professional baseball, and the changes in their profession all mark 1890 as the season sport journalism moved out of the "curiosity shop" for good and started onto the path of the sports media complex we know today.[17]

Prelude
The Player, the Magnate and the Journalist in December

On Saturday, December 13, 1890, the Manhattan Athletic Club became an impromptu Appomattox Court House when *Boston Globe* sportswriter T. H. Murnane followed his journalistic instincts to arrange a meeting between "two great base ball generals." If the year-long internecine conflict had taught him anything, it was the importance of magnate Albert Spalding and player-manager John Ward to the business aspect of the game. While the fighting was all but over, the train wreck had only hurt bottom lines, and any assassinations had taken place in the pages of *Sporting Life* and other papers written for the growing number of baseball enthusiasts across the country. Murnane knew he had a line on a significant story when he learned that National League (NL) magnate Spalding was willing to meet that afternoon with Ward, the leader of the upstart Players' League. Determined to bring the combatants to the table, Murnane left the Albemarle Hotel and demonstrated that he was no "Plain John" journalist who did his work from the comfort of his desk by commenting on the reporting of others. Perhaps the top two candidates for that status in Murnane's mind at that point in the year would have been fellow sportswriters Henry Chadwick and Ella Black. Regardless of the Boston writer's thoughts on his colleagues, Chadwick, Black, and Murnane all made important contributions to their profession during the Brotherhood War of 1890.[1]

In the story that appeared in the *Globe* the next day, Murnane did not elaborate on how he found the player-manager of Ward's Wonders, only that he'd "hunted him up" from somewhere in New York City. The writer may have been familiar with the current player's haunts from the time the two had been teammates in 1878, when Ward won 22 games as

Prelude

a rookie pitcher for the Providence Grays of the NL and Murnane was at the end of a journeyman career. The two of them may have crossed paths as players again in 1884 when Murnane came out of retirement to serve as the player-manager of the Outlaw Reds, Boston's entry in the Union Association (UA), a third major league that had refused to recognize the National Agreement signed by the National League and American Association (AA) in 1883 to protect the rosters of both leagues. Ward, who had converted to shortstop by that point because of arm problems, was not one of the star players who had been enticed by high salaries to "jump" to the new league that year in the short-lived attempt to break the NL's economic dominance of the game. Even so, the fraternity of professional players was still small enough that most of them were on a first name basis and often met one another in the lobbies of hotels that catered to visiting baseball teams. Murnane retired for good in 1885, but he may have covered Ward's formation of the Brotherhood of Professional Base Ball Players, the game's first union, in his own periodical, the *Boston Referee*, or in the content he wrote for the *New York Clipper*. In all likelihood, the sportswriter found Ward at Engel's Home Plate, which was the unofficial office of the Players' League (PL) and was located just three blocks from the Albemarle Hotel.[2]

Once Murnane found Ward, it was unlikely that the writer had an easy time convincing the player-turned-labor leader to sit at the same table as the sporting goods mogul and president of the Chicago White Stockings of the NL. Ward *had* wanted to be present at the negotiations that took place in October of that year, but had been relegated to the hallway with the rest of the players. Rumors—which were the source of the sensational stories that fueled much of late nineteenth century journalism—had Spalding planning to put an American Association franchise in Chicago in 1891. The 27-block trip uptown to the Manhattan Athletic Club, known as the "new temple of Physical Culture," at the corner of Madison Avenue and East 54th Street, may have given the sportswriter the time to pique the player-manager's interest by telling him about the morning meeting between Spalding, Charles Prince, the PL president, and Allan Thurman, the president of the AA. It is likely that both men were aware of the rumors surrounding Spalding's plans to put Ward at the helm of a "Beer, Whiskey, and Sunday Baseball League" franchise for the 1891 season. Recognizing the need to bring fans—especially those from the middle and upper classes—back to the ballparks after the season-long conflict, *Sporting Life* (*SL*) editor Francis Richter was on record as supporting the supposed plan: "That is a deuced clever idea. Ward pitted against Anson would revive interest in Chicago as nothing else could. Great head that of Spalding."[3]

Wherever the sportswriter "hunted up" the player-manager, the two men arrived at the Manhattan Athletic Club just as the NL magnate was finishing his lunch. Waiters in tuxedos trimmed with the Manhattan Athletic Club's cherry diamond insignia moved briskly beneath the high, frescoed ceilings and the Greek revival columns and arches of the fourth-floor dining room. The conversation between the magnate, the player, and the journalist was punctuated by the clink of polished silver on fine china. The leaders of the rival organizations and the sportswriter may have been forced to speak around the sounds of work being done to complete the roof gardens overhead, or they may have been distracted by the noise from the "diaphragm-invigorators, pectoral-developers, dorsal tuners, deltoid-rejuvenators, hand, back, finger, and foot lifting machines, ankle-twisters, [and] toe-stimulators" being operated by the Physical Culture devotees in the third-floor gymnasium one floor below them. Nonetheless, when the three men sat down together, they represented the three key elements that made the 1890 season so influential to the current shape of baseball journalism: Ward for the growing popularity of the players and the game, Spalding for the beginnings of professional sport as a business with economic impact, and Murnane for the developing profession of sports journalism.[4]

If there was awkward silence at the beginning of the impromptu meeting, the lull was not due to a lack of familiarity among the three men. Even though they were occupying three distinctly different positions within the baseball fraternity, they knew each other almost as well as they knew the game from the inside. Henry Chadwick contributed to Spalding's early fame by publishing an account of how the 17-year-old pitcher led his unknown team from Rockford, Illinois, to an upset in 1867 over the juggernaut of the touring Washington Nationals. As a professional player, the Illinois native went on to win championships with the Boston Red Stockings of the National Association (NA) before moving to the Chicago White Stockings when the NL was formed in 1876. The magnate retired at age 27 two years later to focus on his sporting goods business and became the president of the White Stockings in

1882. Spalding knew Murnane as an opponent on the field in the NA and the NL, as well as a part of the outlaw Union Association (UA) in 1884, and then as a sportswriter for the *Globe*. The NL magnate knew John "Monte" Ward as one of the stars of the game, both as a pitcher and a shortstop—and as the lawyer who had spearheaded the "rebellion" that challenged the NL magnates for the control of baseball and cut into the profits of Spalding's sporting goods business.[5]

During the 1890 season, the NL, led by Spalding, and the PL, led by Ward, engaged in a "civil war" to determine who would control the game: the magnates or the players. The conflict is often referred to as "the Brotherhood War" because of the involvement of the union Ward helped found in 1885 with three primary aims: the protection of the players both individually and collectively, the promotion of a high standard of professionalism among the players, and the development of baseball as America's national game. Ward and the Brotherhood objected to the reserve rule, which had been expanded to bind players to their current team and reduced their ability to negotiate their contracts. The professional athletes also objected to the system that the NL and AA magnates used to sell them from one team to another like livestock. While Ward was touring the world with Spalding's group in 1888–1889, the NL owners had instituted the Brush Classification System, which organized the players into several pay classes based on their performance on the field and their behavior off it. Ward left the tour early to address this latest restrictive labor practice, but there was little he could do, which led to even more acrimonious relations between the NL and the Brotherhood during the 1889 season. Although Ward had asserted in his book that "there was no spirit of antagonism to the capitalists of the game, except in so far as the latter at any time attempted to disregard the rights of any member," the actions of the NL magnates led the Brotherhood to believe that the owners cared little for the rights of the players and that it was time for them to take action. By the end of that year, Ward and the Brotherhood created a joint-stock organization with their own capitalist backers, did away with the reserve rule and the other "objectionable" labor practices, and convinced two-thirds of the NL players to join the PL, forcing the older league to scramble to fill their rosters with players who were not ready yet, were past their prime, or were raided from the AA. Given that Ward and the Brotherhood had threatened Spalding's business holdings, it was surprising that the magnate called for a meeting with the player who'd masterminded the rebellion—unless the "sensational stories" were true and Spalding did plan to end all chances of the PL taking the field in 1891 by signing its leader to an AA contract.[6]

Despite the fact that Ward and Spalding had been locked in a "war to the knife" from the first pitch of the 1890 season, the NL magnate began the conversation by reminding the player of their roles as baseball ambassadors who had landed in Melbourne, Australia, on the same date two years earlier. Demonstrating his law background, Ward disputed the magnate's memory and claimed the party had landed on the December 14. Because the expedition had crossed the International Date Line, both men were correct about the day; Ward missed the opportunity to correct Spalding about the city given that the tourist party landed in Sydney in 1888. Murnane must have known that common ground would be difficult to find between the owner and the labor leader, but he refrained from inserting his voice into the story for the moment. As a former player and a partisan for the cause espoused by Ward and the Brotherhood, the sportswriter had contributed more than his share of "hot shot" aimed at Spalding through his work as a reporter for the *Globe* and a *SL* correspondent.[7]

In response to Spalding's reminiscences of the world tour, Ward related a story that the magnate hadn't heard before that day in December 1890. When Ward left the party early and sailed from England to New York on the *Saale*, a steamer in the North German Lloyd line, the ballplayer helped a young German sailor escape punishment for desertion. Perhaps seeing a parallel between the sailor's plight and his own labor battles with the NL owners, the Brotherhood leader presumably arranged for the young man to stow away on the ship by providing him with a suit of clothes, cap, and five dollars cash for spending money once the *Saale* landed in America. Ward went so far as to give the deserter his address and invite him to visit upon his arrival." The player admitted to "being rather nervous himself" about aiding and abetting the escape until they landed in New York, and never heard from the young sailor again.

Leaving his readers to draw their own conclusions, Murnane recorded the anecdote without comment on his part and noted that Spalding had listened to the story with interest, perhaps because of Ward's harsh treatment of Brotherhood deserters who remained in the NL or jumped from the PL before the 1890 season started. If the magnate did note the inconsistency in Ward's sympathies, he did not bring it up that afternoon in Manhattan. One reader who would not have been surprised to learn of Ward's kindness would have been Ella Black. As a Pittsburgh correspondent to *Sporting Life* for the 1890 season, Black defended the leader of the Brotherhood cause on a number of occasions and would have seen the gesture as yet another example of his gentlemanly qualities.[8]

After Spalding finished his lunch, the three men toured the club, which featured many of the same amenities as the six-year-old New York Athletic Club (NYAC). The construction of two athletic clubs in the center of New York City attested to the growing importance of athletic pursuit by the upper classes. Members of the Manhattan Athletic Club (MAC) could spend time exercising in the facility's many venues: 100' × 21' "swimming bath" (40 feet longer and one foot wider than the NYAC's "tank"), Russian and Turkish baths, fully equipped 10,000-square-foot gymnasium, bowling alleys, rifle range, billiards room, boxing room, and fencing room. A detailed list of the equipment provided in the gymnasium included an elevated running track that was just 14 laps to the mile (compared to the 22 laps required at the smaller NYAC facility), rowing machines, ladders, ropes, pulleys, trapezes, horizontal bars, clubs, vaulting horses, punching bags, and, according to *SL*, "a few other arrangements that might be inscribed, 'Erected for the development of unknown muscles.'" Practitioners and promoters of Physical Culture imbued the movement with national importance. *Outing* magazine editor George A. White congratulated America for successfully combining the benefits of the Greco-English amateur athletic movement with the "neglected science of the Greek and the social luxury of the Romans" to combat the drawbacks of nineteenth century urbanization and industrialization:

> America has done this just in time to be of the greatest national service, when the correlative dangers of life in great cities and strenuous exertions of body and mind in commercial affairs threatened to deteriorate the bodily capacity of endurance, and, in consequence, debilitate the mental powers required to meet the strain.

Beyond addressing the physical and mental well-being of its members, the Manhattan Athletic Club could see to their cultural needs as well with musical and theatrical productions in the 1,500-seat concert hall on the second floor.[9]

The Player, the Magnate and the Journalist in December

As a millionaire sporting goods entrepreneur, Albert Spalding would have been at home in the club devoted to amateur athletics despite his association with a professional spectator sport. Given that Ward had gone from being a "poor country boy" to a lawyer and labor leader who commanded "respect and honor" by the age of 30, he was equally at home in spite of his humble beginnings in rural Pennsylvania. Both as a sports journalist and the son of Irish immigrant parents, Murnane was perhaps the least at ease in the opulent club even if he could have afforded the $50 initiation fee and $30 annual dues on his meager journalist's salary of $10 to $15 a week, and found his way to the top of the MAC's 300-person waiting list. If so, this discomfort may have explained why the Boston correspondent allowed Spalding and Ward to do most of the speaking when the magnate, the player, and the sportswriter retired to one of the reading rooms on the second floor to talk among the better class of patrons that all three wanted to bring back to the ballpark in 1891 after the baseball war had hurt attendance in all three major leagues in 1890.[10]

Some of the hard feelings from the negotiations at the end of the season resurfaced when the magnate established that the meeting on that December afternoon was "wholly informal and no way official." Ward's sharp response proved that the treatment of the players by the owners was still one of the main issues between labor and management: "Why certainly: the league couldn't meet a player, you know." Clearly, the PL leader was still upset about being excluded from the meetings in October after the league's representatives were outvoted by the conference committees from the NL and AA. Once the players had been banished to the hallway—again—though they had contributed their own money to the joint stock effort of the new league, the capitalist backers of the PL went on to cut their own deals with Spalding and the NL, which prompted Murnane and other writers to brand them as traitors and the perpetrators of "the grandest throw-down ever known in the history of base ball diplomacy." After the consolidation of the NL and PL teams in Pittsburgh, New York, and Brooklyn, the PL leaders still loyal to the labor cause were floating plans for a four-team league for 1891 with the players who remained loyal to the Brotherhood. Despite the star player's denials, rumors had it that Mike "King" Kelly, who had led the Boston Red Stockings to the PL pennant, was carrying a signed NL contract in his pocket as an insurance policy in case the rebel league

Prelude

folded. Kelly's situation was the exception: most of the former NL players, including Ward, who signed with the PL were wondering if the magnates were going to enforce the blacklist they drew up before the season started.[11]

Beyond settling the player issue, the work ahead to rebuild the sport fiscally and the need to reconstruct the game's image were highlighted when Spalding asked Ward's opinion about improving the present situation in the baseball world. Demonstrating an astute awareness of the negative impacts of the conflict, the Brotherhood leader identified the influence of public opinion on the game's economic viability:

> I should say that settling up the business end of the muddle would be the most important just now, and in doing that you must be very careful how you handle the public. While they are not apparently interested, you will find they are watching with a jealous eye to see that all the arrangements are fair and above board.

In other words, Ward claimed that the fans would not come back in 1891 if they read in the papers that the owners were making reprisals against the players for their actions during the 1890 season. Further, the labor leader's response highlighted the growing impact of the newspapers and sporting weeklies that helped shape public opinion, thus influencing the business of the national sport through the winning—or losing—of audiences of all kinds, from the upper-class patrons coveted by Spalding and the NL to the working-class fans of the AA who attended games on Sundays and drank beer and whiskey in the grandstands. Many of these fans were part of the 40,000 subscribers who read *SL* each week, and the 60,000 who got *The Sporting News*—and the countless others who read the copies found in barbershops, pool halls, and saloons across the country.[12]

In addition to the need for creating a more positive public image, the player-manager showed he was aware of how baseball was benefitting from a critical mass of enthusiasts who had grown to love the game and form attachments to the current players:

> The game of base ball would amount to very little when stripped of its sentimental features. As a commercial business the game would be a big failure. The patrons of the players' league [sic] must be satisfied, or you will have to depend on a new generation for the support of the game. You may replace myself or any of the players at short notice, but you can't replace the patrons of the game.

Significantly, Spalding acknowledged Ward's point about the importance of the identification between the game and its audience when he made a distinction regarding baseball's commercial side and its more intangible elements: "I think every club should have two distinct parts—one the business and the other the artistic." The concerns of both men pointed to the game's unsure footing in the aftermath of the Brotherhood War despite being hailed as America's national game for a generation.[13]

Moving past the impacts of sport journalism and fan identification on the game's future, Spalding proved that he was a quick study when he hinted at the possibility of concessions by asking Ward which "objectionable features" he would end. Listing the underpinnings of the Brotherhood cause by rote, the union leader cited the system that "trafficked" players, decried the reserve rule for its role in the "selling of players and forcing them around at command," and indicted the Brush Classification System for how it regulated the players' salaries unfairly. Spalding answered each objection with equally rote responses that showed how the National Agreement benefitted the minor leagues and ultimately supported the players. Steering the conversation away from the issues that had precipitated the Brotherhood conflict, Spalding sympathized with player-managers who were the victims of interfering, unknowledgeable owners and acknowledged further that a "brainy player" like Cap Anson could direct the artistic interests of a club. While "playing nice" for Murnane and the press, the NL magnate appeared once again to be attempting to shape the future of baseball by putting his opposition on his payroll. He challenged Ward to outshine other respected players and suggested that he wouldn't be interfered with as the manager of an AA franchise in Chicago in 1891.[14]

Resuming his effort to direct the flow of the conversation, Spalding turned to the issue of the players. When the NL magnate asserted that the events of the previous year—namely the defection of the players to the PL—would not be held against them, Ward's response showed that he wasn't afraid of being blacklisted for leading the Brotherhood cause, while revealing his humble background:

> It don't make the least difference to me what is done by the league. I am satisfied to go out of the business and may. I worked faithfully for the principle, and don't know but what now would be the best time to stop. I will enjoy a little country life from now until the first of the year, and then go into a law office here in New York and practice my profession.

"Country life" might have meant hunting and fishing in his home state of Pennsylvania, while the "principle" referred to the rights of the players to determine their contracts as artisans and the ultimate producers of the product that brought the fans to the ticket gates. Taking the risk to praise Ward for the very executive ability that allowed him to lead the rebellion, Spalding said, "Oh, you will play ball for 10 years to come, Mr. Ward, and must naturally get up in the business, as you have the ability." Despite the ultimate compliment of being called a self-made man in the same Horatio Alger mold as the sporting goods entrepreneur, the union leader refused to allow himself to be patronized and remained steadfast in his right to self-determination in his employment: "I am not certain that I will remain in the business. I certainly will not unless I have something to say in the matter." At this point, Murnane could not resist the opportunity to shape public opinion with a plug for his hometown and aimed more "hot shot" at the men who had turned traitor to the PL cause: "The Boston players' league [sic] team is one of the few clubs that Ward is willing to play with. He has already sent word to Pittsburg and other cities that he will do no business with them, and intends to pick out the club he is willing to play with, if at all."

Reading between the lines from both the player and the sportswriter, neither was ready to give up on the Brotherhood cause as an example of the "old Jeffersonian Doctrine." Eight years older than Ward, Murnane perhaps felt the perceived injustices of the capitalists that much more acutely.[15]

Making one last pitch to neutralize his greatest adversary and secure the future of baseball and the National Agreement, Spalding laughed and suggested that the PL would have died along with Ward had its leader passed away during the previous summer. Ward's response showed that he was not amused: "I was almost dead long before that, but struggled along, thinking the other fellow was in a hard way." Glossing over the union leader's self-deprecating stance, the magnate paid him another compliment by allowing that Ward and the PL had given the NL "a hard battle" and blamed other NL leaders for the exclusion of the players from the negotiations in October by claiming he "had no personal objection to having the players put on the conference committee." Ward's reaction to this concession—which he might have recognized as a convenient revision on Spalding's part given the magnate's printed comments in October—was not recorded by Murnane, who reported how the "gentlemen then entered into a confidential talk that it would be a breach of confidence to publish."[16]

By the time the parley ended around four o'clock that afternoon, the electric lights—part of the 2,500 powered by the new facility's "electrodynamo" housed in the basement of the MAC—had been turned on and were "throwing shadows over the carpet." Murnane reported, "the party broke up to go away feeling much better all round for a thorough understanding of the situation." Most likely, the Boston writer was being overly optimistic here. When PL president Charles Prince had met with Spalding and AA president Allan Thurman earlier on the morning of December 13, Murnane learned of Prince's plans to seek an AA franchise in Boston, which apparently signaled his intention to give up the last-ditch effort to operate the PL as a four-team circuit in 1891 after three franchises consolidated with their NL rivals and Buffalo proved to be unviable. Spalding did not succeed in placing an AA franchise in Chicago, but he did continue to work behind the scenes to ensure that the PL cause was not revived. Ward did not give up the principles he had worked for since 1885 until February of 1891, when he met PL Secretary Frank Brunell, Cleveland PL investor Al Johnson, and SL editor Francis Richter at Nick Engle's Home Plate saloon to toast the "treachery, stupidity, and greed" that had doomed their progressive effort.

The player, the magnate, and the journalist all had roles in the shaping of the 1890 season, which they all knew was going to be significant, if not historic, given the Brotherhood effort to change the game and the business of baseball. Murnane did not ask either Ward or Spalding if they would have done anything different with the benefit of the hindsight available to them on that December afternoon. Perhaps Murnane thought he already knew their answers based on his previous experience with both of them: Ward wishing he could have found a way to keep the PL backers from giving up on the cause and negotiating a separate peace with the NL owners, and Spalding wondering if he could find another way to limit the salaries and the growing celebrity status of the players. Or maybe Murnane rushed the end of his story because he was simply on deadline. Either way, the meeting provided an apt illustration of the conflict as a whole.[17]

1

Pre-Season
Taking Sides and Establishing Credibility

After the warmest hot stove season since Henry V. Lucas, Francis Richter, and others challenged the National League dominance with the Union Association in 1884, the 1890 pre-season featured so much baseball writing that Richter expanded *Sporting Life* to 16 pages in early April to allow coverage of the Players' League, the American Association and the National League. "War" correspondents on both sides of the issue fought the battle for public opinion and fan support within the pages of big city dailies like the *Boston Globe*. *Frank Leslie's Illustrated Newspaper*, *Harper's Weekly*, and other illustrated weeklies paid little attention to the conflict, and the *New York Times* remained neutral, but the threat to the capitalist owners was real: Labor had seized the control of production for themselves and was attempting to put on their own show using cooperative principles that struck some as being too socialistic.[1]

The pre-season work of Henry Chadwick, Ella Black, and T. H. Murnane both reflected and contributed to the social, economic, and communication changes that were underway, demonstrating the growing influence of print media. The early *Sporting Life* (*SL*) reports of all three writers featured John Montgomery Ward as they attempted to sort through the headlines, gossip, lawsuits, and sensational rumors aimed at the acknowledged leader of the Brotherhood and the brainchild of their courageous—or dishonorable, depending on each publication's editor—effort to participate more fully in the burgeoning capitalist economy of the United States. Although Chadwick, Black, and Murnane worked as reporters and editorial writers over the course of the season, the coverage they gave Ward during the pre-season illustrated the primary roles they would play throughout the year. As an editorial voice for the National League and baseball's unofficial historian, Chadwick was critical of Ward's "secession" until he had the opportunity to meet with the "rebel" leader in late March. Working to prove that the Modern Woman could write baseball, Black defended Ward's character and noted his popularity in Pittsburgh, while Murnane reported on the spring training trip of the Boston Red Stockings and compared the Brotherhood's cause to that of the founding fathers. In the period that amounted to their own spring training, the three writers worked to demonstrate the various hats they all wore as editorialists, reporters, and professional journalists and provided their readers with an early look at the significant messages they would use to cover the important—and often sensational—season ahead.

"The Base Ball King in the East": Henry Chadwick as an Editorial Voice for the National League

Henry Chadwick was 65 years old in the spring of 1890, living comfortably in Brooklyn as the sporting editor of the *Brooklyn Eagle* and the editor of *Spalding's Base Ball Guide*. Already known widely as "the Father of Baseball," he was almost a Biblical figure, having "been there" in the early days of the game after emigrating from Exeter, England, with his parents and younger sister in 1837. For example, the pioneer sportswriter reminded his 1890 readers that the site of Madison Square was the original home of the "old St. George Cricket Club." After getting his start as a sports journalist writing about the national game of his native country, the son and brother of reform-minded public servants began promoting baseball as both an American game and a "utilitarian" source of healthy exercise. While cricket was as much a part of the sporting scene in New York as baseball in the 1850s, Chadwick observed that baseball's star was rising due to the nationalistic spirit of the decade and the impatience of Americans who would not wait three days to find out who won the contest.[2]

Along with publishing game accounts and essays about baseball's physical benefits in the *Brooklyn Eagle* and the *New York Clipper*, Chadwick began editing *Beadle's Dime Base Ball Manual* in 1860. This established him as the game's first historian and allowed him to set the agenda for the importance of statistics as a measurement of performance and a means of settling disputes among fans of the game at a time that saw

1. Pre-Season

Americans looking for meaning—cultural and otherwise—from objective sources. As part of his constant effort to improve baseball's image and bring the "best class of patrons" to the ball parks, Chadwick's penchant for pointing out the drinking of the players and gambling associated with the game and his role on the rules committee of the National Association (NA) earned him the title he enjoyed, as well as enemies. In 1876, William Hulbert, president of the Chicago White Stockings, reorganized professional baseball to found the National League (NL) with the help of Lewis Meacham, sports editor for the *Chicago Tribune*, and Albert Spalding. While bringing an end to the player-run NA, Hulbert and Meacham excluded Chadwick, whom Meacham described as "a cynical, carping old man" at age 52, leaving Spalding to write a letter of explanation to the game's long-time promoter. Chadwick remained dedicated to the game, and his exile ended when he returned to a position of prominence in 1882 as the editor of *Spalding's Official Base Ball Guide* after Meacham's and Hulbert's deaths. Given the cultural influence of the 50,000 copies of *Beadle's* sold annually and the large audience for *Spalding's Guide* observed by Hardy, Chadwick was well-positioned to use the power of the press to promote the game, its statistics, and its social benefits.[3]

Despite having worked as a sporting reporter since the 1850s, Chadwick's primary role as a correspondent for *SL* in the spring of 1890 was that of an editorial writer. In that role, the veteran journalist saw himself both as a historian of baseball and a guardian of the game's rules, image, and moral qualities. Thus, it was fitting when one of his "New York journalistic confreres" compared him to Alfred Tennyson, the poet laureate of his native England, and generated a reaction from Chadwick that showed he was not without a sense of humor: "Just think of my being called 'irascible,' and adding the taffy of 'lovable.' That last is laughable. How the 'lushers' and 'kickers' do love me. Excuse the egotism, but that about the 'feelings of the poet' is good." No one was about to add "Poet Laureate of Baseball" to his list of titles, but it was clear that Chadwick held himself above the journalists who "loved" him. His use of "lushers" and "kickers," terms he normally employed in editorials intended to admonish and discipline intemperate and rowdy baseball players, pointed to the writer's awareness of the hard-drinking class of hack journalists who aspired to little beyond their next pay packet. Thus, beyond protecting the game's image against behavior that would prevent "the better class of patrons" from attending games, Chadwick sought to reform so-called journalists who produced "sensational" stories that were not concerned with truth, accuracy, or ethics.[4]

Beyond reforming his fellow writers, Chadwick proved that he was willing to "take up arms" in print to protect the game he'd promoted for much of his adult life. Aptly nicknamed "Nestor" by *Sporting Life* (*SL*) editor Francis Richter after the trusted military advisor to the Greeks during the Trojan War, Chadwick was advising just his second generation of baseball players, owners, and writers in contrast to the long-lived figure from Homer, but there were few in the baseball community who weren't familiar with his contributions to the game. Even though he had favored the player-directed model used by the NA from 1871 to 1875, Chadwick had become convinced after working with Albert Spalding for eight years that the capitalistic system of running baseball, with its distinct divisions between ownership and labor, was the only method of operation that would benefit the game. Armed with that and the other two owner messages identified by William Anderson's study, "Nestor" was ready to enter the lists as an editorial voice for the NL "scheme" against the PL with, in the words of Augustus A. Levey while commenting on "the newspaper habit" in 1886, the "greatest vigor," and using a tone to "forbid the suspicion" of an opposing argument's existence. Even though it was not often with the "fewest words," Chadwick's voice followed Levey's precepts throughout the 1890 season as he maintained William Hulbert's "morality crusade" from the 1870s and acted as someone who was, in the description of Davies, a "Victorian moralist to the core." Further, Chadwick's editorial voice dovetailed with the qualities of American Victorianism: rationalism, discipline, didacticism, and morality, all qualities in keeping with the fatherly image of the pioneer sportswriter.[5]

Making use of his humorous and moralistic sides, Chadwick took up his editorial role in a satirical allegory aimed at John Ward in February of 1890. Claiming that Miss Marion Manola, a burlesque and comic opera actress who had achieved some fame on the New York stage while under contract with the company of Colonel McCaull, had "revolted" by breaking her contract to "play" with a new "team," Chadwick marked the dubious act by defining it as "secession—a-la-Ward." After imagining various injunctions and court battles that paralleled actual lawsuits brought against the PL by the NL that winter, the editor of *Spalding's*

Guide closed the piece with a direct comparison and a pun: "The McCaull beauty thought she was a ball player, and could break contracts, etc. adlibitum, but she was brought up with a round turn. She was not 'reserved' enough for the occasion." As the husband of actress Helen Dauvray, Ward may have known that Manola was seeking to join De Wolf Hopper's Comic Opera Bouffe, possibly after the two of them met at the benefit thrown for the New York Giants when they won the NL championship in 1889. It was also likely that the labor leader detected how the light tone of Chadwick's morality play reflected the NL's confidence that the NL Giants would be successful in their lawsuit to prevent him from playing in the PL, just as a judge in 1852 had ruled against an opera singer who tried to take her "special, unique, and extraordinary services" to another impresario. The *Spalding's Guide* editor and media outlets supportive of the NL continued to compare Ward and the Brotherhood to the Southern States for much of the conflict, but the light tone of this satire was not often found in Chadwick's editorials after the court ruled in favor of Ward and the PL in March—much the same as the attitude of the North changed after the first battle of Bull Run was fought in response to another prominent secession.[6]

Chadwick's satire added "Rebel" and "Secessionist" to the character attacks of "John Much-Advertised Ward" and "Judas Montgomery Ward" by other writers while obscuring the labor leader's many achievements at age 30. After being expelled from Penn State in 1877, Ward supported himself as a professional baseball player. Between leading the Providence Grays to a pennant as a pitcher in 1879 and winning the cup sponsored by his wife in 1888 and 1889 by helping the Giants defeat the AA champions, Ward founded the Brotherhood, published a book on baseball, and traveled around the world as part of Spalding's tour. In November of 1889, Ward had acted on the Brotherhood's threats to form their own league and signed more than two-thirds of the NL players to PL rosters. In response to Ward's critics, the *Pittsburg Commercial-Gazette* defended Ward and the Brotherhood by asserting that the players were nothing more than skilled workers who faced expulsion from their profession by "autocratic, monopolistic despots." Ultimately, the article argued that the players were honorable and that they did what they needed to do as men when they formed their own league to break the reserve rule, end the Brush Classification System, and assert their rights as workers and artisans.[7]

Chadwick's pre-season satire was not without rebuttal. Perhaps as irritated by the light treatment of the reserve clause as being compared to an actress who performed in tights while cast in male roles, Ward got the opportunity to return fire when Richter published his letter in *SL* at the end of March. The architect of the PL explained his innocence with regard to recent lawsuits that had been brought against him and took Chadwick to task for attacking the PL without possessing the facts. Contrasting the rebellion rhetoric of Chadwick and other NL supporters, Ward took the spiritual high ground when he compared the spring training trip of the PL teams to a pilgrimage "of 'theologs' on an excursion to some Christian Mecca" and softened the poor play of his largely young, inexperienced team with a humorous refrain from a De Wolf Hopper comic opera bouffe: "'There are some things 'twere better not to dwell on.'" Despite referring to Chadwick as "our quondam good friend" and professing to "have always entertained the greatest respect for Mr. Chadwick's opinions and accepted his advice with the utmost consideration," Ward derided the veteran journalist for "becoming positively sensational" and "going off half cocked upon the slightest provocation" in response to the allegations that Ward had mistreated one of his fellow journalists: "The good father of base ball has mislaid his mental compass and seems to be wandering aimlessly and recklessly as some of the younger brethren. Every one in the Players' League hopes to see him get his correct bearings soon." While honoring the "father" of the game, Ward returned the slight of the Manola satire by comparing Chadwick to more inexperienced journalists who were fueling the conflict between the NL and PL with sensational stories. In the defense of his cause, Ward adopted an editorial tone of his own, and his print feud with Chadwick ultimately illustrated how both men were aware of the issues facing practitioners of journalism to report the news with truth and accuracy and advance ethical opinions as part of the larger movement toward establishing the profession of journalism.[8]

Two apparently chance meetings allowed Chadwick to work as a reporter and conduct his first—and only, until October—player interview for the 1890 season. Perhaps to avoid drawing the suspicion aimed at the gamblers and other unsavory types who were known to be "habitués of the poolrooms," the *Eagle* sportswriter was quick to tell his *SL* readers that he was visiting Maurice Daly's establishment in Brooklyn on March 20 to report on amateur billiards and equally quick to remind his audience of Daly's reputation as a champion player in the 1870s and author of several books on the game. While on assignment, Chadwick encountered Ward and professed to be "surprised to see him looking so well after the heavy strain he must have been subjected to all winter." Two days later, Ward called on Chadwick at his Brooklyn home, giving the writer the opportunity to interview the leader of the Brotherhood.[9]

While journalism historians hold divided opinions about who conducted and published the first interview, most agree that the procedure was used to gather news with growing frequency after the Civil War. Even then, however, the practice was held to be in bad taste by some journalism critics because its coverage of personalities tended to create celebrities of figures that the genteel cultural gatekeepers of the nineteenth century found unworthy of such attention. For anyone to publish an interview with a baseball player—even one as accomplished and educated as John M. Ward—outside of the sporting press would have been regarded as poor journalism. Within *SL*, Chadwick would have been shielded from such criticism since he was writing for an audience that was hungry for news and inside information about the players it admired.[10]

Before the Brooklyn correspondent got to the interview, however, this second meeting precipitated three important admissions that provided insights into his attitudes regarding journalism, the players, and the PL. First, hearing Ward's side of the story allowed Chadwick to address the concerns of journalistic truth and accuracy by recognizing that "there has been some tall lying done this past winter, by writers and partisans on both sides." Ward was evidently persuasive enough that the veteran editor was willing to admit he was "as prone to error as other journalists" and to forgive the younger man's "attack" on him in *SL* on March 26. Second, Chadwick explained his relationship with the players and proclaimed his independence as a journalist. The players, he argued, had not "the slightest claim" on him; what's more, he asserted that the majority of them had been unfriendly toward him for years. That most of the players were not fond of the game's long-time promoter should come as no surprise given the strident, moralistic stance Chadwick had taken toward their drinking and gambling from the time he joined the rules committee of the National Association of Base Ball Players in 1857. Most likely, the same unfriendly attitude of the players had forced Chadwick into the editorial role he occupied by 1890—except when members of the opposition visited him in hopes of setting the record straight. Third, though Chadwick asserted that his opposition to the PL was based on the harm he felt it would do to the game and noted that he was just as critical of the NL leadership for involving the courts instead of addressing the contract issue themselves, his claims of independence were weakened when he closed his self-defense by quoting his employer: "As Mr. Spalding said to me last fall:—'This thing will result in benefit to base ball ultimately. Things will come out all right in the end.' I think so myself." Contemporary baseball fans who were familiar with *Spalding's Guide* may have indeed been aware of Chadwick's editorship, and it was likely that they recognized how the Brooklyn correspondent was addressing a man 26 years his junior as "Mr. Spalding" while giving him the final word in the matter. Even though Chadwick had been present in 1867 to record the triumph of Spalding's Rockport, Illinois, team, the respect the journalist accorded to his employer was based on the younger man's position as a team owner, NL leader, and successful capitalist, not as a former player.[11]

After covering the unpleasant business of Ward's various legal entanglements and claiming his independence as a journalist, Chadwick was free to turn the talk toward the object of their shared devotion: baseball. When reporting on this part of their "chat," he could not resist placing himself into the story by recording his questions along with Ward's answers. Perhaps unaware that he was speaking to a former member of rules committees, the PL leader argued that the players had a better sense of what could be done to improve the game. Instead of being insulted, Chadwick drew Ward out further on the PL's double umpire system (in contrast to the single umpire used by the NL) and the additional foot and a half added to the pitching distance. By the end of the interview, the "rebel secessionist" came across as reasonable, forthright, and well spoken. Chadwick's *SL* reader could have imagined the player leaning forward and heard the enthusiasm in his voice as he talked about his efforts to make the game he loved even better. The pioneer sportswriter's appreciation of those efforts came through as being genuine, which supported his earlier assertions that he was in favor of whatever was best for the game. By the close of the interview, it was clear that Ward's visit had produced a meeting of minds, especially after Chadwick found at least one player who would give some merit to his ideas: "Ward

1. Pre-Season

fully endorsed my view in regard to the advantage of scientific batting as opposed to mere slugging." Chadwick's enthusiasm for the game was illustrated at the end of the interview, along with evidence to demonstrate that baseball was still evolving in the late nineteenth century and that the question of "mere slugging" vs. "scientific hitting" was established well before the advent of ESPN highlights.[12]

As if aware that his readers were seeking information about the business matters of the PL, Chadwick addressed the topic at the end of his report by ducking it. Ever the guardian of the decorum required by American Victorianism, he revealed his formal style when he wrote that "John's conversation with me must be regarded as private and I shall therefore not reveal any part of it which applies to Players' League concerns." The last may have been some self-important puffery on Chadwick's part: even if the labor leader had been speaking on the record, it was unlikely that someone as shrewd as Ward would divulge trade secrets to the editor of *Spalding's Guide* even if he was wearing his baseball historian hat at the end of the interview.[13]

Returning to his editorial role, Chadwick finished his pre-season report with contributions to Ward's growing celebrity status by crowning him as "the base ball king in the East." After nearly 20,000 fans paid to watch a PL exhibition game between Mike "King" Kelly's Boston Red Stockings and Ward's Brooklyn Wonders, Chadwick claimed that the player-manager had dethroned "Ten-thousand-dollar Kelly" as the primary hero of the game due to the success of the Fast Day contest in Boston on April 3. When he coined a new phrase that amplified Ward's earlier religious analogy, "Great is the Brotherhood and Ward is the prophet," it marked the first and only time during the 1890 season that Chadwick put "great" and "the Brotherhood" in the same sentence, except to call the union's efforts a "great failure" or a "great disaster." Demonstrating his familiarity with the work of his fellow journalists, Chadwick quoted the report that captured Ward's response to the huge crowd and promoted the labor leader's emergence as a hero: "What a sight greeted his eyes! And how must the greatest hero of the new League, John M. Ward, have felt when he saw the magnificent crowd which had assembled to pay its tribute to the cause which he had so ably espoused!" Despite this high praise for Ward, Chadwick closed with a somber warning that was similar to the one spoken in the ears of Roman dictators and emperors when they were riding in triumph through the streets of Rome: "The public are very fickle, especially the base ball part of it. Up today, down to-morrow." Like any other gladiator, King Kelly, "the base ball hero of Boston in 1888," had been replaced by Ward, and Chadwick could not resist pointing out that the Brotherhood leader's time as a culture hero could be just as short-lived.[14]

Along with reflecting his established role as the Father of Baseball by virtue of writing about the game for more than 30 years, Henry Chadwick's pre-season reports for SL illustrated how sports journalists of the late nineteenth century operated in more than one mode as the roles of journalism were being established in general. Writing initially with a satiric editorial voice, the *Spalding Guide* editor's comments about John Ward and the PL demonstrated that he was working from the dominant position of the NL. The opportunity to interview a player allowed Chadwick to move into a reporter's role, which operated on a number of levels. On one hand, the interview meant giving more attention to and thus contributing to the celebrity of a baseball player, making it a dubious practice in the eyes of nineteenth century journalism critics. On the other hand, the interview allowed Chadwick to tell a more balanced, accurate, and truthful story, values that journalists of the time were beginning to follow in their work. The Brooklyn correspondent closed his spring training review by adopting his editorial voice to comment on Ward's celebrity status, his effects on the business of baseball, and the role of the press in promoting or evaluating the players and the game. Even though Chadwick identified himself as a non-partisan supporter of "whatever was best for baseball" in the spring of 1890, analysis of his early-season work will demonstrate how he soon developed into a partisan who repeated the NL party line ad infinitum when he—and his employer, Albert Goodwill Spalding—began to feel that the continued existence of the PL threatened everything he had been working to develop since the 1850s.

"A Novelty in Baseball Literature": Ella Black as a Non-Partisan Modern Woman Sportswriter

Writing to SL from the "Smoky City" of Pittsburgh at the end of February, Ella Black used the opening line of her first report to assert her baseball knowledge and the role of women in the approaching "base

1. Pre-Season

ball war": "There is one thing sure, and it is one that is recognized by both the local clubs, and that is that whichever one is a winner in the struggle so soon to commence that one will have to thank the ladies of Pittsburg and Allegheny for having done a great deal to land the victory on its side." While this sentence might not be the most auspicious beginning in "base ball literature" from a syntactical perspective, it did launch the career of a journalist who would have a regular place in *SL* for most of the year before disappearing from the paper's pages at the end of November. Black's print presence in *SL* began with Henry Chadwick and other male sportswriters assuming "she" was actually a man pretending to be a woman and ended in mystery since no trace of her can be found more than a hundred years later. The Pittsburgh correspondent's 38 weekly reports provided Richter's *SL* readers with the unique perspective of a woman's thoughts on the players, the games, the business of baseball and the early development of sports journalism. Abandoning the "Cult of True Womanhood," Black advanced her underlying goals of demonstrating that a "Modern Woman" could write baseball even if contemporary gender restrictions kept her from participating fully while telling the story of the 1890 season as an editorialist, reporter, and progressive reformer.[15]

Prior to Opening Day on April 19, Black wrote editorials about the actions of the owners and the players, news and scouting reports of the Pittsburgh teams, and a human interest story about a local fan club to earn herself a following among the readers of *SL*. Like Chadwick, Black wanted to advance the cause of baseball by making it more acceptable to the "better patrons" of the middle and upper classes; at the same time, she was interested in advancing the cause of women journalists by following the lead of fellow Pittsburgher Elizabeth Jane Cochrane, who was better known to the world as Nellie Bly. To carry out her second objective, Black turned her back on domesticity and submissiveness, two of the four cardinal virtues required by the "Cult of True Womanhood," and invited the same "monstrosity" label that inspired Nellie Bly to first take up her pen in 1885. As a woman writing sports, her transgression would be doubly monstrous because journalism was already a dubious field in the eyes of genteel society, and sports journalism was already established as a male domain, leaving her "embattled" on two fronts. Beyond the pages of *SL*, mainstream journalists and members of genteel culture would have seen a woman writing sports as an oddity on three levels: a curiosity within the curiosity shop of journalists who wrote for "fanatics" devoted to professional spectator sport. Given that Cochrane and other women used pseudonyms in the late nineteenth century while working in the developing field of journalism, Ella Black most likely used one as well, making her actual identity elusive to searches by Jean Ardell, Mike Sowell, and the author of this study. Even if the woman behind the pen continues to remain a mystery, the female sports journalist's efforts to "speak for her sex" in the field of baseball writing demonstrate how the issues surrounding the 1890 season inspired Black to advance herself as a Modern Woman and as progressive a reporter as the contemporary cultural climate would allow.[16]

Francis Richter's use of the term "novelty" in the teaser at the top of Black's first report provided a clue to the editor's initial response to the idea of a woman baseball writer; nonetheless, he went on publishing her reports and by early April he was ready to give her official credentials—the first ever offered to a woman by SL. The Pittsburgh correspondent used her first report to establish the topics she would cover and discuss throughout the 1890 season: the players and the games, the business of baseball, and the experience of a woman trying to break into sports journalism. Her awareness of baseball's need to better "resonate with" and win over upper-class patrons was illustrated when she asserted that the involvement of Pittsburgh mayor George McCallin with the local PL team would win over "the better class of people, and one that before paid little attention to the sport." Some of her male readers may have chuckled in the middle of her inaugural report at her description of female fans gushing over John Ward and other players they found handsome or physically attractive, but the ones who were paying attention should have recognized the depth of Black's baseball knowledge when she predicted that the local fans would not pay out their hard-earned money to "see a lot of 'kids' play ball," which turned out to be the case when the NL franchise in Pittsburgh averaged fewer than 400 fans for their home games in 1890.[17]

Ella Black was back in the pages of SL on March 12 to make good on her promise to provide her readers with insight into baseball's female fans, but it was clear that Richter still thought of her letters as an oddity, curiosity, or "novelty" that would pass within a few weeks. When Black's second outing introduced a serial human interest story about the Young

1. Pre-Season

Ladies of the Diamond (YLD), a local fan club that she had joined, the *SL* editor attempted to generate interest in her story with minor headlines that hinted at the status of the fan club and its economic impact: "The Girls In It" and "A Society of Lady 'Fans' Organized on a Novel Basis—A Stimulus For Pittsburgh's League and Brotherhood Teams." Of note is the fact that the idea of women as "fans" was called into question with the quotes, and not the economic stimulus of the club. Black showed her sense of humor when she labeled the miscellaneous items at the end of her letter as "Pins and Needles." On one level, the subheader acted as a clever bit of editorial apparatus; on another, the female correspondent might have been anticipating the response of the readers in her audience who felt the sewing room was her proper Victorian place.[18]

Turning to a journalistic strategy that had helped spark the success of the penny press almost 60 years earlier, Black used her second report to advance human interest stories that would help win her an audience among the baseball fans reading *SL*. Naming names and hinting at having access to several key figures in the Pittsburgh baseball world despite "being only a woman," she reported that the wives and sweethearts of various players had influenced their decisions about joining the PL or remaining in the NL. Far from being concerned that her audience would find coverage of the female perspective too trivial, the novice sportswriter showed equal confidence that the YLD would provide her readers with a perspective of the baseball world that was seldom glimpsed in the press, and that it would indeed contribute to the coming conflict: "The war between the magnates and their players has resulted in the formation of a society among the members of my sex in this city which will result in a good many dollars going into the treasury of one of the rival clubs." While providing her readers with insight into the activities and mindset of female baseball fans, the larger issues of business and political impact were present as undercurrents, as indicated by Black's use of combative language, labor rhetoric, and economic terms. Over the course of the pre-season, Black covered the club's activities as it grew from 16 to 24 members, passed along the scouting reports gleaned from a "back window view" using opera glasses, and calculated the economic impact on the Pittsburgh Alleghenies when the club planned to boycott the games of a player they found to be objectionable. Given this list of activities, the YLD could be described as a group who had turned away from the Cult of True Womanhood to add "activist baseball fan" to Amy Richter's list of college student, settlement house worker, and suffragist as pursuits of the Modern American Woman.[19]

Initially, Black reported how the YLD had eight "girls" who "were loud in their praise of the team the PL will have here" and eight more young women who "were equally earnest in their admiration of the team the old club will put on the field." After using a tossed penny to decide whether they would attend the first "championship contest" of the PL's Burghers or the NL's Alleghenys, the destination of the YLD's outings would be determined by the play of the home team. For example, if the NL side won the toss, the group would attend the games of the old club until the Alleghenys lost. The losing side would pay the expenses of the winning side, which, as Black noted, "will be the means of turning many dollars into the treasuries of both clubs during the season, as the winning side is to have the privilege of inviting as many friends as it pleases." Later in the spring, she noted how each woman would bring at least two male escorts, making the number of the party for each game at least 48, with the potential to go as high as 80 if each of the eight winners brought at least one female friend who would require two more gentleman escorts. Doing the math, each member of the club was facing a minimum payout of two dollars whenever her team lost to spending more than double that amount if her counterpart brought along additional friends and escorts. Black indicated that she felt "safe" about being on the side that had "pinned its faith on the victories of the Players' League team." Three things would have been apparent to the *SL* readers from Black's description of the YLD: 1) these were serious baseball fans; 2) they had enough free time to plan to attend almost 60 home games over the course of the summer, marking them as some of the "better class" or "finest" fans that she described in her first column; and 3) men weren't the only ones betting on baseball games in 1890.[20]

Despite having significant "secrets" to "give away" in her third letter to *SL*, Black made a rookie mistake by burying that lead story to take an editorial stance defending John M. Ward against the same allegations that he discussed during his conversation with Henry Chadwick in late March. Refusing to believe the story from the "New York organ of the National League" that would "stamp" Ward as "one of the lowest blackguards," Black revealed that she had met him "several times" and attested that "he never appeared in any light other than that of an educated gen-

1. Pre-Season

tleman." Firm in her belief that the *Sporting Times*, which had been purchased by Albert Spalding in 1889 to serve as a source of sporting press for the NL, would not be factual or accurate toward Ward, the Pittsburgh correspondent demonstrated her fairness by acknowledging the counter-argument that he might have been on his best behavior because he was "in the presence of ladies." Remaining "vigorous" in her argument, Black claimed additional evidence due to the fact Ward was "well and favorably known in Pittsburg" and gave anecdotal evidence from a local sportswriter who claimed that Ward "had always spoken as a gentleman, and it was seldom if ever he used an oath."[21]

Beyond emulating Chadwick's use of the editorial stance to guard the image of the players and the game, Black's spirited defense provided clues to her placement as a journalist and the celebrity culture that was developing around baseball players. First, this testimony of an apparent upper- or middle-class, educated woman was based on her numerous meetings with John Ward, leaving *SL* readers to wonder how she become acquainted with him. Equally tantalizing might have been how the female journalist came to overhear a local baseball writer voice his support for Ward. Even before she revealed in September that she "was thoroughly acquainted with" an informant who was "intimately connected with some of the old club officials," it should have been clear to her readers that Ella Black had the opportunity to meet baseball players on "numerous occasions" and was well situated enough to be in the right place at the right time to overhear the opinions of baseball writers and significant inside information about the game's business operations. Secondly, while some of her argument was based on unsubstantiated gossip and hearsay very much in keeping with the journalistic style of the day, the rookie writer's use of the phrase "well and favorably known" indicated Ward's celebrity status.[22]

The latter half of Black's editorial defense of Ward was weakened by a bandwagon argument and a hasty generalization; nonetheless, she returned to her progressive mission to present her readers with more coverage of the feminine view of the game. Without indicating her sources, the rookie writer claimed, "all the boys here who know Ward speak in the same way of him" and "no man with such a sweet little woman for a wife as he has would act that way." As usual, "all the boys" can still be wrong and a man with a "sweet little woman" for a wife is nevertheless capable of straying. Other accounts of Ward and his wife,

Helen Dauvray, paint different pictures: Ward as a player in more than one sense of the word and Dauvray as possessing the caprices and attention-seeking foibles of stage folk. Nonetheless, Black went on to suggest that "Mrs. Ward" had a leading role in the inspiration behind the PL after overhearing Ward say that she had given him "many good ideas and had been a great help in preparing his book." By identifying Dauvray as "a base ball enthusiast" who "can score a game as correctly as—well, as I can," the rookie writer's readers may have smiled at her aside about scoring a baseball game, which once again revealed a stylistic and personable flair to her writing. Beyond going against the Cult of True Womanhood, Black's ability to "brag herself up" demonstrated a self-awareness that was consistent with the contemporary development of reporters, and at the same time perhaps made her even more interesting to her male audience and fellow writers. While her generous compliment identified the actress as a fellow fan, the donor of the Dauvray Cup would have needed no introduction to the regular readers of *SL* who may have been further impressed with the story of Ward's wife as the muse for the PL. Among her efforts to promote the role of women in baseball, Black's use of "Mrs. Ward" when the actress had kept her maiden name stands apart as perhaps one idea that was too modern for the Modern female journalist.[23]

Black's advancement of Helen Dauvray as part of her mission met with mixed success. Unfortunately for her project, the female sportswriter's report is the only source of these stories about the actress' influence on Ward's ideas and work. As the sole suggestion that the celebrity couple may have worked together, Stevens offered that Ward and Dauvray might have collaborated on a letter she wrote to New York newspapers in 1888. While Di Salvatore is silent on the matter, it is possible that Black may have heard these stories first-hand from Dauvray when the two of them met while traveling together on a train, but she did not indicate whether Ward had corroborated his wife's influence during the "numerous occasions" they had met. To relate the influence of another player's wife—and perhaps to discredit Albert Spalding, Black told the story of the sporting goods magnate's treatment of Ned Williamson after his injury during the 1888–1889 world tour. When Williamson's knee became too infected for him to travel, he remained in England to allow it to heal, but Spalding was only willing to advance Nellie Williamson barely enough money to cover their expenses—hence the reason

1. Pre-Season

Williamson had signed with the PL instead of the NL, according to Black. What the female sportswriter did not reveal, however, was that Williamson had sent unflattering reports back to *The Sporting News* during the trip, which may have precipitated Spalding's stinginess.[24]

Ultimately, Black's support of Ward and Dauvray was not reflected by their lives outside of the press. If they had access to New York newspapers, Black and her readers might have been aware that the couple had stopped living together in January of 1890—at the same time that Jessie McDermott took out a restraining order against her husband after he assaulted John M. Ward on a New York street. Di Salvatore and other writers speculate that Ward and Jessie had become lovers while the ball player was rooming in the McDermott house before his marriage to Dauvray in 1887. While Black perhaps deserved praise for wanting to believe—and cover—the best about Ward, her somewhat naïve defense may have caused Chadwick, Murnane, and other sporting writers who might have known about Ward's involvement with McDermott to charge her with another rookie mistake.[25]

In contrast to her attempts to defend Ward and advance the influence of players' wives, the scoop found in Black's third letter marked a significant moment in her development as a reporter. While riding in a streetcar with two members of the Pittsburgh Alleghenys management, the female reporter overheard their discussion of how the NL was planning to drop two franchises and go to an eight-team format while redrawing its schedule to go head-to-head against the configuration and the dates of the PL. Even more significant to her was that the men chose to speak of these matters in her presence because they discounted her gender: "'It makes no difference, she's only a woman and won't understand.' Allow me to say, my friend, women are not usually dull of comprehension, and 'only a woman' may have an interest in base ball matters." As yet another instance of when Black was in the "right place at the right time" to obtain a scoop, the anecdote would have left little doubt about her effort to work as a reformer for the profession of journalism and show men, like the ones she overheard, that women could indeed be players of some kind on the baseball stage. This incident illustrated a second progressive element to the female reporter's efforts, that of "uncovering the economic and political facts of industrial life more boldly, more clearly, and more 'realistically' than anyone had done before."[26]

Reporting the scoop in the manner Black used was not without risks. Given that riding streetcars was known to be an activity for working girls, often described as "man mashers," to pick up a man, or "catch a mash," it was brave of Black to mention the streetcar ride as the source of her scoop. Even though Henry Chadwick might have chided her for eavesdropping, while T. H. Murnane might have been equally upset she didn't ride longer to overhear more inside information, Black's ability to turn the activity into a source of information for her job attested to her resourcefulness and resilience as a journalist. Her scoop was vindicated when the NL met at the end of the month to dissolve the Indianapolis and Washington franchises and redraw their schedule, which validated Black's work because she could no longer "be credited with sending out false reports," even if her methods were somewhat indirect and unconventional.[27]

After advancing her argument that women could write significant baseball stories, Black returned to her serial human interest story to report how the activities of the YLD were beginning to hit the same fever pitch as any other baseball fans and expand her editorial role as a guardian of the game's image. The Pittsburgh correspondent had observed on March 26 that the YLD had inspired the formation of a sister club in Cincinnati; she revealed more of her competitive side when she couldn't resist sniping, "From what she says, though, I don't think their club will either be as enjoyable or as successful as the one here." Black could say this with some confidence because her YLD club had grown to 24 members by early April, and all of them were reportedly prepared to boycott the games of John "Pebbly Jack" Glasscock, who had been one of the former Indianapolis players moved to New York and who would replace John Ward at shortstop for the NL Giants. While this action was aimed at Glasscock's games in "this city or elsewhere" with the expressed purpose of preventing ladies of all ages from being exposed to Glasscock's habitual "use of language during the progress of a game that would have put the meanest tough in the country to shame," Black's objections were based on deeper issues.[28]

Pebbly Jack's penchant for swearing in the presence of ladies wasn't the only example of his behavior that was hurting the image of the game. As one of the first "double jumpers" banned from the Brotherhood after he signed with Indianapolis of the NL in November of 1889, Glasscock might have earned some of the same scorn Black heaped on Jake "St.

Jacob" Beckley for being "unfaithful," "dishonorable," and "wavering." In 1878, Glasscock played 26 games for the Pittsburgh Alleghenys of the International Association before finishing the season with the Forest City club of Cleveland, but if a much younger Ella Black had the opportunity to see him ply his trade one year before he broke into the majors, she made no mention of it in her reports. The future sportswriter had scorecards for local games dating to 1877, but 1878 may have predated her attendance at Recreation Park, or Glasscock's demeanor at 21 was nondescript enough to fail to draw her attention. Black also might have taken him to task for having a history of jumping contracts, as he did in 1884 at age 27 when he left Cleveland for the Cincinnati Outlaw Reds of the Union Association, giving the oft-quoted motto of "I have played long enough for glory, now it is a matter of dollars and cents." Instead, the female sportswriter compared Glasscock to John M. Ward and found him lacking as a gentleman—even if he had the "ability to hit a little the hardest," as evidenced by his .352 average with Indianapolis the year before. Further, she noted how he had "managed to get the entire audience down on him" at Recreation Park in Pittsburgh during the previous season and how he would not be "any credit" to Mr. Day's New York team.[29]

Beyond protecting baseball's image to draw a "better class of patron to the game," Black highlighted the economic consequences of their boycott pact:

> Probably the magnates may laugh at this and say they can stand such a loss without much effort. True enough, but just the same we will try to keep every one we can away from those games. There are now twenty-four of us girls in the club, and each one will be able to keep at least two gentleman away from the games in addition to themselves. Now that makes a total of seventy-two people who would have otherwise gone to the games. They will average fifty cents each to the club or thirty-six dollars each game. New York will play ten games here, so that will mean three hundred and sixty dollars the club will not get that it might just as well have.

Perhaps Black was correct that the magnates weren't reaching for Glasscock's newly minted New York contract to tear it up in response to the home-grown protest of the YLD, but Spalding and company may have taken more notice if they could have predicted audiences as small as 200 for some of the Pittsburgh NL games that summer and a total attendance of just over 16,000 for Alleghenys home games. Demonstrating a sense of the business end of baseball as well as the game's need to win over new and affluent audiences of ladies and their gentlemen escorts, Black was clearly working her way into her role as a progressive reporter.[30]

One week after announcing that she had received her credentials from *SL*, showing the temerity to take O. P. Caylor to task for the vulgar language he used in the *Sporting Times* to support the cause of the NL, and returning to her unorthodox method of using "back window views" and opera glasses to scout "Hecker's Youngsters," Black received perhaps the greatest validation of her career to that point, the notice of the game's first sporting journalist:

> While I highly appreciate all the kind words that have been said of me since I began writing in the columns of THE SPORTING LIFE, there has not been any of these that touched me as much as the kindly mention given me last week by Mr. Chadwick. I have heard of him ever since I first heard of the game, and have been taught to regard him as the writer of all writers on that subject. ... I cannot thank him sufficiently for what he said of me and only trust he will again find some of my work worthy of mention.

Although she carefully worded her response, Ella Black was clearly thrilled as a novice journalist to be recognized by the "writer of all writers" on baseball. Chadwick's lukewarm, faintly patronizing praise of her "characteristic" method for gathering news by "riding the cars" and his tepid response to the fact she wasn't any stronger in her "allegiance" to the PL may have indicated that the rookie writer was putting the best spin on the faint praise of the veteran scribe. In the end, she appeared to be taking validation where she could find it from someone who had been linked to the game long before she began to learn "its mysteries."[31]

After appearing in the pages of *SL* less than two months before the beginning of the 1890 season as an unknown, untested, and untried journalist, Ella Black wrote her way into a position of relevance by the first pitch. Working with an avowed mission to prove that a woman could write baseball, she demonstrated that she could take on the roles of editorialist, reporter, and professional journalist. Black was not able to interview John Ward as Chadwick had, but she did not let that keep her from adopting an editorial voice to defend him. She was not able to ask questions directly of local NL officials, yet she did not let that stop her from showing her skills as a reporter by breaking a significant story about the changes in the NL business model. Her range was limited and

1. Pre-Season

her methods were unusual out of necessity, and Black still demonstrated that she was aware of the issues facing the field of journalism as its practitioners attempted to improve the image of their profession. Facing skepticism from editors, doubts about her actual gender from her fellow writers, and mixed praise from the Father of Baseball, Black made a name for herself, weathered the trials and doubts to take her place as a baseball writer, a Modern Woman, and a relevant voice from a previously marginalized perspective.

"The old Jeffersonian Doctrine": T. H. Murnane as Players' League Reporter

As a former major league ball player turned sportswriter, Timothy Hayes Murnane was unique among *SL* correspondents during the spring of 1890. Understandably, Murnane's stance on the PL was influenced by the treatment he received in his own playing days during an eight-year professional career, and his background contributed to his pro-labor fervor during the Brotherhood War. Born either in Tipperary County, Ireland, or in the industrial town of Naugatuck, Connecticut, in 1851, Murnane got his start in baseball as a semi-pro player with teams in Norwalk (1869) and Stratford, Connecticut (1870). He became a major leaguer when the Middletown Mansfields joined the National Association in 1872, and went on to play for the Philadelphia Athletics (1873–1874), Philadelphia White Stockings (1875), Boston Red Caps (1876 1877), and Providence Grays (1878), where he was a teammate of John Ward. Murnane made little mention of this last fact in his writing for *SL*, perhaps because he hit just .239 while Ward won 22 games and posted a 1.51 ERA in his rookie campaign.

After being out of the major leagues for five years, Murnane got first-hand "war" experience when he served as player-manager and minority investor for the Boston Reds of the Union Association (UA) in 1884. Because the St. Louis Maroons ran away with the league title, Murnane's 58–51 club provided little threat to the ticket sales of the Boston Beaneaters that season, just as the UA did little to threaten the NL—except perhaps to harden the resolve of Spalding and the other magnates to maintain their economic control of the game. Murnane made little or no direct reference to the early chapters of his life during the 1890 season; nonetheless, the perspective of the third-year reporter for the *Globe* was significant because he was an eyewitness to the 1876 "coup" of the NL that ended the player-directed NA, and he was a business rival of the NL in 1884 as a part of the UA. Thus, even if he was a biased witness, his journalism was important as one of the few—if not only—sustained voices that could speak for the players.[32]

Similar to emblematic qualities found in the writing of Chadwick and Black, T.H. Murnane's work for *SL* and the *Boston Globe* (*BG*) during the pre-season illustrated how the reporter's role was developing within the profession of journalism in the late nineteenth century. In the former player's initial *SL* appearance, his description of the Boston PL franchise's spring training trip established his role of covering baseball news, sniping at the opposition, and promoting the Brotherhood. Reacting to the threat by the NL to blacklist any college players who scrimmaged against teams from the outlaw league, the Boston correspondent employed a "colorful," "personally distinct and popular" writing style that mixed poetic prose with war rhetoric and told stories in support of the players' cause. The lead of his April 2 report painted a positively idyllic word picture of the southern hospitality experienced by Mike "King" Kelly's team in Charlottesville, Virginia: "Here, where the solemn looking undertaker has to face a starvation business and the blush of the peach is on every cheek, the professional ball player can exercise daily and sleep like a schoolboy at night." Whether or not Murnane was seeking to counter the invasion and rebellion rhetoric used by Henry Chadwick and other NL supporters, the Boston correspondent's untutored, style nonetheless contrasted with the older writer's formal approach. Murnane's florid prose was present in the second paragraph as well, even as he turned to his own war rhetoric:

> The men have received many compliments for their honorable stand in the late base ball war, for it now looks as if the danger line has passed. The Players' League has passed the shoals. No longer will the Will-o'-the-wisp lights lead the boys astray. The monopoly is routed and from this out it will be impossible for a half dozen magnates to say who shall invest their time and money to bring out the best points in our glorious national game.

Beyond his use of "honorable stand" to highlight how the PL had weathered the repeated efforts of the NL to keep it from taking the field, Murnane made a point of commenting on the anti-monopoly and pro-labor elements of the Brotherhood cause. Returning to poetry to perhaps add more "sparkle" to his style, he used two metaphors to create images of the "ship" of the Brotherhood effort reaching safer waters despite the spectral misguidance of O. P. Caylor, Harry Palmer and the other NL journalists who were using Spalding's *Sporting Times* as a platform for attacks designed to scuttle the new league with false promises and threats of lower salaries. Further, the former player and manager clearly took pride in his co-ownership of baseball through his participation both on the field and in the press box when he added "glorious" as an intensifier to the more familiar phrase of "our national game."[33]

While in camp with the Red Stockings, Murnane covered their spring training regimen to provide *SL*'s readers with an inside look at the daily existence of ball players. The routine included a one-mile walk out to the field at 10:30 each morning for a two-hour practice, and a slow run back to the hotel for lunch, "thus getting up a good sweat." After lunch, the team rested for an hour and then went back out to the field for a game with the "University men" or another two hours of practice. According to Murnane, the University of Virginia nine benefitted from crossing bats with the professionals: "They are now a stronger team than was the Harvard team of last season. They handle themselves more like professionals than any college team I ever saw, except perhaps the old Harvard team of '76 and '77." What's more, the Boston correspondent referenced the moral and ethical response demonstrated by the players on the university's team when they took a "manly stand" against the "dictates of the League" by scrimmaging with the Red Stockings despite the threat of being blacklisted for going against the National Agreement. In response to the defiance of the college men, Murnane could not resist taking a shot at Spalding and the other NL magnates in light of the successful "rebellion" of the Brotherhood and the PL to that point: "The League has always looked at base ball law as a child of its own brain, and the many rebuffs it has received during the last three months must have made it feel very uncomfortable."[34]

On the return trip, a chance encounter between King Kelly's Red Stockings of the PL and the Brotherhood "deserters" who remained with the Philadelphia Phillies of the NL allowed Murnane to expand his reporter role to that of PL promoter and sniper. Simultaneously answering the critics who called the character of the new league into question and entertaining his readers with a dramatic extended narrative, the story showed how the *Globe* sportswriter helped lay the foundations for future baseball writers with his use of the anecdote, one of the literary techniques identified by Robert Park in 1923 as the hallmarks of New Journalism. Further, the tale certainly met Charles A. Dana's definition of news as "anything that will make people talk" or Arthur McEwen's corollary that served as the source of the "Gee Whiz!" school of sports journalism. Eschewing Kelly's aristocratic nickname and putting his readers on the train platform to experience the tension between the players of the rival leagues, Murnane held up the Boston captain as a man of character and used the showdown to invert the dominant baseball culture. After learning that the "deserters" had been stranded on a side track, the Red Stockings decided to "pull the curtains" in their car and avoid all contact with the men who had turned their backs on the Brotherhood. Later, however, they decided to form a gauntlet for the Phillies to pass through on their way to dinner. Because it illustrated the tensions between the PL loyalists and the "traitors" who remained true to the NL while featuring a cast of five eventual Hall of Fame players, the story is significant enough to be given in full here:

> Harry Stovey came out of the car in the middle of a shave and carried a razor. Dan Brouthers said he would not miss Sam Thompson for a farm.
> "Let us hiss them," suggested one of the boys.
> "Not for a thousand dollars," sang out Mike Kelly.
> "Every one a gentleman," said Billy Nash.
> "Look into their very souls and see them flinch," was Jim O'Rourke's advice. "Here they come."
> Sure enough, with big Sam Thompson in the lead. As he caught sight of the Boston men his cheeks turned crimson and his chin went up. He looked over the heads of the men in line, after first looking for recognition and finding nothing but a cold stare.
> Myers passed, but never turned his head or lifted his eyes from the platform. The color seemed to leave his face and his step was uncertain. The young players of the party looked bewildered, but the Boston men had only eyes for the deserters, as they said, and paid no attention to the inoffensive players. Clements came along with his head bobbing up and down and his face turned in the opposite direction. Schriver was an object of pity; his face changed color, and he went by with bowed head. Gleason came last, looking straight at the Boston men and a smile on his face, but the cold stare he got in return made the smile look like a ghastly bluff, and he turned color. Not one of the deserters looked back. Harry Wright and his wife came along soon after and was cordially greeted by all his old acquaintances, who had a pleasant word for the old veteran.
> After that the Boston men paid no more attention to the men who had

sold their honor. Several of the young players of the Phillies came back and had a pleasant talk with the Boston men, and were assured that there was nothing but the kindest feeling entertained for them. This seemed to have pleased the boys, and they were not backward in expressing their good will for the Players' League.

From what I saw I am sure that the young men now going into the League ranks will soon detest the players who sold out their fellow players just as much as the regular Brotherhood men do now.

Kelly's refusal to hiss at the deserters' even "for a $1,000" would not have been lost on Murnane's readers. That fellow Brotherhood player and noted third baseman Nash equated Kelly's position with the behavior of a gentleman made Kelly look even better and served as a rebuttal to attitudes like the one adopted by Chadwick that Kelly was "merely out for the stuff." Contemporary readers may have been surprised to see Orator Jim O'Rourke keep his comment to a mere nine well-selected words.[35]

As an example of how late nineteenth century journalists were making use of drama even as they attempted to avoid sensational rumor, the event allowed Murnane to return fire in the "moral war" being waged against the PL by Caylor, Palmer, and other writers loyal to the NL. To further demonstrate the good character of the Brotherhood men, Murnane highlighted their respect for Phillies manager Harry Wright, who was one of the game's earliest professional players, as well as their lack of animosity toward the younger players who filled their spots in the NL rosters. Even though this event was small in its own right, Murnane's narrative both affirmed the importance of loyalty among the fraternity of baseball players to his Victorian audience and illustrated his use of that value to promote the virtues of the Brotherhood members who supported the PL. Because the story was told from the player's perspective, it showed they could be every bit as virtuous as Thompson and the other men in the NL who were being touted by Chadwick as model citizens and gentlemen for remaining loyal to their employers, even though the reserve clause gave them very little opportunity to do otherwise when it was extended to the entire roster in 1889.[36]

With *SL* expanding from 12 to 16 pages to cover three major leagues, there was certainly room for "Murnane's Missive" to appear in the April 5 issue. Most likely, the former player was too preoccupied with reporting the Fast Day game on April 3 for the *Boston Globe* (*BG*) to write a "screed" for Richter's paper. Murnane's coverage of the PL exhibition game took up more than two full-page columns and included several illustrations. While Fast Day had lost much of its religious significance by 1890 and was soon to be replaced by Patriot's Day in 1894, Murnane indicated that the crowd "eventually observed the religious spirit of the day" even if they "worshipped at the diamond shrine." Continuing to work with a "colorful," "distinctive" style, he returned to his mix of metaphor and religion in his lead while adding military history when he described how the Brotherhood was "baptized Thursday in the rays of the very sun of Austerlitz" that kissed the "swift foot" of "the Only Kelly" and the "massive brow" of Ward. Historically, the "sun of Austerlitz" burned through the fog at a key moment in the 1805 "Battle of Three Emperors" and helped bring victory to Napoleon, who had crowned himself emperor the year before. Given Murnane's pro–PL stance, he was likely referring to the Napoleon who was credited for serving the French Republic; however, his analogy certainly opened the door for Chadwick and other NL supporters to compare John Ward to the Napoleon who led the disastrous march to Moscow in the winter of 1812.[37]

Working once more to report the event in a way that would put his readers into his coverage, the former player described how the sun brought forth spring grass from the cinders of the new Congress Street Grounds, and overwhelmed "with gladness the somber purpose of Fast day" to call out "a greater mass of people than ever before surrounded a Boston diamond." After making this allusion to the nearly 24,000 who turned out for both major league games in Boston that day, Murnane captured another slice of 1890 baseball culture with his characterization of the local fan: "[Shedding] his winter shell, the indelible base ball crank walked abroad once again in all his bounding enthusiasm, fairly rolling in the novel luxury of two games and two leagues to choose between." The players traveled from the Tremont House in "tally-ho coaches" with a bugler leading the way in a fashion that perhaps called to mind the fox hunts of the English countryside. Murnane went on to describe the slow progress of the procession along various city streets as the coach drivers picked their way through crowds of supporters and stopped briefly to allow the players to get down and pose for the "ubiquitous photographer." Without going into as much detail as he did in *SL* about the chance meeting between Brotherhood loyalists and deserters, the

1. Pre-Season

former player noted that "[s]everal times the procession met or passed the ever memorable band of the old League in its circus barge of faded glory, but there was no bloodshed." The PL players must have still been on their best behavior because there apparently was no hissing either during these encounters.[38]

Once the players reached the new ball park, Murnane continued to set the scene for his readers as he spared no words in enumerating the scalpers, hawking venders, the "great banks of humanity" in the park, the spectators on the roofs of nearby buildings, the "climbers like squirrels up a line of new telegraph poles," and the workmen who brought their own ladders. According to the *Globe* writer, the only "neglected opportunity" was the one view furnished by "the masts of the vessels that rose on three sides of the peninsula" that housed the new park. Before the game could start, the crowds roaming the field had to be removed, and the police were ineffective at this task. Hinting at the growing status of some ball players, Murnane described how Captain Mike Kelly came out and at once, the throng "fell back before him with such meek, gaping awe that he needed no manly physical force."[39]

In the second column of his long story, Murnane returned to his role as PL promoter when he went to almost as much length to describe the atmosphere of the park: "Brotherhood, by the way, was in the air, and pervading every part of the grounds was a sportive kindliness and delight that is sometimes absent from the diamond and the grand stand. One man bubbled over in his glee: 'We are all in it,' and apparently this was the controlling idea." After missing an opportunity in the opening of his story, the former player-manager took a poke at Spalding and company when he noted how "the pleasure of the crowd seemed to be heightened by the thought that the old league had not such a grand attendance up at the South End, a sample remark being, 'I'll bet a frost has struck 'em today.'" Murnane supplemented his argument that the Brotherhood was on top by noting that the "candy butchers" who sold their wares at the rival grounds in past seasons were at Congress Street on Fast Day in anticipation of better business. To show that they were right, he reported that their trays were "patronized with reckless good nature," thus providing further proof that Fast Day in 1890 was largely a symbolic holiday. The presence of the "unwearied," "bewhiskered warrior," "General" Arthur Dixwell, a trust fund baby and early baseball convert from the ranks of Boston's Yankee elite, and his cry of "'hi! hi!

for the brotherhood!" was another sign that local fans were ready to support the new league. What's more, Murnane observed that the game was "subordinate among the attractions of the day" because "[t]he people had come to a housewarming rather than to a contest." In the end, the crowd met the defeat of the home nine without the usual regret found among Boston fans, and "enjoyed seeing the ball knock off a policeman's helmet almost as much as any run that was made."[40]

The Boston crowd's surprisingly good-natured reaction to a loss did not stop Murnane from describing "the features of the game" in some detail. He praised the play of Billy Nash at third for the home team and John Ward at shortstop for the visitors from Brooklyn. Due to the overflow crowd, both sides benefitted from the ground rule doubles that were awarded to hitters who reached the cranks in left and right. Without apologizing to his audience, Murnane made use of several slang phrases, including "big card," to describe Dave Orr, "stone wall," for Con Daily, who handled the "ugly drops" of pitcher Van Haltren "with ease." Father Chadwick would have been pleased to learn that "[n]ot the shadow of a kick was made on either side." Befitting his large salary, King Kelly scored the first run of the season for Boston as he tried to rally his team from a seven-run deficit. The Boston writer's "colorful" and "personally distinctive" style may have resonated with his readers who were baseball enthusiasts, but it also would have drawn fire from E. L. Godkin for being too sensational in the French style of journalism—if, that is, the journalism critic bothered to read the sporting page of the paper.[41]

Given that the size of the crowd was judged as a preview of the coming "war" between the NL and the PL, the players' reaction to the turnout was significant and thus an important component of the coverage. As a passenger in the special train, Murnane was afforded an upclose observation of the responses of the "old guard" and the "new men" on the Boston team: "There was a look in their eyes that plainly showed they were agreeably surprised at the unlooked-for reception." Ward in particular was especially pleased by the crowd's reaction:

> John M. Ward was completely taken aback when he got on the grounds and had to elbow his way up to the player's bench.
>
> "What do you think of this, Mr. Ward?" sang out an enthusiast. "It completely knocks me out," answered the little Napoleon of base ball: "but I always had a good opinion of Boston."

1. Pre-Season

Ward's eyes feasted on the immense crowd, as if it was the realization of all his hopes, and it was something for him to feel proud of.

This passage illustrated Ward's growing status as a celebrity and advanced the perspective that his progressive, anti-monopolistic cause was a worthy pursuit. Similar to Black's assessment of baseball and the labor issue in Pittsburgh, the extent of this coverage showed that Murnane was fully aware of the significant events unfolding in front of him as a prelude to a significant season.[42]

With no ball game to report for Monday's paper due to Boston's Blue Laws, Murnane adopted Chadwick's editorial voice to extol the history of baseball along with the game's present and future importance at the national level:

Base ball is our national game as much as the stars and stripes in our national emblem. All that is necessary to make the sport a grand success for 100 years to come is honest play among the professionals.

The National League was formed in 1876 for the purpose of purifying the sport and succeeded. Like great political parties, after fighting for principle and winning a victory, they often forget the watchword of the pioneers and lose sight of other people's rights to make money, and try to convince the people that all streams should flow gently into their sea of prosperity.

The players' league has started out with nothing but the best interest of the game at heart. The gentlemen who are back of the eight clubs comprising this organization are of the highest standing, and the players engaged need no recommendation for honesty.

Within this succinct summary of American capitalist culture, Murnane's political stance on the magnates of the NL was softer here, perhaps due to the middle ground taken by the *Globe*, but it is clear that he felt the need to defend the virtue and the character of the PL in the same terms used by Chadwick to support the NL. Beyond promoting the good character of the players and their backers and addressing the ongoing issue of honesty in the professional game, the former player highlighted the importance of the Brotherhood cause by reasserting the labor rights of the artisans on the field to make decisions about their livelihood.[43]

Writing to the *SL* during the last week of the pre-season, Murnane expanded the role of reporter to being a critic of the players and the action soon to take place on the field. Due to the response to his pre-season analysis of the two Boston teams, he spent the greater part of his report defending his assessment of the Beaneaters against the rebuttals of journalists who supported the NL. Taking advantage of his ability to speak with the players on a regular basis, the *Globe* writer gave Arthur Irwin, Red Stockings shortstop and fielding glove entrepreneur, the opportunity to tell his side of recent contract infractions alleged against him. Murnane's undertaking of the former task contained some insights to his opinions of fellow writers, while the second was significant due to the amount of space he gave to a fellow player. Taken together, the report helped define Murnane's pro–PL stance while demonstrating his access to the players as a sports journalist.

Murnane closed his final pre-season "screed" with a few last salvos aimed at the old League and boosts for the new one. Reporting that the Boston National League team had sent out "a couple of thousand invitations" to the opening game, he answered Chadwick's earlier "secession-a-la Ward" allegory with a barb of his own: "This papering the house is an old business for the theatres but something new for the League." In contrast to this metaphor, Murnane reported that similar invitations to local government officials for the PL opener were returned "in most cases" because "the parties said they would rather help the boys along." Reporting how the Kansas City franchise in the AA wouldn't give a local player his release, he used the example to compare the players with the patriots of 1776 who declared American independence: "This is a sample of National Agreement methods, and one of the very acts that drove the players to fight on the old Jeffersonian doctrine." Closing with a series of stirring images, Murnane emphasized the readiness of the players for the fight that was ahead and his unequivocal support: "There goes a band of music advertising the game. The PL is not dead, but muchly alive. On with the dance and let the soda water sizzle."[44]

The pre-season work of Chadwick, Black, and Murnane saw them tuning up for the long grind ahead while illustrating the changes underway in the profession of journalism. Further, their early work demonstrated the respective roles of editorialist, progressive journalist, and reporter, as well as the key issues of style, content, and accuracy that were present both on the surface and between the lines of their *Sporting Life* correspondence. In the months ahead, each of the writers would work within all three roles and address each of the issues, but to varying degrees depending on the point in the long season, which would in turn bring out changes in how the writers delivered significant messages while

1. Pre-Season

telling the story of the 1890 season. All three responded to the first pitch of Opening Day with the same celebratory spirit implied by Murnane's closing ballroom metaphor, but soon "upped their games" once the conflict between the National League and the Players' League became a "war to the knife."

2

Early Season
Identifying the Issues and Defining the Conflict

When the 1890 season started on April 19, *SL* correspondents and sports journalists compared the National and Players' Leagues on a number of levels; other elements of the press, however, paid little attention to the conflict. The upper-class media reflected the genteel skepticism of giving journalistic attention to something as trivial as men earning their living playing baseball—especially if those men were immigrants or of immigrant stock. *Harper's Weekly* and *Frank Leslie's Illustrated Newspaper*, publications aimed at upper- and middle-class audiences, rarely covered professional baseball. The only time *Leslie's* deigned to mention the Brotherhood War was in early May when it showed the NL and PL parks side by side at the foot of Coogan's Bluff in New York City. The conflict received a one-paragraph explanation; in contrast, the illustrations contained five crowd scenes, indicating a greater interest in the fans than the game.[1]

Another example of upper class reservations about the growing celebrity of baseball players was found in "The Enchanted Baseball," a satire published in *The Cosmopolitan*, which was aimed at a more Victorian audience in April of 1890. The short story featured Algernon de Witt Caramel, who was part Connecticut Yankee and part comic opera hero—without apologies to Twain or Gilbert & Sullivan. Other elements included a beautiful fiancée, a mustachioed melodramatic nemesis, travel to an enchanted kingdom, and last-minute heroics en route to a "yearly income of several millions." As the "champion shortstop of America" for the New York Brobdignagians who played at the Polo Grounds, he was easily recognized as John Ward, the shortstop of the champion New York Giants, though no upper-class audience of *The Cosmopolitan*

2. Early Season

would have believed in 1890 that a lowly baseball player would ever earn a million dollars, let alone several. These examples illustrate the upper-class bias that Chadwick, Black, Murnane, and other sports journalists were working against as they attempted to improve baseball's image during the 1890 season.[2]

Given that the PL comprised roughly two-thirds or about 125 former NL players, the quality of the play served as one of the primary criteria for judging the strength of the two leagues. Sports journalists identified Cap Anson of the NL and John Ward of the PL as representatives for their respective leagues, while King Kelly became a celebrity largely by virtue of being "well-known." To improve the quality of play and the audience, both leagues instituted rules to reduce instances of "bulldozing" (stalling with a lead to win by virtue of the game being called due to darkness) and "kicking" (arguing with the umpire's decision). These rules were designed to make the game more appealing to the genteel patrons who found such practices objectionable. At the same time, however, star players were given special treatment by the press, such that when the player-manager of Spalding's Chicago Colts argued with the umpire, it was just a case of "Cap being Cap."[3]

The sporting press also spent considerable time comparing the business practices of both leagues. From the start of the season, the attendance figures were used as the other primary criterion for judging the economic strength of the leagues as businesses. As with evaluating the quality of play, the attendance numbers became a largely subjective evaluation tool by the middle of the summer. Members of the sporting press covered the front office decisions of both leagues, including the practice of moving games to cities with better home attendance and lowering ticket prices to compete with neighboring teams in battleground cities. Other journalists compared the business models of both leagues, demonstrating a more progressive interest in the game that went beyond results and statistics.[4]

Concurrent with the comparisons between those two leagues, baseball journalism benefitted from the advent of a third major league in 1890. Some big city newspapers in the battleground cities doubled their coverage by assigning reporters to write about both the NL and the PL. Sports journalists demonstrated that they were following each other's work, illustrating the fraternity of baseball writers that led to gab sessions in the press box, mutual praise and criticism, and occasional print feuds.

Working as editorial voices and reporters, baseball writers expanded those roles as guardians and prophets of the game, critics, snipers, and promoters of baseball as a business, as well as observers and reformers of their developing profession.

Collectively, the April and May reports of Chadwick, Black, and Murnane reflect and record the early excitement, developing conflicts, and growing disappointments of the season's first quarter. By the end of May, as observers on both sides saw that the PL was going to be able to compete with—if not surpass—the NL, Chadwick's editorial voice became strident and filled with a sense of urgency that reflected the tone of his employer's Memorial Day interviews. On the other side of the conflict, Murnane's reporting illustrated a growing confidence in the PL as the Brotherhood realized they could indeed compete with the NL magnates. Despite having gone on record with her support for the PL cause, Ella Black remained more objective than the other two in her reporting and editorializing as she advanced her own progressive cause. While immersing the reader in the early days of the 1890 season, the week-by-week analysis of Chadwick's, Black's, and Murnane's work will illustrate the initial qualities of their coverage, as well as their significant messages.

Week 1—April 19–25: Opening Day Heroes, Business Figures, and the "Fraternity" of Baseball Writers

The first week of the Brotherhood War saw the NL drawing 29,010 fans for its first four dates, rebounding from a weak opening of just 17,886 in 1889; however, the figures for the PL were nearly double at 50,453, making it clear that the fans were voting with their pocketbooks early in the season. Even so, the 1890 numbers for the NL indicated they were on par with the figures from 1888, which were not hampered by weather and the need to use smaller venues. While it was too early to know whether the nearly 200 percent surplus tickets sold for the PL games indicated an increased interest in the sport or whether the "fickle" baseball public was drawn to the novelty of the new league, Spalding and the NL magnates no doubt were aware of the disparity. After the long winter of discontent and discord, Chadwick, Black, and Murnane led their reports of the season's first week with festive descriptions of the Opening Day parades, but soon turned to the business side of the game coverage, and illustrated the sense of fraternity that existed among baseball journalists.[5]

Reprising the warm welcome of the Fast Day game earlier in the month, Boston fans treated John Ward to a repeat hero's welcome on Opening Day, greeting him with yet another floral display as the founder of the Brotherhood. T. H. Murnane had high praise for Ward's team, which won two of their five games with Boston during the opening series. Promising that Ward's team would be "well patronized for Bostonians know good ball playing when they see it," the player-turned-sportswriter had further praise for Ward's skills and attitude, noting how his "base-running and plucky up-hill work would make him a loss to any team." If contemporary readers recognized "plucky" as the watchword for the self-made man of Horatio Alger's novels, Murnane would have been successful in advancing his argument that the Brotherhood leader was worthy of press attention.[6]

As a *Boston Globe* sportswriter, *SL* correspondent, and official scorer for the Red Stockings, Murnane was on hand to assess the level of play and comment on the business side of the game. The Red Stockings won four of their first six games and the former player-manager was speaking to PL critics when he noted how the contests were played "without the semblance of a kick of any sort." Changing roles from defender to prophet, he predicted the same good behavior on a regular basis due to the business model of the new league: "The players now have a common interest and I look for the best discipline ever exercised since the league was formed." Reporting the gate receipts as more evidence of the PL's strength, Murnane noted how local interest in the new league and its cause had earned the Red Stockings almost $13,000 "before a championship game was played" and netted them almost $19,000 in gate receipts when 23,000 fans attended the first six games of the season. Crediting the new league's structure, he saw it as a way to draw the elusive better-paying audience: "No wonder the players feel delighted with their new venture, and try to put up an article of ball that will attract the best people of this part of the country." After praising the PL for operating with the strategy of providing a superior product instead of attempting to run another organization out of business, Murnane was not shy about warning the NL of the "boomerang effect" of their confrontational, winner-take-all business strategy.[7]

Identifying Tim Keefe as "one of the original Brotherhood men," Murnane used an interview with him to continue to tout the PL business model. Quick to highlight the fast start for the PL cause, Keefe noted how the new league was outdrawing the NL by almost three to one in the battleground cities. Comparing Buffalo and Cincinnati as the two single-team sites, Keefe recognized how Cincinnati had boosted the NL attendance figures, which was accurate since "Porkopolis" drew over 13,000 for the opening series, the highest total for any NL city (Boston was next with just under 8,000), but he qualified the early numbers by saying, "everyone knows that Cincinnati is anything but a good weekday ball town" in the summer when the weather became warm. Keefe strengthened his argument by pointing to the drawbacks of the Reds' $4,000 manager and high-priced veteran lineup compared to Buffalo's low team salary of more talented players. Ward's brother-in-law concluded the interview by illustrating the "live-and-let-live" strategy of the PL when he revealed how they drew up a non-conflicting schedule based on the NL's usual scheduling practices and sent the draft to their rivals. This move had the opposite effect when the NL dropped two of its franchises and drew up a new schedule with the express purpose of driving the PL out of business. The interview demonstrated how the business side of the game would command at least as much coverage as the games and the players. The amount of space given to the interview further illustrated Murnane's access to the players, his (and Richter's) willingness to cover potentially controversial perspectives, and the former player's project to "boost" the PL and "down" the NL at every turn.[8]

The presence of Keefe's PL Giants at the Congress Street Grounds inspired Murnane to adopt Henry Chadwick's baseball historian role as a one-man nineteenth century Elias Sports Bureau. Continuing his project of promoting the strength of PL lineups and identifying individual players as men worthy of particular praise, the Boston correspondent reported that six of the nine men who had won the previous 14 batting titles were present at the Congress Street Grounds, with five of them being active: Mike Kelly and Dan Brouthers for the Boston Red Stockings and Jim O'Rourke, George Gore, and Roger Connor for the New York PL Giants. The sixth was Ross Barnes, who had won the batting title in the first year of the league's existence and was umpiring that day. The three not present were Abner Dalrymple, who was playing in Denver, Jim White, who was with Buffalo of the PL, and Cap Anson of the Chicago Colts, the lone title winner currently playing in the NL. Murnane combined this fact with his sense of the PL as a democratic, joint business venture that didn't involve the usual high-priced sale to move a player to a new team: "Just think of it! Here was a concern starting into the business with over 30 men, the pick of their profession, and not one dollar of purchase money was put out for the lot."[9]

Working as both an editorial writer and a reporter, Henry Chadwick made the trip to Boston to be on hand for the Opening Day contest between the Brooklyn Bridegrooms and the Beaneaters. Although he would have said he was in Boston to bring the "best patrons" a new appreciation of the game, Chadwick's pro–NL bias was evident in his report of the opening week. While in town, he did pay a professional courtesy visit to the home of the Red Stockings on Congress Street, but had little to say beyond suggesting that it would be "a handsome ball ground"—when it was finished. In contrast to the Brotherhood park, which the *Spalding's Guide* editor noted as being in a recently reclaimed portion of the city that was already "covered by factories, wharves, and railroad depots," the Beaneaters' South End Grounds were "very convenient for the wealthy residents of the many suburban villages" which were "rapidly becoming part and parcel of the city itself." The advantage of being more accessible to upper class patrons was evident in the crowd on hand for Opening Day: "A finer assemblage of the best class of patron of the game than filled the grandstand on the occasion I have never seen outside of Washington Park, Brooklyn, the number of ladies occupying the reserved seats being a specially attractive feature." Chadwick judged the crowd at "fully four thousand," demonstrating a practiced eye given that the published number was 3,884. What he didn't note, however, was that the crowd at the Congress Street home of the PL game was more than double, at 8,334. Chadwick's assessment of the Boston fans illustrated his refined perspective and his desire to draw the "best patrons" to the game, as well as how little has changed in Boston after more than a century:

> I have to record the fact that the assemblage in the grandstand was far more of a partisan character than I had expected to find in the city of culture. I am so accustomed to the impartiality exhibited by the grand stand occupants of the Washington Park grounds at Brooklyn that the partisan feeling exhibited at the South End grounds seemed to me quite of the country town order.

Anyone who has attended a baseball game in Boston and had the temerity to wear the colors of the opposing team—or any opposing team for that matter—knows that the partisan crowds are still attending games there; however, they would still bristle at being called a "country town" akin to the backwaters described in Jane Austen novels.[10]

Boston's fans received almost as much attention as the players when Chadwick described the events on the field in the middle of his report. The veteran sportswriter's formal style was evident in his opening line: "The game was contested in a manner which raised the crowd to quite a pitch of excitement at times." The fervor of the "best class of patrons" was evident when they reacted to the play of their Beaneaters: "the grand stand occupants became wild with enthusiasm, and they were at fever-heat as they saw Long throw out the first two Brooklyn batsmen in the second part." The game itself, a back-and-forth battle that the Beaneaters ultimately won, 15–9, was indicative of "the glorious uncertainty of base ball" when the decisive moments of the game turned on the Brooklyn pitcher being struck in the back by a thrown ball while running the bases and Beaneaters star John Clarkson settling down to "finished work in the box" after giving up a 8–3 lead to make the Boston crowd, in Chadwick's tepid baseball slang, "very chilly."[11]

The organizational climate among the journalism fraternity was warmer when T. H. Murnane, "that old experienced hand," joined Chadwick in the press box at the South End Grounds for the end of the game. In contrast to the high-scoring NL contest, the PL game at Congress Street was a 3–2 affair that evidently allowed Murnane to travel across town to scout the opposition and check the accuracy of his pre-season assessment of the Beaneaters. Some of that brotherly sentiment was present in Chadwick's playful description of Murnane, who was almost 30 years younger and the same age as the Brooklyn correspondent's daughter, as well as his pleasure that he and Murnane had picked only three games right out of eight on Opening Day. The spirit of bonhomie among the sporting journalists extended to the following day when Murnane and his wife visited Chadwick at the Dorchester home of George Wright, former player and current sporting goods entrepreneur. The three of them "compared notes, related anecdotes, discussed events of the past as well as the present, and settled the question of the day to our mutual satisfaction." The Brooklyn correspondent was even willing to take Murnane's and Wright's advice "in regard to a scurrilous and lying attack"

2. Early Season

that had been made on him. If there was history of bad blood between Murnane and Chadwick, as the Boston writer would allude to in one of his October reports, there was no hint of it at the start of the season. Before long, however, the two sportswriters would find themselves on the opposite sides of a bitter conflict, and there would be no spirit of "mutual satisfaction" between them when the negative feelings resurfaced in print.[12]

The 3–2 start of the NL's Pittsburgh Alleghenys eclipsed the 2–3 opening week of the PL's Pittsburgh Burghers, yet Ella Black reported that the PL was already in the lead prior to the first pitch due to the superior quality of their pre-game parade. Two bands supported the PL, compared to just one for the NL, and the female sportswriter described the reporters who attended the Allegheny game as being "compelled" due to a short straw or editor's punishment. As per the agreement struck by the Young Ladies of the Diamond (YLD), Black attended the Burghers game at the brand-new Exhibition Park, where "the grand stand and bleaching boards were both filled so it was almost impossible for any late comer to get a seat." Across the Allegheny River, fewer than 1,000 spectators attended the NL game at Recreation Park, where they could hear the enthusiastic applause from the PL game. Black's NL information matched Clarence Dow's *Boston Globe* figure of just 730 fans for the Alleghenys' opening game. The total for the remaining three games in the series was 917, pointing to the local NL franchise's early inability to draw at home. In contrast, Dow's figure for the Burghers' opening game was 8,413. The PL drew only 3,291 for the rest of the series, but still outpaced the NL club by just over 10,000, or seven to one. Black showed her competitive tendencies while advancing her cause to promote the New Woman: "Best of all there was a big attendance of the weaker sex and they were by no means slow with their applause, but cheered and shouted almost as much as the men."[13]

The product on the field for both Pittsburgh teams, however, was another matter. The Burghers lost to Charles Comiskey's Chicago Pirates on Saturday, playing "worse than a crowd of children," though Black conceded that the condition of the field contributed to some of the errors. The rookie journalist demonstrated well-developed reporting abilities when she described the "discomfiture" that settled over the crowd: "It may have been there was too many flowers or too many ladies looking on, or too big a crowd, or—well, it was too much something."

After an off-day to observe the Blue Laws designed to prevent business from being conducted on the Sabbath, Black switched to the Alleghenys for Monday's game, where she saw a similar error-filled exhibition by the "colts" of the NL clubs, who played like recently promoted amateurs, which is what they were.[14]

Ironically, Monday's game at Recreation Park also marked the end of the YLD, the group of female baseball fans the Pittsburgh correspondent had described for the readers of *SL* during the pre-season. The club attended Saturday's game at the Exhibition Grounds as per the coin flip, and each member paid her own expenses. Because the Burghers lost, the supporters of the Alleghenys appeared at the NL park on Monday with their gentlemen escorts, only to find out that every Brotherhood girl—other than Black—"had to go away or some sort of an excuse," leaving the NL girls in a pretty fix. Despite this less than sporting ending that may have reconfirmed some of *SL* editor Richter's attitudes about female fans, the club nonetheless served Black well by providing her with compelling copy to whet her reporting skills during the pre-season.[15]

Black did not have access to the players and could not discuss baseball matters with the other sporting journalists in hotel lobbies, but these handicaps did not prevent her from breaking additional stories or commenting on the business side of the game. Black's opening week report broke a story about the local NL team's plan to boost their attendance by lowering ticket prices to 25 cents, a move that would put them almost on par with the "beer and whiskey" league of the AA. Similar to the streetcar scoop she reported in March, the female sportswriter happened to be waiting in the box office of a local theater behind two loose-lipped members of the Alleghenys management. Even though Black defended herself against potential eavesdropping charges, the box office story could have been another subterfuge to hide her reporter's news instincts and her desire not to show up her male colleagues. Black's report that "The local officials have always claimed they never made any money in former seasons" revealed that some things, like poor weekday attendance in Cincinnati in the summer and partisan fans in Boston, would not change in the baseball business for at least another 100 years.[16]

Furthermore, the Pittsburgh correspondent proved that she was not afraid to cover events that her male colleagues chose to ignore. Even as he was being hailed as the prophet of the PL and the "Base Ball King of the East," word of John Ward's separation from his wife, Helen Dauvray, reached the press. Murnane and Chadwick ignored this detail from the player's personal life, but Black made a point of defending the labor leader and the actress who had once cared for her on the train while she was "as miserable as a woman could be": "there has been a misunderstanding somewhere that time will unravel and bring them together again." If the rumors surrounding Ward and Jessie McDermott were true, the Pittsburgh correspondent's optimism might have been as inaccurate as her assertion that "no man could have been more devoted and loving to a wife than her husband was," but her opinion was nonetheless based on her meetings with both parties and few could argue against her call for outsiders to leave the couple alone. By discussing the matter at all, Black supported her project to provide *SL* readers with a different perspective on items in the sporting news.[17]

In contrast to the spirit of fraternity that Chadwick and Murnane demonstrated in Boston, Ella Black was still defending her right to participate as a baseball writer at the beginning of the season. Leading off her last April report, Black responded to Joe Pritchard, *SL*'s St. Louis correspondent. In one of his columns, Pritchard had expressed his doubts that Black was who she claimed to be or whether women possessed the capacity for writing news. Alluding to a trip she planned to take to Philadelphia, the card-carrying correspondent promised to meet with *SL* editor Richter to prove that she wasn't misrepresenting herself. Pointing to the handicap of not having the "privileges of a man" when it came to reporting, she promised that if she did, she would "give the St. Louisian an idea of how much superior to *some men* a woman could be." Further rebuttal came in the form of Black's appreciation for the support she had received from other *SL* correspondents: "Kindly words such as have been given me by Messrs. Harris and Chadwick are highly appreciated, but—oh, no, it cannot be the rotund Mr. Pritchard is actually growing jealous of a woman." (See the full text of Black's April 26 report in Part 1 of Appendix A.)[18]

While the week one reports by Chadwick, Black, and Murnane all demonstrated the excitement generated by the opening of the baseball season, the focus of their coverage differed. Chadwick offered more commentary on the partisan quality of Boston's fans and his visits with fellow journalist T. H. Murnane than on the action on the field. Murnane promoted the PL cause through his discussion of attendance figures and gate receipts, as well as his interview with Brotherhood leader Tim Keefe. Without direct access to the players, Ella Black nonetheless covered more baseball than the other two while concluding her human interest story about the Young Ladies of the Diamond, supporting John Ward and his wife, breaking a story about a reduction in ticket prices, and defending her right to write about the game. With the "baseball war" between the NL and PL underway, the focus and the messages of sporting journalists soon turned away from game stories to weightier matters.

Week 2—April 26-May 2: Player Business, Baseball Business, and Journalism Business

After two weeks, the total PL attendance was 127,623, while the figure stood at 71,965 for the NL. The jump in attendance could have been spurred by the better weather, or both sides could have started padding their figures once it became clear the size of the crowds was going to be used as a measuring stick for the "baseball war." With the heady rush of the opening week behind them, sporting writers turned to covering the game once more—through the lens of business. Despite the good news for Spalding's sporting goods due to the amateur baseball league being formed in England and Ella Wheeler Wilcox's assessment that allowed men to demonstrate "a certain intellectual acumen with physical strength and agility" that she saw as "essentially American," the *Rochester Herald* predicted that the "golden egg" of salaries ranging from $2,000 to $10,000 would not be "picked up freely by professional base ball players" in the years ahead. While Murnane found little to argue with about the 8–3 start of Mike Kelly's Red Stockings, Black and Chadwick both saw room for improvement in the middling performances of the Pittsburgh and Brooklyn teams, as well as the methods of sport journalism employed by their peers. At the same time, all three writers demonstrated the effects of the Brotherhood War through their interest in the business of the game beyond the scores and statistics: Black continued to report on ticket prices in Pittsburgh; Chadwick editorialized about the effects of kicking on the image of the game; and Murnane promoted the benefits of the PL format as a business model.[19]

2. Early Season

In Pittsburgh, the Alleghenys were drawing so poorly after just 2,477 people attended the first six games that the NL moved the games scheduled with Spalding's White Stockings to Chicago with the hope of higher ticket sales in Cap Anson's hometown. The Alleghenys front office claimed the schedule was changed so that the installation of opera chairs and other improvements could be made at Recreation Park, but Black was not shy about pointing toward the flimsy quality of the excuse by noting that the renovations could have just as easily been made when the team left for the road four days later. Interpreting the change as evidence that the NL might give up the fight in the battleground city of Pittsburgh, she speculated that persistent poor attendance might cause the Alleghenys to be moved to Indianapolis, where John T. Brush still held a franchise. Even though the NL franchise started the season by winning three out of four from the Cleveland Spiders, the Pittsburgh correspondent was not impressed because the Spiders "had so many young bloods in its ranks that it was about on a par with the local men." In contrast, Black judged that the veteran Cincinnati Reds, under the management of Tom Loftus, outplayed the local NL team at every position except second base and right field, which were manned by returning players Fred Dunlap and Billy Sunday.[20]

Pittsburgh baseball fans were treated to another surprise when the PL Burghers announced that they were cutting ticket prices in half to 25 cents, perhaps to scoop their rivals, who soon followed suit. Drawing on her knowledge of local attendance since Pittsburgh joined the NL in 1887, Black noted that the team averaged just over 2,000 fans for non-holiday games. With two teams competing for that limited number of fans, she reasoned that the PL stood to lose more ground business-wise because they were still paying for their new facilities and were looking for profits to share among the team's stockholders, which included private backers and the players themselves. After ten games, the Burghers were averaging just over 2,100 fans per home date, but that average had dipped considerably after the team had averaged almost 3,000 spectators per game for the opening series when local enthusiasts came out to see Comiskey's Chicago Pirates. Despite the moved NL games, the combined average in Pittsburgh was up from the previous year; however, both front offices were likely starting to feel nervous in the battleground city of Pittsburgh.[21]

In contrast to T. H. Murnane and other male journalists who could speak directly with players, managers, and team officials, Ella Black once again found herself being held back due to social conventions and attitudes toward female journalists. Despite the reporter's instincts that led to a significant scoop and *SL* credentials, the Pittsburgh correspondent bristled at her inability to work directly as a journalist: "I only wish that now when there is so much news going the rounds, that I was able to do some interviewing, for I think I might get some things that the others miss. You know a woman's ideas are often different from those a man will have." Without the restrictions placed on her as a woman baseball writer, she would have been able to ask Alleghenys President Nimick about the likelihood of the franchise moving to Indianapolis instead of being relegated to "Madame Rumor." Instead of only being able to comment on the "rather amusing row" caused by Allegheny Director J. P. O'Neill's status-driven remark that the Opening Day crowd at Exhibition Park was "composed of servant girls with aprons over their heads, women with babies in their arms and men wearing blouses," the *SL* correspondent would have been able to ask Burgher officials about their assessment of their fan base. Perhaps she knew she would have no defense if T. H. Murnane were to accuse her of being a "Cheap Jane" journalist because she had little more than the work of other writers as the source material for her "screeds" when she wasn't riding the cars with or standing in line behind local baseball officials.[22]

Contemporary social conventions and propriety, however, could not prevent Black from borrowing a page from Chadwick's role as baseball historian. After attending the game between the Reds and the Alleghenys, the female sportswriter provided her *SL* readers with personal background and more insight into the development of baseball players as local celebrities. The sight of Tony Mullane took Black back to the first time she saw the 31-year-old "relic" pitch during the 1884 season, when Moses Fleetwood Walker was Mullane's catcher on the Toledo Blue Stockings of the AA:

> What a favorite he was then with the ladies! They all used to rave about his good looks. One girl, since dead, the daughter of a well-known hotel man of that time, was so badly smitten with him that she managed to secure an introduction, and the result was that Mullane's "lines were cast in pleasant places" during his stay in the city. She took him buggy riding and to the theatre, and, in fact, devoted herself to him completely while he was here.

Beyond illustrating an unlikely romance between a ball player and an

2. Early Season

upper middle-class young woman (who was not alive to defend herself in 1890), the anecdote provided the rookie writer's readers with a sense of Black's personal history to help establish her credibility as a baseball writer and further advance her project of covering the game from the feminine perspective.[23]

After the New York Giants of the NL forfeited a game when the umpire exercised a new rule designed to end disputes over their calls, Henry Chadwick editorialized on "kicking" and the practice of using substitute umpires. The eradication of "kicking," or arguing with the umpire, was a particular pet project of Chadwick's because he felt it hurt baseball's image with "the best class of patrons of the game." When a local substitute umpire was used in the second game of the Boston-Brooklyn series, the former rules committee member reasoned that the substitute should have been disqualified as a former employee of the Boston club, and judged that it would have been a "merited punishment" if the Brooklyn team forfeited the game through their "insulting" behavior. Beyond the bad publicity, the moral element, and the rulebook, Chadwick pointed out that it was impractical for pitchers to "kick" against the judgments of the umpire:

> I don't care how determined an umpire may be when he goes into a match to do his duty with thorough impartiality, he can not help feeling irritable and angry when the pitcher charges him with either being a knave or a fool— a knave for rendering partial decisions, or a fool in not using judgment in his position—and that is what every pitcher does who kicks against decisions on balls and strikes.

This early display of spleen on Chadwick's part—along with the number of times he brought up kicking in the report—showed how strongly he felt about the practice. He was quick to assert the fact that not a single kick was heard from the Bridegrooms after Byrne, the team's president, ordered the practice stopped, thus showing that it could be controlled. Black seconded Chadwick's notion about kicking by supporting the AA's decision to grant umpires the power to eject players for arguing a call. Citing "many a disgusting display" and "disgraceful exhibitions of rowdyism," she reasoned that players would think twice about protesting to avoid the "disgrace" of being sent off the field.[24]

Despite the restrictions placed on Ella Black, baseball journalism was evolving in response to the changes in the game. Chadwick used the platform of *SL* to note that the game had become important enough that two Boston papers, the *Globe* and the *Herald*, were printing "double reports" in the sense that each paper had reporters covering PL and NL games. He noted how each of those reporters was a strong partisan of the league he was covering, including Murnane as the "Brotherhood backer" for the *Globe*. In case some members of *SL*'s readership were scratching their heads at how such papers could appear to support both leagues at the same time, the veteran journalist pointed out that these "double reports" were the source of stories from the same paper that were reprinted in the League or Brotherhood organs in New York without bylines as per the custom of the day. While he was no doubt pleased with the increased coverage of baseball in newspapers from a major city, Chadwick appeared to favor the neutral stance he found in the *Boston Journal*, perhaps because he viewed himself as a non-partisan supporter of the game.[25]

Because of the *Boston Globe*'s commitment to provide coverage of both the local NL and PL teams, Murnane accompanied the Red Stockings on the road. After traveling to Philadelphia to take two out of three from the Quakers, Boston's PL franchise went to Brooklyn for a three-game set with Ward's Wonders. Having no game on Sunday to report on for Monday's paper, Murnane checked in with John Ward, who was pleased with the performance of his team on and off the field, despite their middling 5–5 record to that point:

> I had to come here, into the home of the [American] association champions, with a new team, new grounds, and about everything new a manager could have to look out for. I had to depend wholly on the article of base ball my team put up, and I find they are coming out our way to see the best the market affords.

While contending with the Gladiators of the AA, Ward was battling with the Bridegrooms of the NL in a three-way race for the patronage of local fans (Philadelphia was the other battleground city with NL, PL, and AA teams in 1890). Ward didn't mention the Bridegrooms in his interview, but they were off to a 5–4 start and were drawing slightly better at home than the Wonders after a miserable opening series. Addressing the joint venture structure of the PL, Ward illustrated his awareness that the central tenets of the Brotherhood's effort required constant publicity: "It may take time, but I am satisfied that the boys will make a good round sum besides their salaries this season." Additionally, the quote shows that the business side of the Brotherhood venture was foremost in his

2. Early Season

thinking. Murnane closed the interview by adding "The Great Hustler" to Ward's many soubriquets.[26]

Building on the joint-stock element of the PL business model, Murnane expanded his promotion of the new league with an observation of how its shared profit structure was already translating to better play on the field: "The men are taking more interest in their work than ever before. They are evidently out for business and not a man of them needs looking after. The handsome dividend they are sure to receive at the end of the season has made the livelier ones of the party more thoughtful." Despite the undertones of public relations with regard to "handsome dividend," Murnane's use of "work" and "out for business" pointed to an increased concern for the economic side of the game. He didn't name names; nonetheless, it was significant that he alluded to the "livelier ones of the party" who were giving baseball a less than salutary image among the "better class of patrons." That point may have been reinforced indirectly when he asserted, "Capt. Kelly was never in such condition for his work as he is this season."[27]

Black, Chadwick, and Murnane covered the games in their second-week reports, but each of them held different views about what the quality of the action on the field foretold about the future of the game. The inability of the Pittsburgh Alleghenys to draw at home concerned Black about the team's overall viability as a business, while Chadwick advanced his argument about the link between the players' behavior and baseball's ability to improve the quality of its audience. Proving more optimistic than the other two writers, Murnane used the quality of the play by the Boston Red Stockings and his interview with Brotherhood leader John Ward to promote the strength and promise of the PL to provide a more economically sound and incentivized brand of baseball. As the early focus of the sportswriters shifted from game stories to business operations, the conflict between the NL and PL was about to infect the fraternity of sportswriters.

Week 3—May 3–9: Conflicts All Over: On the Field, in the Front Office, and in the Press Box

By the end of the third week, the initial excitement of Opening Day had faded and the routine of the baseball season was settling in: daily games, road trips, player injuries (both actual and euphemistic), and front office decisions all led to the inevitable conflicts found in any social situation. With its own daily grind of deadlines to meet, headlines to write, and papers to sell, the sporting press reflected and helped shape the larger conflict between the NL and the PL. As another illustration of the baseball player's growing celebrity status, an unsigned editorial in *SL* credited "American Hero Worship" as the reason why the NL attendance was dropping. By documenting how the Red Stockings were out-hitting and outslugging the Beaneaters, Clarence Dow's weekly statistical roundup in the *Boston Globe* supported the *SL* editorialist's argument that the baseball hero was worth the high salary paid to him. The strong starts by two PL pitchers, Boston's Bill Daley (5–0) and Chicago's Silver King (5–1), demonstrated the "hero worship" quotient of the upstart league, while Kid Gleason (6–0) served as an example of the new heroes the NL needed to develop to compete with the PL. To further establish the player's status, the editorialist argued that the baseball hero was a "formidable figure" in his own age even if he might not "go thundering down the ages to dwell with that of Caesar or Hannibal." In their week three reports, Murnane and Black were both attuned to the conflicts found on the field, in the front office, and among sporting writers.[28]

Still traveling with the team for the *Boston Globe*, Murnane renewed his praise and support of John Ward—until the fortunes of his hometown team were threatened. Leading the PL with an 11–5 record after 16 games, the Boston Red Stockings were in the middle of their first eastern swing, taking two of three from the Philadelphia Quakers and Ward's Brooklyn Wonders. Returning to his argument about the advantages of the PL model, Murnane observed that Ward was "putting up a much better game than he did last year" and suggested the Brotherhood leader could be forgiven for hitting just .250 since he was managing a hastily assembled team in a newly created league while competing with two other Brooklyn franchises for the local fan dollar. The *Globe* writer had further praise for Ward's new ballpark, calling it one of the "handsomest pavilions in this country," and promoted the success of the PL by reporting how the Wonders left Boston with "$10,000 velvet" after the opening series in April. When calls starting going against his Red Stockings, however, Murnane adopted a more combative tone. Revealing his more partisan side, he criticized PL umpire John Gaffney for giving Ward the benefit of "about every close decision and a good many that were not close" in the nine games played between the Wonders and the Red Stockings to that point in the young season.²⁹

When it came to the fraternity of baseball writers, Murnane was equally willing to pay compliments to his "brothers"—and then take them away. He noted Henry Chadwick's presence at the first contest he saw played at Brooklyn's Capitoline Grounds in 1870 and honored the Father of Baseball by writing that he was already recognized as "the great authority on the national game" 20 years earlier. In the next paragraph, however, Murnane "called down" Chadwick twice, and he added a third attack by the end of his report. A visit from John Ward allowed Murnane to take "Chad" to task for printing information about the alleged disharmony between Fred Pfeffer and Charles Comiskey. Murnane also took issue with Chadwick over the positive influences of the NL's practices to admit "the fair sex who get in on their shape" for free. Finally, Murnane accused the Brooklyn correspondent of putting a misleading face on the attendance at a recent NL game in Chicago by reporting that only 3,000 attended the two games in the Windy City on a cold day to avoid having to address the embarrassing fact that there were only 125 people in the stands at the NL park. Clearly, Murnane was not one to let honorific titles get in the way of good sports journalism. (See the full text of Murnane's May 10 report in Part 2 of Appendix A.)³⁰

Everything was quiet on the field in Pittsburgh because there were no games in the Smoky City until the beginning of June due to the conflicting schedule drawn up by the NL. Both the Alleghenys (5–9) and the Burghers (6–8) had losing records, but the fans were continuing to support the PL team because the Alleghenys management was unpopular with the press and the public in the union town of Pittsburgh. Anson's colts outplayed Hecker's youngsters and took three of the four games that were moved to Chicago. After two losses and a tie in Cleveland, Paul Hines was sent home, and Ella Black singled him out by reporting that he was "indignant" because he thought he was "playing as well as anyone" on a team where there were "too many players for every position." The conflict generated by this and other internal weaknesses would lead to the long losing season the Alleghenys were to endure.³¹

Despite Connie Mack's Buffalo Bisons having recently lost two of three to the Burghers, Black predicted that they "will do some great playing before the season is ended," but her prophecy was premature since Mack's team went on to win only 31 more games that year. The

Pittsburgh correspondent credited the "clockwork" fielding of the Burghers and was pleasantly surprised when they handed Silver King his first defeat after losing twice to him and Comiskey's Pirates earlier in the season. Pitcher Ed Morris returned to the Burghers lineup on May 2 in an outing that "showed his arm had regained all its former cunning" and would have resulted in a win if "he only exercised a little judgment and not persisted in using a slow ball." Far from protecting the pitcher's local reputation for being fond of alcohol, Black offered pointed criticism that included the hope Morris would "avoid the rocks on which he was wrecked before" by taking better care of himself off the field and avoiding his tendency to act like a "baby" when he "sensed the calls were going against him or his teammates were not supporting him enough."[32]

While the ballparks in Pittsburgh were quiet, there was no shortage of conflict in the front offices of the local teams. Perhaps reacting to the predictions made by Ella Black the week before, Alleghenys President Nimick came out in the local press with a statement that "the club will not be transferred, but will play here this year, and for many more to come." The Burghers were planning to seek legal action to bar George Miller from continuing to play for the Alleghenys, based on the court case that supported the legal right of the Kansas City franchise in the Western League to enjoin John Pickett from playing with the Philadelphia Quakers of the PL. Black demonstrated her reporter's instincts once again by reproducing the strategizing of two Alleghenys officials, while revealing some of her shyness in an anecdote that bears extensive treatment here:

> "I hear we are to be made to suffer," said one, "by them trying to take Miller from us."
>
> "That will be all right," responded his companion, "for it will give us a chance to get in our work."
>
> "How will that be done?"
>
> "Easily enough. I have just seen a lawyer to-day and he tells me that our contract with Beckley will come in ahead of the first one the Players' had with him. They did not live up to their contract and so it was made void. Then we made one and fulfilled it. This one Beckley broke and, if we are forced to take such a step, we can compel him to live up to our contract with him. So, if we lose Miller, we will be sure of getting Beckley."
>
> This was all I could hear, as the gentlemen were so unkind as to move on, but as I have not seen anything of this in print before, I thought I would give it to you just as I got it. I was very strongly tempted to speak up and ask for some further information, but could not muster up enough courage.

2. Early Season

Mirroring the fact that Pickett played 100 games for the PL Quakers in 1890 because the court that ruled in favor of the Kansas City franchise did not have jurisdiction in Philadelphia, George "Doggie" Miller and Jake "St. Jacob" Beckley both played out the season on their respective teams. Thus the plans for legal wrangling and the lawyer consultation went for naught. As the two officials spoke like villains from a vaudeville skit, perhaps Black felt more secure about quoting them. Whoever she was and whatever she did to overhear the conversations of local NL officials so regularly, it must have been clear to her that she would have been out of sources if any of them started reading her *SL* column and became more careful about what they said in public.[33]

Black's reluctance to address the Alleghenys officials highlighted the ongoing conflict she faced as a writer for *SL*: the printing of rumors due to the restrictions placed on her as a female journalist even as she worked to be reliable and avoid sensationalism. Addressing the rumors found in the sporting press, she claimed that "People get tired seeing the same thing dished up day after day, especially when they soon get to know it is nothing but a rumor that has really little or no foundation." Given that the rumor in question was whether or not various NL teams—including the Alleghenys—would be moved due to poor attendance, the conflict became apparent when the novice correspondent saw the effects of her earlier speculation in print. That same realization may have caused Black to continue to bristle against the societal restrictions that prevented her from going to President Nimick, Secretary O'Neill, Manager Hanlon, or Secretary Tener directly to put questions to them even if they might refuse to give her an answer because they "might laugh and think it all nonsense to talk base ball to a woman."[34]

Despite distancing herself from Dr. Mary Walker and other suffragists, Black reaffirmed her goal to advance the progressive cause of female sportswriters and win over her male readers: "I only hope some day, unless THE SPORTING LIFE should remove me from its staff, to be able to force some of the brilliant (?) masculine members of humanity, who have seen fit to ridicule the idea of a woman writing base ball, to admit that I am competent to do it." As if to prove her integrity as a sports journalist, Black followed this declaration with a decidedly unflattering anecdote of a female fan attending her first game who wondered when the umpire would take his turn at the bat and credited every batter with too many hits because she used the literal meaning of the word.[35]

The week three columns of Murnane and Black demonstrated sport journalism's constant need to balance the hero worship often involved in celebrating the exploits of the players with the coverage of the conflicts found on the field and in the front office. Through his praise of John Ward and his Wonders, Murnane developed his pro–PL stance, while contributing to the same hero worship identified by the *SL* editorialist. Black, on the other hand, refused to take the side of the insulted veteran Paul Hines and went so far as to admonish pitcher Ed Morris to behave better both on and off the field. Both writers exposed internal conflict to advance their own causes: Murnane further promoted the PL cause by taking Henry Chadwick to task for his pro–NL stance, while Black covered the front office intrigue and commented on the social restrictions of the time to advance the cause of female journalists. Following this pattern of focusing on the business of the game and the manner in which it was reported at least as much as the action on the field, the work of the editorialists and reporters covering the Brotherhood War both reflected and shaped the tone of the larger conflict as the 1890 season progressed.

Week 4—May 10–16: Good Player-Manager, Bad Business, and Ugly Future

One month into the season, Albert Spalding shared his views about the good and the bad of the baseball business. Arguing against the perception that fans were drawn to the skill exhibited by the players, the president of the Chicago Colts advanced identification as the best reason for fan involvement: "Each set of men is supposed to represent the highest degree of skill that its particular city can get together and residents of that city become identified with, so to speak, and interested in the success or failure of their team." Spalding noted how the Union Association's (UA) attempt to place two teams in one city had failed in 1884 and how it wasn't working in 1890. Bad weather had caused poor attendance for Comiskey's Pirates, whose receipts were estimated at as much as $3,000 below expenses, and Anson's (and Spalding's) Chicago Colts, who were thought to be as much as $2,000 in the red. Despite the NL leader's assertions that only one league could live, Murnane remained optimistic about the PL's operations, while Black's and Chadwick's reports were shaped respectively by the bad fortune of local teams and a dark and dire sense about the future for the members of the "professional fraternity" of baseball players.[36]

The "real surprise of the week," according to Murnane, was the sweep of Comiskey's Chicago Pirates by Ward's Brooklyn Wonders. Resuming his editorial role as PL promoter, the Boston correspondent once again employed culturally coded words and metaphors to imbue the labor leader's performance on the field with a greater significance: "This plucky player deserves great praise for his uphill fight in getting such a team together and handling them the way he is doing at present." Bringing the Brotherhood struggle back to his local scene, Murnane's comparison of the two Boston teams was more detailed as he argued "records go for very little" and analyzed both lineups position by position. Using his experience as a player and a manager, he excused the recent struggles of the Red Stockings with the assertion that "Every team will run up against a snap during the season." Murnane's perspective as a former player also shaped his overall assessment of the differences between the drawing power of the two leagues and the advantages of the PL modifications to the game: the "old stars" who moved to the PL were keeping their "old friends and admirers," the livelier ball of the PL was the source of the increased batting, and that extra 18 inches of pitching distance was leading to a "considerable difference in the curves" being thrown in the PL. To promote the advantages of the PL business model, he previewed the upcoming series between Kelly's Boston Red Stockings and Comiskey's Chicago Pirates that was scheduled for Memorial Day weekend, announcing the plans for special trains from Lowell and Lynn, Massachusetts. Promising a gate of "nearly $5,000," Murnane claimed "the four games will be for blood in dead earnest."[37]

Beyond discussing dollar figures, Murnane remained in his editorial mode as he commented on the way baseball business was being practiced in both leagues. First, he claimed that prior to 1890, only the "magnates" cared about the attendance figures, whereas "[n]ow every ball crank is interested in the number of people who passed the turnstile, and the little table furnished each morning by THE GLOBE is the first thing sought." Contradicting Spalding's opinion and the NL policy, the PL partisan argued that there was enough room for both leagues in the country. In an early recognition of the differences between large and small market teams, he noted how Pittsburgh and Cleveland could not expect to support two teams as effectively as the battlefield cities of Boston, New York, Chicago, and Philadelphia. Still in editorial mode, Murnane noted how the NL attendance was down by just over 100,000 from the previous year and balanced his observations by pointing out that the NL was doing somewhat better because Cincinnati and Brooklyn were improvements over Washington and Indianapolis as baseball towns.[38]

Working in a progressive editorial vein from the labor-friendly Smoky City, Ella Black observed that both Pittsburgh teams were experiencing early-season hard luck, and that no one in either front office was making good decisions. Guy Hecker's Alleghenys youngsters were playing better than before; their games were "splendid examples of good playing but bad luck, and every bit of the bad luck has been traveling in a Pittsburg uniform." Practicing her use of baseball slang, Black described how manager Hecker had been "'finding' the ball as though his eye had been 'on it,'" but an injury had put him on the "retired list," thus giving the veteran Paul Hines another chance at first base. Pitching was the problem for the Burghers: James "Pud" Galvin and Harry Staley had "managed to pitch only two or three good games between them," John Tener had "been hit all over the grounds," and it turned out that Ed Morris "was by no means in the excellent condition he claimed to be in." In fact, many observers thought he had "about run his race, and will either have to give up the diamond for good or else seek the seclusion of a minor league." Black's scouting report was accurate given that Morris went 8–7 with a 4.86 ERA in 15 starts in 1890, his final season in the major leagues.[39]

Meanwhile, as she worked to build her career, Black was doing her best to stay in Chadwick's good favor. The female sports journalist quoted the "most charming" personal letter she received from a well-known "veteran base ball writer" who praised her for her stance against kicking: "I am glad to see that you 'go for the kicker.' Sustain the umpire all you can. If they do not do well keep silent, if the reverse give them praise. That is my way." Perhaps feeling encouraged and confident in the face of such fatherly support, Black closed her column with a sweeping editorial stance regarding the business decisions being made by leaders on both sides of the conflict and a prophetic statement of her own: "The puzzling thing in all of this to me is why it is that good common-sense business men, who in regular business would be careful to do what they knew to be for the best, yet when they get into base ball they commence a throat-cutting suicidal policy, that means their ruin in a very short time." To provide an example of this dangerous policy and show that she was not a partisan writer even though she favored the PL, the female sports journalist disapproved of how the Burghers "tried hard" to arrange a game in Pittsburgh to draw fans away from the Alleghenys-Reds game that was set to take place on one of their off days. Like Murnane, she seemed to be saying that there was room for both leagues to exist without the "petty spite" of driving each other out of business. Once again, the nature of the 1890 conflict encouraged sports journalists to advance their careers by writing about more than just the game on the field. Even the "Gossip" at the end of Black's report could have worked in her favor as she disagreed with Cincinnati writer Ren Mulford over whether her comments about how well admired Tony Mullane was in his bachelor days might upset Mrs. Mullane and promised to send a photo to the editor of *SL* so that her fellow sportswriters might be able to recognize her.[40]

In contrast to the baseball business covered by Murnane and Black, Chadwick's weekly report focused on baseball journalism and provided his *SL* readers with a preview of the persona he would adopt with regularity in the middle of the season. Demonstrating his awareness of the importance of the press, his lead paragraph illustrated how other venues were paying more attention to the significant season of 1890:

> No more striking illustration of the growth in influence and importance of the national game in public estimation could be well afforded than is shown by the attention the proprietors of the leading daily newspapers, the weekly illustrated papers, and the prominent monthly magazines, are devoting to the subject of base ball this year.

Chadwick was especially impressed that "staid magazines like the *Century, Harper's, The Cosmopolitan, Lippincott,* etc." had chosen to devote their pages to discussions and illustrations of baseball. *Harper's* covered only the amateur game and *Cosmopolitan's* baseball offerings were limited to Nichols' satirical short story and an article by his employer; nonetheless, the *Spalding's Guide* editor used this attention from the upper-class monthly magazines as a springboard to launch an editorial stance about the status of the national pastime based on the "latest returns from the seat of war":

> The game is here to stay. "It is not for a day, but for all time," and even the madness of a small minority of its votaries, urged on by leaders who look only to self-aggrandizement in their efforts to "elevate the game" cannot long prevail in temporarily retarding its brilliant career of progress to the point of perfection in its club management, which is bound to be the ultimate result of the labors of the game's best friends in the future.

What started as an observation of the positive influence of journalism quickly evolved into the company line that the NL were the saviors of the game who would prevail against the usurping rebels led by Ward and his band of self-seekers. As the season wore on and the dangers to the game posed by the continuing success of the PL became more apparent to him—and his employer, Albert Spalding—Chadwick would adopt the strident, chiding, and shrill tone of a modern-day Cato the Elder with greater and greater regularity in his editorials.[41]

Working to both get the facts right and support the NL cause, Chadwick advised his colleagues as well as the players. Noting how he had "laid down the law governing double and triple plays in 1859" when there were nearly as many "strikers" playing cricket as "batters" playing baseball, the veteran writer publicly disagreed with Murnane's interpretation of a play and took PL supporters to task for rewarding good hitting when the lively ball used by the rebel league was the source of the higher scoring games. Offering another hint of his "Cato the Elder" persona, Chadwick passed along some fatherly words to the players of the PL:

> My advice to players who want to get in out of the cold weather of the ensuing season of 1891 is to secure a situation on the first thoroughly reliable club financially that they can find, either by renewal of their present engagement or by obtaining a new one, for the fall in salaries that is bound to come next year, as a result of the Brotherhood revolt, will fall like a sudden storm on the great majority of so-called star players.

Anticipating that the market would be glutted with younger, less expensive players who had been seasoned during the costly war, he addressed the rebels, whose "engagements" were not with what he considered to be "thoroughly reliable" clubs financially, to "get in out of the cold, boys, while you can and when you can." Somehow, when Chadwick used the familiar term of "boys" for the players, it had a different feel to it than

2. Early Season

when Murnane used the same term. The veteran writer's use of "so-called" further demonstrated the cultural resistance to the idea of players as celebrities.[42]

Four weeks into the season, Murnane, Black, and Chadwick settled into the roles they would play and the topics they would discuss in the weeks ahead. Working with the assumption that the PL model was a good one, Murnane acted as a promoter for the new league. Following Spalding's policy that most cities could only support one team, Chadwick began to adopt an editorial role that would soon have him calling for the destruction of the PL with each of his weekly reports due to the bleak future its presence created. Faced with covering two under-achieving teams, Black criticized the play and front office decisions of both teams, as well as the leadership of both leagues. Whether or not sportswriters adopted T. H. Murnane's avowed (though not always practiced) strategy of covering the good they saw in baseball that year, the stances and messages would show more change in the weeks ahead.

Week 5—May 17–23: Comparisons on the Field, in the Front Office, and in the Press

Near the end of May, both the PL and the NL saw the beginnings of interesting pennant battles. In the PL, three different teams occupied first place over a three-week span; Ward's Wonders lived up to their name by leaping over both Boston and Chicago. In the NL, Philadelphia led the standings, with Brooklyn, New York, Chicago, and Cincinnati all within two games of first. Despite the benefits of American hero worship and Richter's assertions that the PL was financially sound and operating a model campaign, the new league's per-game average attendance dipped to just 2,373, while the NL's held steady at just over 1,500. Even as the total PL average declined, New York (+ 88 percent), Pittsburgh (+ 50 percent), and Philadelphia (+ 24 percent) experienced total growth compared to the year before, according to Clarence Dow's weekly statistical roundup in the *Globe*, while Cleveland (-19 percent), Chicago (-10 percent), and Boston (-6 percent) all supported Spalding's assertion about the inability of battleground cities to support two teams. With

Chicago proving to be a "dead card" due to an average attendance of just 861 and Pittsburgh's PL attendance hovering just over 2,000 compared to the embarrassing NL average of 413, these conflicting data, along with the assertions that the NL was "working" their attendance figures in contrast to the paid tickets being counted in PL cities, led Black, Chadwick, and Murnane to advance their various causes by making active comparisons between the two leagues as the 1890 season neared the quarter pole.[43]

Traveling to Brooklyn to visit a sick relative did not prevent Ella Black from editorializing about decisions made by both Burghers backer George McCallin and J. Palmer O'Neill, who, as the "nominal head" of the local NL franchise, suggested that the two leagues would benefit if they could be induced to "pool their issues." Naming particular examples, the Pittsburgh correspondent compared the listless, discouraged play of the NL club to the effective fielding and hitting of the Burghers and commented on the poor press given to Alleghenys second baseman Fred Dunlap and the lack of attention given to Pud Galvin's non-existent support during his starts. Black questioned O'Neill's decision to release Dunlap to save $2,000 in payroll, as well as McCallin's move to rent Exhibition Park to a circus that damaged the infield. Not satisfied with meting out criticism for local officials, she accused magnates in both leagues of talking too much and once again expressed surprise at their cut-throat policies: "Now it strikes me it would be much more to the point if these gentlemen would leave the talking to the women, and instead devote themselves to trying to lift base ball back to the place it used to occupy." Echoing O'Neill's suggestion, Black stepped into the role of peacemaker when she suggested that both leagues would be better served by an "amicable arrangement" that would allow them to "work harmoniously together." Perhaps the Pittsburgh correspondent was still upset from her unsuccessful attempt to use her *SL* credentials to get into Brooklyn's Washington Street Grounds. The ticket taker was familiar with her work and expressed surprise that she was indeed a woman, but wanted to check with President Byrne or some other official before letting her in as a member of the press. Since it was close to game time, she paid her way in to avoid further "red tape."[44]

In contrast to Black's evaluation of both leagues, Chadwick and Murnane drew comparisons to promote the league they favored and to rebut each other. Chadwick reported that more of the NL games were

2. Early Season

won by smaller margins: by May 21, the NL had 56 single-digit victories and 19 double-digit victories to 35 and 41 respectively for the PL. Once again, the *Spalding's Guide* editor blamed the livelier "Brotherhood ball" and argued that a greater number of the NL games were more interesting to watch due to the smaller margin of victory. Writing for the *Globe* one day after Chadwick's comments were published in *SL*, Murnane appeared to be offering a direct rebuttal to his Brooklyn colleague when he asserted that the ball in 1889 seemed "plenty lively" and that the PL, "with the greatest ball players the game ever produced, find it impossible to play one of these [1 to 0] games, showing how foolish it is to try and compare the leading organizations of the country unless pitting them against each other for a series of games." Murnane went on to distinguish the established players of the new league from the NL's "colts." Observing how "Batsman are born, but fielders can be educated to a certain extent," the player-turned-sportswriter went on to answer Chadwick's comments with a close analysis of the batting styles of Kelly, Brouthers, Anson, and other stars to show that "it has often been tried, and always found to be a big mistake, to try and change a batsman's style." Concluding his rebuttal, Murnane argued that while the young players coming up in both leagues had the makings of able fielders, they "have much to learn before they make the ninth part of a combination necessary to get the best results."[45]

All three writers had criticism for their fellow journalists. Extending his PL promotion to the press, Murnane admonished Boston writers for giving too much unwarranted attention to the Beaneaters: "Take, for instance, a team at the bottom of the list, playing a losing game, and yet getting columns in the daily papers. Making mountains out of mole hills is just about as reasonable as making phenomenal ball players out of second-class men." The "double journalism" practiced by the *Globe* and other Boston papers could have been the source of what Murnane took to be over-coverage, thus marking the beginnings of today's "sports media complex." Proving himself a one-man forerunner of the Elias Sports Bureau once more, Chadwick could not help pointing out an oversight made by *SL*'s editor, Francis Richter: "I see that you forgot to make the correction in my last letter relative to the New York 13-inning game being the next best record to that of the 24-inning Harvard-Manchester game. I forgot the game I witnessed in 1879 when the Providence and Chicago clubs played 17 innings without a run." At that point in his career, Chadwick could no doubt claim he had forgotten more than most of the second-generation writers had learned to that point. Reminding her readers of the social restrictions that kept her from mixing with ball players, Ella Black replied to Ren Mulford's allegations that she was unknown to the Pittsburgh players and offered a hint to her eventual disappearance from the pages of *SL*: "So long as I can write base ball and not make myself conspicuous, all right; when I cannot do so I shall stop writing."[46]

One month into the 1890 season, Chadwick, Black, and Murnane all honed the underlying messages of their *SL* reports to compare the action on the field, in the front office, and in the press. Even as she advanced her cause as a female sportswriter, Ella Black remained impatient with poor play and bad decisions by both leagues. Despite offering a sound argument that numbers alone could not serve as an adequate basis for comparison of two very different products, both Chadwick and Murnane were guilty of cherry-picking statistics and other evidence to support their arguments and comparisons that promoted their separate partisan causes. As the season's first holiday approached, both leagues looked to large turnouts on Memorial Day to revive ticket sales and cover gate guarantees, creating expectations that led to even more pointed comparisons and judgments about the health of the game.

Week 6—May 24-30: Quarter Pole Assessments by Players, Magnates, and Writers

At the end of May, both leagues brought out their big guns to turn up the war rhetoric. *SL* devoted almost two full columns to the "hot shot" exchanged between Albert Spalding of the NL and Frank Brunell and E. B. Talcott of the PL. Spalding cited the NL's 14-year history and made dire predictions, while Brunell and Talcott answered their rival magnate point by point. The standings of both leagues did not compete for press attention because Boston and Brooklyn were distancing themselves from the rest of the PL while Philadelphia, Brooklyn, and Cincinnati sat atop the NL. Given the net gain of almost 100,000 fans from 1889, Clarence Dow refuted Chadwick's claims that interest in the national game was declining. As the leagues moved past the landmark

2. Early Season

of Memorial Day and prepared for the middle of the season, Chadwick took cues from Spalding's views while Murnane looked to the players to assess the progress of the conflict.[47]

Spalding's uncharacteristically extensive and gloomy remarks to the press borrowed terms from the editor of his *Guide* while providing a model for Chadwick's *SL* reports for the remainder of the summer. The magnate stood by the NL's record, citing its successful campaign against "demoralization" in its "many guises—crooked base ball, dirty work on the field, rough elements, want of discipline, lack of confidence," which had characterized the NA in the earliest years of professional baseball according to Chadwick. Spalding's dire fears for the future of baseball were later echoed by his loyal employee, and the magnate also predicted that the PL would blend the distinctly different business models of the AA and the NL:

> I can see clearly the outlines of the future. If the PL lasts there will be 25-cent base ball, Sunday games, beer will flow in the grand stands, and the industry will be ruined by utter destruction as the grand finale of the play. The League, I promise you, will hold on until it is dashed against the rocks of rebellion and demoralization. I stand ready to go out of the business and wash my hands clean of it all when the hour comes.

While equating the PL with the lower-class operation of the AA, Spalding contributed to the tone for Chadwick's new persona by claiming that only the complete "withdrawal of the PL from the field" would lead to the salvation of the game. The usually taciturn sporting goods magnate went on to admit that the best-paying NL teams were only making "about enough to pay traveling expenses, advertising, and other incidentals of putting the game on the field, exclusive of salaries." Finally, his prediction that rain on Memorial Day would sink the PL by the end of June invited Richter to compare him to Ezekiel Stone Wiggins, a theorist and educator who was known as "the Ottawa Prophet." Despite threatening weather in Boston on Memorial Day, 1,802 fans turned out for the game between Kelly's Red Stockings and Comiskey's Pirates, while just 340—"the smallest crowd ever seen at the South End grounds"—came out to see the Beaneaters take on the Reds. Contrary to Spalding's predictions, it was the Boston Triumvirs who lost money on Memorial Day because the gate receipts failed to cover the guaranteed money that was given to the visiting team. The crash that Spalding was looking for did not occur because the Memorial Day attendance of the two leagues combined to bring in 26,243 more fans than the year before, with the PL playing to 11,408 more fans, perhaps leading to an even greater sense of urgency in the missives of the magnate and his editor.[48]

Replaying the sentiments expressed by his employer earlier in the week, Chadwick filled his editorial with praise for the NL and stepped up his attacks on their rivals. Illustrating his contribution to the contemporary culture's love of numbers with an extensive analysis of the NL pitching that ignored the PL altogether, the *Spalding's Guide* editor continued to treat the NL's counterpart as if it did not exist, except to denigrate its "double umpire system," lively ball, and recent lawsuits, or to advance his argument against "picked nines" after Comiskey's Pirates lost seven of eight games in the east. In contrast, Chadwick had much nicer things to say about Cap Anson, who was in town to play the NL Giants:

> What a right royal welcome Old Fidelity Anson received from the friends of the League last Saturday at the Polo Grounds. It had such an effect on him that he almost forgot to kick. Had he gone through the game without a talk with the umpire the patrons of the game would have said "that can't be Anson, surely." When Anson retires from the base ball world his last words will be:—"Mr. Umpire, I object."

Ironically, Chadwick followed this bemused tolerance of Anson's most well-known trait with an expression of his desire for umpires to regularly invoke the one-minute rule designed to curb kicking. Beyond providing an early example of special treatment for star players, Chadwick promoted Anson as an employee who had showed the proper appreciation to his own employer by remaining loyal to the NL. The *Spalding's Guide* editor demonstrated his loyalty to the same employer and the prophet function within the editorial role by making a dire prediction of his own about the business of the game: "Not a dozen leagues will be in the professional arena in 1891, where there are twenty now, and hundreds of players will be seeking employment at one-fourth the salaries they are now getting. Verily the sowers of the Players' strike in 1889 will reap the whirlwind in 1891." Adding a Biblical element to the voice of the ancient Roman senator, Chadwick thus stepped into his Cato the Elder persona to call for the end of the PL, but not before offering a backhanded compliment to the Philadelphia Quakers of the PL for holding a benefit to help Harry Wright with his medical bills, calling it "the one bright spot in their brief record."[49]

2. Early Season

While Spalding and Chadwick were shaping the NL rhetoric for the summer months ahead, Murnane conducted interviews that functioned as attacks on the NL and promotions for the new league. When interviewed during a trip to Boston to play the Beaneaters, Cap Anson adopted his employer's company line: "'The Brotherhood can't possibly live,' said Ans, 'as they are losing money too fast, and can't stand it like the old League.'" Loyal Anson refused to budge from his position even though Murnane could name "a couple dozens" backers of the PL who were prepared to support the new league. The Boston writer had more "hot shot" for Anson later in the same report when he compared the relative strengths of the Chicago teams: "When I think of the vast difference in the playing of the two Chicago teams, I am sure that my old friend Anson is a dead bird. Anson would be lucky to win one game in five against the Brotherhood team." Murnane further slighted the Chicago captain by appearing to question his resolve on the field: "Hutchinson, Burns, Wilmot, Anson and Cooney are good ball players, but even they lack the nerve to play good, hard ball, with the exception of Anson and Cooney." Despite Murnane's last-minute qualification, his "old friend" could not have been pleased to be lumped with rookies (Cooney), four-game wonders (Hutchinson), and aged veterans (Burns).

The Boston writer reported a similar Spalding-directed argument by Gus Schmelz, who was in town to lead his struggling Cleveland Spiders against the middling Beaneaters: "'We've got you dead. You can't live. The League has the money.'" In response, Murnane "gently called him down" by refuting the NL's company line again:

> You must have been reading Al Spalding's interviews where he is trying to keep the League's spirits up. You don't want to think I am going to print the "gush" you are now giving out so freely. Oh, no. You might cut it out and send it to the Cleveland magnates. Gus, old man, as the little boys say, you are talking "tru" your hat.

Providing his readers with a view of the game that Black could not and Chadwick chose not to use except in rare occasions, Murnane's interviews served as groundwork for future sports journalists even as they may have earned him censure by the profession's critics for giving extensive press to men associated with a trivial endeavor.[50]

In contrast to his work to counter NL rhetoric, Murnane's interview with Fred Pfeffer, who was pitching for Comiskey's Chicago Pirates, promoted the PL while revealing inside information about the business of baseball and the formation of the Brotherhood. In 1889, Pfeffer held stock in Spalding's Chicago team at the same time he was a player. Pfeffer claimed that "A. G. Spalding knew all about the classification scheme while on the trip around the world" between the 1888 and 1889 seasons. Since he was a stockholder, Pfeffer was privy to various schemes planned by Spalding, even though the player maintained that his "interests were with the players first, last, and all the time." Once the plans for the PL were formed, Pfeffer claimed to have lost money because he was afraid the sale would attract attention and tip off the NL to the Brotherhood's plans. After the new league was announced, he said he was happy to get $300 per share even though he took a total loss of $2,500.[51]

Once the initial excitement and novelty of the new season wore off, the worst fears of the NL magnates were confirmed: the public preferred the known quantities of the star players found in the PL to the untried personnel of the NL, despite its pedigreed history. As much as the attendance numbers could be trusted, they supported that observation in places like Boston, where almost four times as many fans turned out for the PL games on the Saturday and Monday of Memorial Day weekend. In addition to "papering the house" with free tickets and inflating attendance numbers to make their positions appear stronger, both leagues took the fight to the press, even though the strategy threatened to "talk base ball to death," in PL Secretary Frank Brunell's words. The NL maintained their stance as the established league and questioned the origins of the PL, and the PL maintained their attack on the reserve rule, the classification system, and other labor tactics that limited the options of the players. Both were equally adamant that only one league would be standing in 1891. Due to the impatience of the "moneyed men" backing the PL, Spalding's prediction was ultimately correct, though his timing was off by five months.[52]

As their early season reports progressed, the roles that Henry Chadwick, T. H. Murnane, and Ella Black would play in the conflict became clear. Chadwick would champion the NL in all ways, as exemplified by his blind assertion that Ella Black would have been treated well had she mustered the courage to speak to Bridegrooms President Byrne during her visit to Brooklyn in late May: "She should have asked to see Mr. Byrne, who would have been glad to show her every attention, as he is the most gallant of the League magnates." Murnane's faith in the PL was equally strong as demonstrated by his use of a boxing image to credit the new league for providing the players with a greater stake in the business of the game: "I tell you the season is young, and the League will quit when losing money before the PL, for the simple reason the cream of the talent have their heart in the fight, and won't quit while they see their opponents staggering in the ring." While Chadwick and other members of the "baseball writer's fraternity" appeared to have accepted Ella Black as a fellow member, Murnane was among the scribes who still questioned the legitimacy of her efforts, forcing her to take every opportunity to prove them wrong. Even though she remained loyal to her cause to prove that women could indeed write about the game with the same level of intelligence and insight as men, she proved to be less of a partisan than either Chadwick or Murnane despite her avowed support for the labor cause of the players. As the season of 1890 wore on week by week, all three sporting journalists advanced their positions, demonstrating the significance of the Brotherhood War to the development of the players' celebrity status, the business of the baseball, and the evolution of sports journalism—all while helping to write the game into American culture.[53]

3

Mid-Season

Going to Extremes and Staying the Course

When May gave way to June, sportswriting partisans for the NL and PL went into attack mode as both leagues started to lose money. Rumors had the Pittsburgh Alleghenys moving to Indianapolis or anywhere else that they could draw better, and the debts of the club were reported to be as much as $65,000. The team's ownership group was ready to sell if a buyer could be found, and the NL directors were called to New York to discuss the situation. A. G. Spalding was in enough of a dither to be credited with asking nonsensical questions: "Am I I, or am I somebody's first cousin?" and promising that the NL would fight the PL "until one or the other was dead." By the end of July, the Brotherhood War had dragged on long enough that the game's fans grew weary of the conflict. The situation in Pittsburgh had gone from "worse to worse" with the average Alleghenys attendance dropping to 376 per game in contrast to the reported 2,452 of the Burghers. Worst of all, allegations that the players in both leagues were imbibing "too freely," especially when on the road according to reports from Cincinnati, did nothing to improve baseball's public image. The PL was determined to carry on with the fight; Ward, Ewing, and Kelly reportedly laughed at any talk of compromise with the NL. In response to the ongoing conflict, sportswriters became more critical on all three fronts: the players and the product on the field, the business decisions being made in the front offices, and their fellow journalists.[1]

As the 1890 season settled into the familiar daily grind of games, travel, and deadlines, baseball journalists worked to find stories to cover. Stacked teams like Comiskey's Chicago Pirates, the questionable customs of "kicking" and "bulldozing," and controversial players, like NL Giants shortstop Jack Glasscock and King Kelly, remained as targets for ink. The presence of the Brotherhood War, however, upped those stakes as the season progressed. The performance of highly touted teams and the presence—or absence—of "kicking" was linked to the attendance figures. Writers also questioned whether certain players were worthy of the press attention they received. In battleground cities, partisan writers used all of these elements to play the local teams against each other, often blending fact and opinion at will in the custom of war correspondents. As the attendance figures started to drop, the critiques of the players and the game became higher in urgency and tighter in tone as some of the writers worked to make baseball "resonate with the dominant social classes."[2]

The sense of urgency was additionally reflected in the work of the sportswriters when they turned to covering and editorializing about the business of baseball as much as, if not more than, reporting the action on the field. Writers examined the gains made by amateur baseball in response to what Chadwick termed the "Kilkenny cat business" to describe the conflict between the NL and the PL. Others reported on syndicate rumors, compromise talk, and stories that looked ahead to the 1891 season. Given the larger trend within the field of journalism toward covering news with economic impact, the shift toward extensive coverage of front office affairs marked an important transition in sport journalism. Further, the cooperative nature of the PL in response to the restrictive practices of the NL capitalists gave some of the coverage a progressive flavor as the sports journalists worked to uncover the economic and political power structures at play within the game of baseball that were highlighted by the Brotherhood War.[3]

In the pages of *Sporting Life* (*SL*) and the daily newspapers in the battleground cities, the middle of the season brought an increased awareness by sportswriters of each other's work. Whether writers met in the press boxes or in hotel lobbies or engaged in print feuds that no doubt helped drive up the circulations for Richter and other editors, the fraternity of sportswriters was as close-knit as the community among ballplayers before the 1890 conflict. Contributing to the development of journalism as a profession, the sportswriters battled the genteel bias against giving undue attention to something as trivial as baseball and baseball players while working to combat gossip and sensationalism with truth, accuracy, and a sense of ethics. Just as the Brotherhood War acted to remove baseball from the curiosity shop largely occupied by "fanatics" and "cranks" of the game, the more serious subject matters lent a new gravity to baseball writing and sports journalism within the larger efforts of the practitioners of the profession.[4]

In keeping with the above trends, Chadwick, Black, and Murnane all mounted special attacks to advance their individual agendas. Using his Roman persona to prevent permanent harm to the game, Chadwick went on the offensive in an attempt to return baseball to the path toward a "millennial age" where it would be accepted by the "best class of patrons." Becoming equally as aggressive in his criticism of Spalding and the NL magnates, Murnane advanced the complimentary ticket issue as a barometer for measuring the unreliability of the opposition. Remaining non-partisan as she evaluated both the NL and the PL, Black sought legitimization by meeting with Chadwick and entering into a print feud with Murnane. While the business side of the game was the focus of all three writers during the middle of the season, they all worked for validation: Chadwick for his ideal future of the game, Black for her social project, and Murnane for the PL in general and the Red Stockings in particular.

Week 7—May 31–June 6: Picking on Comiskey and the Alleghenys' Front Office and Picking-Off Miss Ella

The attendance figures in early June refuted Spalding's and Chadwick's claims that interest in the national game was on the wane: Overall attendance for both leagues to that point in the season was up by 116,000. If, as T. H. Murnane and others contended, the NL was indeed "papering the house" to inflate their figures with free tickets, the practice only kept their per game average at half of what it was the year before (1,468 in 1890 vs. 3,028 in 1889). Memorial Day came and went and, despite the dire predictions, the PL was still afloat, so Spalding and the NL began looking for signs that the new league would founder by Fourth of July, the next milestone date on the game's business calendar. Each of the *SL* correspondents maintained a critical stance toward the game and its players; however, they took different routes toward expressing their individual messages.[5]

3. Mid-Season

Trading his Greek toga for Roman robes, Chadwick attacked what he saw as the weaknesses and failures of the Brotherhood cause. The veteran sportswriter denounced what he called "the picked nine" of the Chicago PL franchise, blaming the slow start of Comiskey's team on the fact there were stars at several positions from the previous season's St. Louis Browns of the AA and Chicago White Stockings of the NL. The Chicago Pirates were just above .500 at 15–14 and the supposed all-star team was not drawing well at home, averaging just over 1,650, far below the PL average of 2,420. These numbers perhaps lent merit to Chadwick's analysis, yet Murnane's report that the Pirates "took away $3,300 for their share of the three games" in Boston would have countered NL partisans' claims that the PL teams were not meeting expenses. This example illustrates how both writers combined references to a star player with the performance of his team at the box office; only Murnane, however, had regular access to dollar figures from the front offices due to his more consistent role as a reporter.[6]

Remaining in an editorial mode, Chadwick blamed the new league indirectly when he suggested that the "quarreling professional base ball factions" were opening the door for an increased interest in amateur baseball. Building on that allegation, the Brooklyn correspondent indicted the PL further when he argued that the different policies between the two leagues created "a divided interest," interfered "with the catering to the best class of patrons," and left "the professional issue in a demoralized condition, with ultimate bankruptcy staring the majority of the clubs in the face." The threat of insolvency prompted Chadwick to play the prophet and predict a time in the near future when there would be "two great National and American leagues in the West and two in the East, each playing for its own pennant up to the close of August." Although he was eventually proved correct about the two leagues, the cost savings and the shorter season he imagined were not realized. Training his sights on members of the press who supported the PL, the Brooklyn correspondent decried the practice of sportswriters taking issue with the calls of the umpires: "The newspaper attacks on umpires is not criticism; it is simply vulgar, prejudiced abuse by red hot partisans, who, for the life of them, cannot see a fair decision or a correct one which tells against the home club." Chadwick might have had Murnane in mind because the *Globe* writer had remarked that NL umpire Sandy McDermott "couldn't make the League men win, as their hits were 'as scarce as hair on a blacksnake's back'" in his previous report. Working both explicitly and implicitly, Chadwick thus sought to discredit the new league on all three fronts: players, business, and press.[7]

Writing from Boston while the PL-leading Red Stockings were on their second eastern swing, Murnane went on the offensive as well. After the Pittsburgh Alleghenys lost three out of four to the Beaneaters in Boston, the player-turned-sportswriter called Hecker's Alleghenys "the weakest team that ever took the people's money at the South End grounds." Murnane's *SL* column mentioned the presence of Alleghenys Director J. P. O'Neill in Boston, along with a mysterious figure named Randall, but his *Globe* column was much more critical, claiming the Alleghenys' debts to be $65,000 with O'Neill aspiring to be the manager. Murnane profiled "Detective Randall" as well, describing him as being in the NL's employ for the purpose of "keeping tabs on the Pittsburg management in the interests of the league."[8]

Turning away from the dime novel plot, Murnane came out strongly against the leaders of the NL, laying the blame for the conflicting schedule at their feet and offering a commentary on Albert Spalding as a self-made man: "While the PL go along doing the best they can, their old masters are hunting for a place to 'load the mine.' "Rather see the game go to smash than allow the Players' quarters," is Al Spalding's cry. That is generally the way with a man who started out empty handed." Speaking with direct experience about how the Horatio Alger story candidate had been looking out for himself since organizing the first baseball exhibition tour to Europe in 1874 to scout the sporting equipment business opportunities there, Murnane pointed out how Spalding was declaring war against some of his fellow players and responded as a former player himself:

> "It's now war to the knife," says Spalding. Who ever thought that such a level-headed business man could make such a declaration? I'm not a player, but if I was you can bet I would play until my toe nails dropped off before I would weaken or give one iota to men who shoot off their feelings in the above manner.

The *Globe* writer concluded his analysis by claiming there was enough room—and enough cities—in the country to support both leagues, with the larger markets of Boston, New York, Chicago, and Philadelphia being

3. Mid-Season

home to two teams, and the smaller ones "looking out for one team each." Brooklyn clearly fell in the latter category. Due to the efforts of Chadwick, Donnolly and other NL scribes who were writing against Ward and his Wonders, the City of Churches was a "dead cock in the pit" to Murnane, perhaps because there were not enough upper-class patrons there to support teams from two top-flight leagues. In the end, the *Globe* writer assured his readers that the men connected with Ward were "not easily frightened, and will stay long enough to see Ward and his team get the patronage they deserve."[9]

Perhaps to prove that he was not writing his "screeds" as a pure PL partisan, Murnane editorialized that he was "fully satisfied" that Ward and Ewing were making a big mistake in adopting the new practice of ladies' day in Brooklyn and New York: "The fair sex pay to go to the theatre, and why should they expect to see the high-priced base ball games without paying for the privilege? The ladies have always attended the games well in this city, and would scorn the idea of a free blow-out." Elsewhere in the same column, Murnane showed he was aware of Black's presence by asking *SL* editor Richter what his "lady correspondent" thought of the new practice. Even though he asked for Black's opinion, the question was likely rhetorical, as future exchanges between the two sportswriters would soon illustrate.[10]

When the Alleghenys went 5–19–1 on an extended road trip that lasted more than a month and then lost three straight to Anson's Chicago Colts, Ella Black did not bother to hide her sarcasm. Perhaps because it was the only baseball in town until the Burghers returned, Black occupied "her old seat" at Recreation Park even though the Alleghenys led both leagues with fewest wins (nine), most losses (27), and lowest average attendance (441), and reported the depth of their inept play: "Such a magnificent exhibition of fumbling, muffing and weak hitting it has not been my lot to see very often in this world, and such a dose as that of last Monday I do not care to have repeated if I can help it." Demonstrating her neutrality as a sportswriter, she praised Anson's team for being "made up of *real* ball players, while the Pittsburgh team—well, it is better to draw the curtain and say nothing at all about the larger part of its make-up."[11]

Black was equally critical of the local NL club's business situation. The *SL* correspondent claimed that John L. Sullivan was outdrawing the Alleghenys, even though the boxer was appearing for only a few minutes each night on a Pittsburgh vaudeville stage. Not impressed with the promised changes brought by "Mr. Director J. Palmer O'Neill," who had recently taken over control of the Alleghenys, she found fault with how he was bringing in new players, releasing old ones, playing George Miller all over the diamond, and sending "Sir Guy Hecker" into the box to pitch for his spot on the team even though the player-manager was primarily a first baseman at that point in his career. Help did not come from the NL front office either; four more home games with the Reds were moved to Cincinnati, which was outdrawing Pittsburgh by eight to one at that point.[12]

Still seeking validation as an aspiring sports journalist, Black defended her identity and her work against attacks by her fellow writers yet again:

> So an Eastern paper has announced that another of our local writers is the party responsible for my letters. Well, if they only keep it up long enough they will have all the Pittsburgh writers blamed for doing it. In the meantime I am compelled to stand to one side and see others get credit for my poor efforts.

With a little less wry humor, she answered Chadwick's previous questions directly, claiming she "did not have the courage to face the press box in Brooklyn" during her recent trip to the East. Revealing that she would be in Brooklyn again the following week, she mentioned her plans to call on him, proving that Chadwick, Murnane, and Black were keeping tabs on each other.[13]

At the start of the summer months, all three writers also sharpened the focus of their commentary on the season unfolding before them, naming players, dollar figures, and fellow journalists. Chadwick's attack on Comiskey's picked nine and Murnane's disparaging remarks about Spalding's background, however, were designed to discredit their respective oppositions. In contrast, Black's analysis of the Alleghenys' poor play and questionable management were the work of a neutral observer. At the same time, with a female sportswriter was advancing that opinion, her readers would have noted the tone and degree of her critism. The attacks of baseball writers moved toward white heat along with the conflict between the leagues as journalists began picking convenient data for ammunition and picking fights with each other.

3. Mid-Season

Week 8—June 7–13: Pittsburgh "Surprise" Players, Brooklyn Cherries and Boston Roses for the Front Offices, and Fraternity Fights Within the Press

Boston, Brooklyn, New York, and Philadelphia led the PL in alphabetical order, as noted by Clarence Dow in his weekly statistical roundup for the *Globe*. The Cincinnati Reds were leading both leagues with 30 wins while battling with Philadelphia and Brooklyn for first place, so the NL magnate's cries of "dead game" seemed unwarranted. If anything, the NL needed to look to its own house. Dow's statistics demonstrated how the PL was "having heavier batting and fewer strike outs," while more of the series between the NL teams were marked by batting averages below .200. Charlie Comiskey's fifth-place Pirates were just breaking even at 21–21, but a writer signing himself "Anti-Monopoly" wrote to *SL* to question Chadwick's attack on Chicago's "picked nine" with a spirited defense that the PL Giants could be called the same thing since they were essentially the same team as the 1889 NL Giants. Richter poked further fun at Chadwick with the letter's heading: "A Correction. A Probably Unintentional Mistake by Mr. Chadwick Set Right." The anonymous writer known as "Anti-Monopoly" provided a valuable clue to baseball's "better class of patrons" when he described himself as someone who has "carried the interest in the manly and wholesome sport from his college days into his professional life." Thus assailed from a number of fronts, Chadwick began to be more selective in the material he brought to bear against the PL, while Murnane alternated between promoting the business decisions of the PL and attacking the front offices of the NL. Remaining neutral in her Smoky City seat, Black advanced her case by reporting on the surprises she observed at Recreation Park.[14]

The news in Pittsburgh regarding the Alleghenys was not improving. For Black, the product on the field was proof "that the young blood theory is by no means what it is held up to be," an argument that was supported by the team's last-place 10–32 record. In contrast to the consistent lineups used by Neil Hanlon of the rival Burghers, the few fans in the stands at Recreation Park were treated to a "constant succession of surprises, and no one can tell just what will be done with them next." Nominally, "Sir Guy" Hecker was still the manager, but director J. Palmer

O'Neill apparently continued to try his hand at arranging the players on the field. Fueling "Madame Rumor," Detective Randall was in town and told *SL* that "positively he was here after the managership" of the club. To complete the melodrama developing in the front office of the local NL franchise, there was some confusion over whether the NL or the local directors owned the club. After losing four home dates—and six straight games—to Cincinnati, the Alleghenys lost three more home dates—and three more games—to Anson's Chicago Colts, where the per-game average of 861 had not improved, but was still almost double Pittsburgh's anemic total of 441. Staying with her business coverage, Black reported that O'Neill was planning to petition the league for 20-cent tickets, which would allow him to undercut the PL by a nickel.[15]

In Brooklyn, Chadwick promoted the NL by reporting cherry-picked business data that put the old league in the best light. Returning to the line of attack initiated by Spalding at the end of May, the veteran writer used anecdotal evidence to place more implicit blame on the PL for starting the conflict that led to the decline in attendance because "a large number of the patrons of the professional fields, having become disgusted with the Kilkenny cat business which characterizes the professional leagues now, have gone over to the amateurs." According to the figures published the week before, overall attendance in New York for both leagues had almost doubled from the year before (more than 101,000 in 1890 compared to just under 55,000 in 1889). It was true, however, that attendance was way off for the NL in New York since their Giants were averaging just 945 people per game, well below the 2,389 average from the year before. That fact did not stop Chadwick from disparaging the attendance figures given by George Dickinson of the *New York World*, who was a supporter of the PL: "These are Mr. Dickinson's figures, and, of course, must be correct, for George never, etc. etc." Despite this sarcastic, if not snide, tone with regard to one of his journalistic "brethren," Chadwick showed that he was willing to quote Dickinson at length when the matter suited the NL cause, as was the case when the comparison between the balls used by the two leagues showed that the NL players were able to hit the PL ball as much as 100 feet farther. Dickinson's observation allowed Chadwick to conclude, albeit conveniently, "This does away with the absurd talk about 'the superior batting of the P. L. teams.'"[16]

Moving from covering the players to reporting on the box office,

3. Mid-Season

Murnane alternated between defending the PL and attacking their rivals. In direct refutation to Chadwick's criticism of Comiskey's "picked nine," the former player speculated that the rest of the PL was "laying for them" after the press labeled the Pirates "pennant-winners" and "world-beaters" before the season started. Observing that the Chicago players were discouraged, the former manager further promoted the PL when he blamed the local press for giving so much attention to Anson's Chicago Colts, who were facing a "fifty per cent weaker organization to win from" in the NL. Still in attack mode, Murnane turned to business matters when he observed that "the NL has the Pittsburgh Club to look out for and must stand the losses there this season," even though the Smoky City was usually a good baseball town. Staying with dollars and cents, he quoted Director Billings of the Boston Beaneaters triumvirate as saying, "We are ready to lose $100,000." Murnane liked the chances of that prediction coming true, especially if Boston had to continue to support weak-drawing NL teams like Pittsburgh, Cleveland, and Chicago.[17]

Beyond an increased interest in baseball business both on and off the field, the three writers were watching the practice of their profession—and each other. Murnane answered Chicago sportswriter and NL supporter Harry Palmer's refutation of his statements about the salary of Anson's Colts and the losses incurred by the Alleghenys of Pittsburgh. In doing so, the Boston writer couldn't resist taking a shot at Palmer's boss by questioning his sources and his independence as a journalist: "I would like to know how Harry could expect to get any authentic information, as the only place he goes for ball news is into Magnate Spalding's office, and must naturally write about as Albert says." Continuing to watch the exchange between Black and Chadwick, Murnane wrote, "I would like to see that meeting between Henry and Ella on the Brooklyn grounds. The young lady will find Col. Byrne a gentleman who is not afraid to put himself out to make it pleasant for a representative of the press."[18]

Black proved that she, in turn, was watching Murnane's column. First, the Pittsburgh correspondent defended herself again by claiming it was "hardly fair" to ask a woman what she felt about ladies' day (as Murnane had done the week before) when he had already made up his mind against the practice. Undaunted by the deck stacked against her, she indicated she was in favor of the practice and put her questioner on the spot: "By admitting them free the clubs lose nothing and the presence of the fair sex serves as a magnet to draw many a one of the male gender who would otherwise never think of attending a game of ball. Now, Mr. Murnane, confess that I am right?"[19]

Still demonstrating the communication among sporting journalists, Black documented an unexpected source of validation when she revealed that she had received a letter from "one of the best-known base ball writers in America." While she did not name the author, anyone who was paying attention to the "dead game" rhetoric of the NL would have recognized Chadwick's work. When the Pittsburgh writer quoted the passages advancing the NL line of how the PL had killed the game and warning the Brotherhood players that they would suffer the most in the end, she further demonstrated how the *Spalding's Guide* editor used his Roman persona in private correspondence as well as in letters to *SL*. Mindful of her impending visit with Chadwick, Black nonetheless possessed the confidence in her opinion to question his attack of the PL: "This is the opinion of an authority and while I cannot claim to have had anything like his knowledge on such matters, still I think he is putting it a little too harshly, and the PL will yet show up in better shape than he gives it credit for doing."[20]

While his anti–PL stance was making him a target from a number of perspectives, Chadwick commented on current journalism practices in his *SL* report by adding a verse to a "pome" about the journalist's lot:

> Who writes up all the base ball "stars"
> And gets for them increase of pay?
> Who never tells of their working the bars
> And in return is abused each day?
> The reporter.

Beneath the surprising whimsy of this poetic turn, there was a certain amount of disaffection about the work sportswriters were doing on the behalf of the so-called "stars" to promote them in the press while protecting their public images. Recalling Chadwick's earlier admission that the players did not like him much, it would appear from this poem that the feeling was mutual. What's more, the poem must have done little to endear the players to the veteran writer. Further, the "pome" illustrated the one-sided nature of the press-player relationship. The nature of that relationship would change over the next 25 years to one where the writers were treated better by the owners—in exchange for better press.[21]

3. Mid-Season

The week eight reports showed the 1890 season's journalistic impact on a number of fronts. Turning to alliteration ("Kilkenny cat business") and selective use of statistics, Chadwick further expanded his offensive against the PL by turning the analysis of their own supporters against them. Murnane adopted a similar strategy, both blaming and questioning the Chicago press. The lines between the three writers drew tighter as well with the planned visit between Chadwick and Black and the exchange between Black and Murnane over the practice of ladies' day. Both the tone of the rhetoric and the degree of proximity between the writers would increase in the coming weeks, thus mimicking the conflict between the two leagues.

Week 9—June 14–20: More Brooklyn Cherries for NL Players, Pittsburgh Business Onions, and "A Capital Journalistic Find"

After winning six of eight and traveling 1,000 miles in a seven-day span, the Boston Red Stockings opened up a five-game lead in the PL standings. Murnane's missive did not appear in *SL* that week (likely because he was traveling with Kelly's team); however, his *Globe* report demonstrated the same PL promotion and NL criticism found in his correspondent work. The player-turned-sportswriter praised Old Hoss Radbourn for learning a new pick-off signal and used an interview given by Brotherhood deserter John Clarkson as a source of nineteenth century bulletin board material. When Clarkson claimed that the "slavery cry" did not go over well with the public, Murnane gathered rebuttals from Mike Kelly and Billy Nash. Kelly pointed out how the triumvirs were none too pleased with Clarkson's work (the Brotherhood deserter was injured at that point in the season), and Nash revealed how Clarkson had "worked on him last winter to shake the brotherhood": "Finally, I told Clarkson that I had my price, and when he asked for it I told him $1,000,000 for three years and all of it in advance. That was the last thing I ever heard from this man who was getting well paid for his dirty work." In 1890, a million dollars was not a number that was bandied; that winter, an anonymous bidder had offered that sum to buy the entire NL, and the only baseball player to receive that kind of money was Algernon de

Witt Caramel, a fictional version of John Montgomery Ward who, as mentioned above, appeared in the pages of *The Cosmopolitan*. For Murnane's purposes, the amount was more than enough to make the Brotherhood deserter look bad for doing the "dirty work" of Spalding and the NL. Ella Black's visit to Brooklyn dominated her and Chadwick's reports. Despite the mutual validation they found in this meeting, Black expanded the scope of her evaluation of both leagues and Chadwick resumed his cherry-picking in support of the NL.[22]

In response to Clarence Dow and other writers citing the telling fact that two former teams from the weaker AA were leading the NL standings, Chadwick's answer was to do some more cherry-picking. Paying more attention to the PL than he had up to that point, he created tables for the pitchers in both leagues to demonstrate the superiority of the NL hurlers. Returning to the folly of "picked nines" and the "plight" of the baseball "slaves," the veteran writer answered "Anti-Monopoly's" letter by reiterating his position that significant seasoning is required because teamwork is not additive in nature. In other words, Comiskey and stars from the 1889 St. Louis Browns, plus Pfeffer and stars from the 1889 Chicago White Stockings, did not immediately equal a superior finished product in the Chicago PL franchise of 1890. Showing the same snarky side he displayed with his earlier "Secession a la Ward" satire, the *Spalding's Guide* editor went on to "pitch some hot shot" into the PL tent when he suggested that the following question be added to the list of those asked by census takers: "Were you ever a base ball slave at $5,000 for seven months' play on the ball field etc., etc." As with the snarky attack on PL partisan George Dickinson, Chadwick's use of "etc., etc." stood in for the reminder of a spurious argument that did not merit full explanation.[23]

Back in Pittsburgh after her second visit to the New York City area in less than a month, Ella Black had positive baseball news to report when the Burghers beat the PL Giants to achieve a .500 record. The female correspondent only mentioned attending a Bridegrooms game at Washington Park, but it is likely she attended a PL game in Brooklyn because her report echoed Murnane's praise of Ward's handling of his hastily assembled team. After noting how neither New York team had found an adequate replacement for the Brotherhood leader at shortstop, Black questioned Buck Ewing's signing of his brother John, who had pitched for the Louisville Colonels of the AA in 1889 when the team set a major league record for 111 defeats. At that point in the 1890 season,

3. Mid-Season

John Ewing's 3–6 record wasn't the worst in the league (John Tener of the Pittsburgh Burghers held that distinction with an 0–4 mark), but it did support her assertion that he was "as easy a pitcher as the batsmen of the PL will have to face this year."[24]

Using her visit to Brooklyn to gather information for a rebuttal to Murnane's take on ladies' day, Black quoted Charlie Byrne as a result of her only interview of a team owner: "Why, I would rather have six ladies in my grand stand, than twenty policemen. Where there are ladies you will always find that good order will be kept, and that with but little trouble." According to the president of the Bridegrooms, as many as 400 ladies had been in the stands the day before Black's visit. Speaking from experience, Black maintained her rebuttal of Murnane's idea that ladies' day was bad business by reasoning that "many a one" who got in free "would return and buy tickets in the future once they began to understand the game." What's more, if Black's earlier math was correct, each female visitor from the "better class of patrons" would bring two male escorts, thus making "ladies day" a sound practice on both the business and promotional levels.[25]

Upon receiving a letter from a Cleveland woman who wanted to know how she "ever managed to remember all about the players and what has been done in seasons gone by," Black validated her work by offering insight into her journalistic process. Reflecting the cultural bias against a woman's intellect or perhaps wanting to avoid being labeled a "blue stocking," the female sportswriter called her brain a "very poor one." Claiming to leave the "heads as a store-house" strategy to male baseball writers, Black relied instead upon reference materials she'd collected:

> I have all the various League and Association guides for many years past. I also have a score of every game played by a professional club in this city since the first game played by the famous 1877 team. Then I have several files of old papers, a number of scrap books filled with base ball matter and a large amount of other stuff of a like nature, so it is easy enough to find any point I may want to refer to.

Guides and scrapbooks would have been easy enough to acquire and collect, but the detail about having "a score of every game played by a professional club" in Pittsburgh since 1877 might have raised questions in the minds of her 1890 readers: did she score the earliest games herself or did she acquire them from a sportswriter or a family member (or perhaps someone who was both)? As with many other details—such as being a bad traveler—Black revealed just enough to pique the imagination of her audience.[26]

Beyond making rebuttals, Chadwick and Black each reported on the visit they shared the week before, thus granting Murnane's request to be present for the meeting. After observing how Chadwick was "as quick and active as though thirty years younger" than his actual age (66), Black had the highest praise for how much she learned about baseball in the few hours she spent with the father of the game. Chadwick led off by telling Black he almost thought she was a man. Black forgave him for this observation, even though it was in keeping with the prevailing attitude in which "no one will give a woman credit for knowing how to hold a pencil, hardly, while if she talks about writing, O dear, no, that's an utter impossibility." After complimenting Black's "conversational powers" and "genial disposition," Chadwick tempered his praise of *SL*'s "capital journalistic 'find'" with a back-handed assessment of her support for the PL: "Woman-like, her sympathies are with 'the poor oppressed slaves of the professional arena.' She does not know them yet, but she is not of that narrow-minded partisan class who can see nothing good in the opposition." The ultimate irony here is that the *Spalding's Guide* editor was already well on the way toward establishing himself as just that class of partisan with his new mid-season persona. Perhaps forgetting that the Pittsburgh correspondent had already revealed that she knew how to keep score, Chadwick could not resist the teaching moment and gave her "an insight into the mysteries of shorthand for movements" that she was most likely too polite to refuse. Black's willingness to serve as a pupil matched Chadwick's interest in her work, making the meeting mutually gratifying. As important as this meeting was to each writer, it remains historically significant as the first and only eyewitness testimony to Black's existence and identity.[27]

Week 10—June 21-27: Local Boy Made Good, Chadwick and the Capitalists, and Defending the Cause

By the summer of 1890, Billy Sunday's popularity as an evangelist was "as national as his base ball reputation," according to an unsigned article in *SL*. The fleet right fielder spoke about "the desire of all men for peace and happiness" at Y.M.C.A. meetings in the various NL cities whenever the Alleghenys were on the road, which was often given the number of their games that were moved that season. Sunday, however, was not the only member of the baseball community who mixed religion with the national game. Recognizing Sunday's club as the owners of the worst record in both major leagues at 13–40, Black reported on the conflicted and unhappy dispositions of the local NL fans and broke additional stories in *SL*. While decrying the loss of a millennial age, Chadwick's editorials identified the key issues that he would return to regularly until early September. Stopping just short of preaching the PL gospel, Murnane nonetheless defended the Brotherhood cause in general and the Boston Red Stockings in particular.[28]

Writing from Pittsburgh after her travels, Black reported that nothing seemed to be working, no matter what the Alleghenys management tried. The NL finally approved the 25-cent admission and "one of the best crowds" of the season showed up at Recreation Park, only to be turned away because the arrival of the Cleveland Spiders had been delayed due to a train wreck. More of the home dates with the Phillies were moved to Philadelphia, where attendance was better, but two games were kept with the intra-state rival for Saturday, only to be rained out and replayed on a Monday when far fewer people were able to attend. Worse yet, after weeks of rumors in the papers, no one seemed to know who was in charge of the Alleghenys. The Pittsburgh newspapers had club owner William Nimick in charge, but when Black returned to her "riding the cars" method of journalism and happened to overhear an unscheduled interview of the "little president" by a local reporter, Nimick denied all reports that he was running the club. Reporting how Director O'Neill had been "reduced to the capacity of a manager," she was "alarmed" at the rate he was moving players all over the field and trying out new prospects. Lamenting that Richter would not have the opportunity to see one of the more promising Alleghenys pitchers take the box in Philadelphia, the Pittsburgh correspondent explained how Will Gumbert had "an excellent office position" and was "chary about letting it go to adopt the professional diamond as a regular business." Consequently, the local product planned to pitch only in home games. Gumbert started ten games and won four of them to lead the Alleghenys staff in victories—all the while maintaining his more secure, and thus more appealing, day job.[29]

At the end of June, Chadwick supported his validation cause by going into full attack mode. Adopting his Cato the Elder persona, the *Spalding's Guide* editor once again blamed the players for the revolt and the strife it brought, and claimed they were still slowing "the advance of the professional class toward a millennium period." As if it were not bad enough that the ungrateful employees had disrupted baseball's progress toward the ideal age parallel to the paradise promised to good Christians, Chadwick's tone became more dire and strident when he borrowed from Shakespeare to compare the Brotherhood men to a tragic figure from English history: "By the time the fall season is reached the poor duped players will be exclaiming with Richard:—'Now is the winter of my discontent,' without the sequel of the 'glorious summer' King Dick referred to." Taking up his favorite cudgel, Chadwick went into the breach once more against the "kicking which has characterized the contests of the PL clubs" and attacked the cooperative arrangement of the PL as a "false sentiment." Further, he asserted that "the capitalists must have exclusive control of their clubs" and that "any other plan renders financial success impossible." Citing the total attendance figures from June 20, he put the average attendance for both leagues at 1,658 compared to the average of nearly 3,000 per game for the year before. His data conflicted with that published in the *Boston Globe*, which showed a drop in per-game average for both leagues, but a combined average of almost 3,400—and thus a net gain of almost 400 people. Chadwick returned to his amateur baseball argument with figures to show that an average of 3,000 more people per game attended the championship series between Harvard, Yale, and Princeton due to the "Kilkenny cat business." Arming himself with Biblical and Shakespearean references, economic theory, and alliteration, the *Spalding's Guide* editor made use of any and all rhetorical ammunition at hand to deliver his editorial message that the PL must be destroyed if baseball were to return to the path that would take it to the peace and happiness of the golden age he envisioned for it. (See the full text of Chadwick's June 28 report in Part 3 of Appendix A.)[30]

While traveling with Kelly's Boston Red Stockings, T. H. Murnane changed from PL reporter to a defender of the new organization's image against unscrupulous journalists. Kelly's team played an exhibition game in Elmira, New York, on their way west to Cleveland and opened the door for attacks in the press that indirectly promoted the NL by putting the PL in a bad light. The *Globe* writer answered charges made by W.

H. Cahill, *SL*'s local correspondent, that the "rank" play of the Red Stockings caused half of the 1,200 spectators to leave after the fifth inning, which prompted the players to quit the field before the game was finished. Murnane defended his team, his league, and their cause against the "newspaper men" who "thought they saw a chance to kick and send out a few lies that might please the enemies of the PL." From what he saw in the *New York Sun* and the Cleveland papers, they succeeded—as did Cahill, whose report was published right under Murnane's in *SL*. Pursuing the truth and accuracy as journalistic standards, the *Globe* reporter wrote that, as the official scorer of the game, he wanted to "nail" for Richter and his readers the "false statements" that the game was called in the eighth inning and wasn't scored. Further, Murnane indicted the Elmira fans and writers when he opined about how much more difficult it was "to please these backwoodsmen than the most critical lovers of the game in Philadelphia or New York." As if to demonstrate his objectivity as a journalist, the *Globe* writer closed his report with "hot shot" for Secretary Hart: "I am inclined to think it bad business management to play anything but championship games during the season." Providing his readers with another inside look at baseball operations, Murnane reported that some Elmira officials wanted to arrange an exhibition game between the Red Stockings and the PL Giants at a later date and that Hart was nearly "prevailed on" until "the boys kicked and the arrangements were not made."[31]

The week ten reports from Chadwick, Black, and Murnane provided further proof of the hypercritical tone that was developing in baseball journalism as the tensions of the 1890 season mounted. Whether defending her position on ladies' day against male and female colleagues alike or breaking news about the dubious decisions being made in the front offices in both leagues, Black stood her ground and advanced her position as a journalist. Illustrating his partisan qualities, Chadwick drew on references to his fellow English writer to blame the players for derailing a golden age. Remaining more practical, Murnane was changing his stance of PL promoter to Boston Red Stockings booster as Kelly's club looked more and more like league champions. The nature of the conflict, on the field, in the front office, and among their fellow writers, caused all three to sharpen their pencils and do their best work. If the readers of *SL* were looking for these writers to become less partisan as the season approached the Fourth of July, their optimism was premature.

Week 11—June 28–July 4: Calling Down "Pebbly Jack" and "King" Kelly, Syndicate Rumors, More Criticism, and Globe Rebuttals

As the 1890 campaign neared the midway point, observers noted the strength of the eastern teams in both leagues. Once the invasion of the western cities was complete by the end of week 11, the weakness of the western teams in the NL held up as they combined for a 24–37 record at home. More parity existed in the PL, where the western home teams went 31–25, led by Comiskey's "picked nine," who dominated during a 13–2 home stand to move within a half-game of Kelly's first-place Red Stockings. In the attendance war, the PL still held a commanding lead. As much as the attendance numbers could be trusted due to the "papering of the house" and the "cooking of the books" allegedly committed by both sides of the conflict, the new league had just under 60 percent of the total tickets sold as published and was outdrawing the NL in head-to-head competitions in every "battleground" city except Brooklyn, which put them in control of the field on almost every front. The NL was already embarrassed by published reports that had creditors besieging the Alleghenys front office in Pittsburgh for ballpark rent, equipment costs, and advertising fees; nonetheless, Albert Spalding was not too proud to admit women and professional actors to counter the promotions being offered by his crosstown rivals. With the NL appearing to be in trouble, Black maintained her investigative and editorial stances, while Murnane dug in to defend "Kelly and the Boys," who were becoming targets as PL front-runners.[32]

Observing the product on the field in both Pittsburgh ballparks and scouting teams from the New York area, Black showed confidence in offering her opinions and observations about leading players from both leagues. After "several writers saw fit to take up the cudgels on behalf" of John Glasscock in response to her criticism of "Pebbly Jack's" behavior on the field, the female sportswriter held her peace, trusting that "the past would bear out all." Glasscock did not disappoint: during a dispute with the umpire, the NL Giants shortstop "grew so angry over it that he became very profane and was finally ordered out of the game." Aware of baseball's need for a public image that would bring out the "best class of patron," she noted that "Pebbly Jack" was showing bad

3. Mid-Season

judgment to behave in such a way at that point "in the history of the national game when there should be nothing done to disgust the spectators"—especially in a park where such a small turnout would allow every fan there to hear every single oath.[33]

Having gotten a first-hand look at the Boston Red Stockings, Black showed more confidence in her opinions when she assessed the team's travel arrangements and King Kelly's handling of his players. Likely aware of the fact the PL leaders were in the middle of a 6–8–1 road trip, the Pittsburgh correspondent looked to the team's accommodations: "Too much style seems to be the stumbling block." That impediment included the special train car that the team traveled in and the observation that manager Kelly was "too much 'one of the boys' himself to ever be able to hold the others in check." Uninfluenced by Kelly's star status, Black critiqued the Boston manager's habit of making defensive changes in the middle of the game: "To me this looks like a very bad policy, as a man becomes nervous and plays poorly when he knows he is likely to be taken out of the game. It is also hard on the man that is brought in, as he is minus the practice of the man he replaces." Adding more sting to her analysis, Black noted that Ned Hanlon, the manager of the middling Burghers, avoided Kelly's mistake by adopting a policy of leaving a player in the game to redeem his mistake instead of giving him a quick hook.[34]

Rumors of a syndicate and grumblings about the mismanagement of the Alleghenys were in the news in Pittsburgh. John B. Day, the president of the NL Giants, was in town and had "talked very freely, according to the local papers" about the formation of a syndicate within the NL. Without naming which newspapers printed the story, the *SL* correspondent was able to contradict Day's syndicate claims by learning through a proxy that there was no truth to the rumors that the Alleghenys were being kept in business with the help of the league. Once again, Black's journalistic instincts proved accurate since protests of "there's no fire" often indicate the exact opposite. Such was the case as Day's team was losing enough money by the beginning of July that it had to be supported with secret payments from the NL. Noting how the Alleghenys were typically playing to fewer than 200 fans in the home games that were held at Recreation Park, the *SL* correspondent added the lack of off-season efforts to re-sign its players or find better talent to her list of the local management's failures. The talk around the league was that the club had assumed that the other teams would settle for amateur talent or sign older players past their prime to fill in the gaps. Local reports had the Alleghenys planning to keep their home dates for the rest of the season, starting with a series against the Brooklyn Bridegrooms. In order to compete for the fan dollar, the Burghers were planning a "balloon ascension and parachute jump" promotion after the afternoon game on the Fourth of July to boost attendance on that key holiday in the baseball calendar.[35]

In contrast—and perhaps in response, given the date of his *Globe* column—to Black's observations about Kelly and the Red Stockings, PL observer and promoter Murnane had mostly positive things to say about his "boys." The Boston correspondent blamed the poor western swing on the "hard luck" that touches every team over the course of a long season and noted how the sickness of shortstop Arthur Irwin had cost the team the lead they had enjoyed through most of June. Indirectly referencing the accusations of dissipation by the PL, Murnane resumed his argument that the players were taking better care of themselves on and off the field than ever before and praised Captain Kelly in particular for keeping "himself in excellent condition" while "playing the best game of his base ball career." Illustrating the growing celebrity status of baseball players, he related an anecdote in which John W. Kelly, the composer of "Slide, Kelly, Slide," gave an impromptu oration at the train station in Chicago: "'Gentlemen,' he shouted in a loud voice, 'you are God's people, and every one among you is entitled to a kiss from the lips of Chicago's fairest daughters.'" Murnane offered another vote of confidence for Kelly by asserting that he was "such a universal favorite everywhere" because he is "not mercenary and never slow to help any poor fellow in distress." What's more, Kelly claimed that umpires around the country spoke highly of him, even as the King was more effective than any other captain at getting the most from the umpire for his team. By the middle of the season, the Boston correspondent's validation of all things Red Stockings would be tempered somewhat even as the former player identified more strongly with the team, proving that there was "cheering in the press box" in 1890.[36]

As the season neared the midway point, Black and Murnane (and Chadwick, who apparently took the week off), established their journalistic approaches to the stories unfolding before them. In order to be taken seriously as a sportswriter, the Pittsburgh correspondent asked the difficult questions—albeit through a proxy interviewer—and refused to allow her reports to be blunted or colored by the harsh language of a "Pebbly Jack" Glasscock or the growing celebrity status of a "King" Kelly. In contrast to the critical stance of Black, Murnane was moving from PL promoter to Red Stockings booster, both offering excuses for their poor play and contributing to Mike Kelly's growing prominence as a culture hero. As the "Kilkenny cat business" of the baseball war dragged on, the sport journalism of 1890 became more and more relevant to larger social issues as it moved further and further away from the quaint aspects of the "curiosity shop" it had occupied for much of the nineteenth century.

Week 12—July 5–11: Amateur Players to the Rescue, Secret Signings, and Print Feuds

With both sides being accused of using complimentary tickets to "paper the house," commentators were beginning to call the attendance numbers into question, but everyone could see that attendance was down. Commanding 57 percent of the published ticket sales, the PL had proved Spalding wrong by lasting past the Fourth of July, but its per-game average was down by a third from the opening of the season to just under 2,100. Even though the combined daily average was up by almost 25 percent from the NL average in 1889, teams in both leagues looked to cover little more than their expenses in the weeks and months ahead. T. T. T., *SL*'s Baltimore correspondent, suggested "interchange games" between the American and Atlantic Associations to provide the novelty required to bring fans to the ballparks. While this "inter-league" idea was 100 years ahead of its time, it was not of practical help to the NL and PL, who were unwilling to halt their "war to the knife" to schedule exhibition games with each other. The premier leagues had to rely on the pennant races, which were interesting as far as they went. In the PL, Boston lost its hold on first place for just a day to Chicago; the race was more encompassing in the NL, where four teams had at least 41 wins. By week 12, the need to put fans in the seats was on the minds of all three writers, though they addressed the issue differently. Chadwick looked to amateur baseball; Black scooped a story for the 1891 season, and Murnane feuded with the NL and his fellow sportswriters.[37]

Turning away from the "Kilkenny catfight" of the professional circuits, Chadwick reported on the amateur contests he witnessed at the Staten Island Athletic Club on the Fourth of July. The delight he took there in witnessing two pitchers' duels did not prevent him from taking aim at the PL once again:

> In these days of abusive kicking against the decision of player umpires by player magnates; of dirty ball playing and pugilistic encounters and of vulgar rowdy yelling called "coaching" on the professional ball fields, it was a great treat to me to see such a gentlemanly conduct at the hands of the amateur players.... Keep it up gentlemen, and we will soon have an era of amateur ball playing which will make the professional players sorry that they ever entered upon their war against the National League.

As cheered as the Brooklyn writer was by the sight of "a game played on a model diamond field; before an assemblage of society people of the Island" and "the spirit of honorable rivalry" demonstrated by the amateurs, he could not help mourning his belief that the "millennium of professional play is yet in the dim future." Ever concerned that the professional game lacked the quality of audience and character of play he witnessed at the amateur contest, Chadwick looked to an ideal baseball world that included the best patrons in the stands and the best character on the field, as evinced by his praise for Billy Sunday: "Not only is he Sunday in name, but Sunday in his high moral character," marking the speedy orator as a valuable component within the Brooklyn writer's moral war on the Brotherhood that echoed other contemporary press wars.[38]

The Fourth of July gate receipts had swelled the coffers briefly; nonetheless, commentators were beginning to discuss ways to achieve a peace between the warring factions and bring the fans back to the ballparks. After reminding her readers that Spalding and the magnates had created long periods of no baseball in the battleground cities by changing the NL schedule to compete directly with the PL, Black called for the "old league" to "pull in its horns and try to effect a compromise by which both bodies will start the next season in such a way that neither need have a fear of what the outcome will be." Perhaps the most significant sign that the NL was losing ground came when the newest members of the league took Henry Chadwick's advice—and looked for better situations in the PL. Breaking the story that "the present members of the Cincinnati NL Club have all signed PL contracts for the season 1891," the Pittsburgh correspondent went on to report that the other newcomers to the league, the Brooklyn Bridegrooms, were reportedly eager to do the same, but they had "such a kindly feeling" for the team's owner, Byrne, that "they will all be willing to stay as they are now situated." Black did qualify the story by saying that her informant, who was "fortunate enough to wear that article of apparel known as trousers," got the story "from such a source that I cannot help but believe it is true in every particular." Despite missing the opportunity to meet him during his recent trip to Pittsburgh, Black still had the highest praise for the Brotherhood leader: "Ward himself is about the entire team. He covers almost the entire field in doing his field work, and is always to be found where a man may be wanted."[39]

Back in Boston where the Red Stockings were playing host to the western teams of the PL, Murnane editorialized about the attendance situation and took issue with the public's support of players who had deserted the Brotherhood. Claiming that local fans had "no earthly use for the old League" in Chicago and Pittsburgh, the former player joked how the situation was bad enough that "talking base ball to a League magnate seems like rubbing it in." Even the stalwart, dependable Anson was "so thin and drawn up that it would have taken a Turkish bath to have opened his pores." Referring to the Reds and Bridegrooms without the benefit of Black's scoop, Murnane predicted that the NL was "sure to lose some of their best men as soon as their contracts run out." Addressing the "comp" policy, the player turned journalist did not hesitate to call out the NL leaders:

> While the attendance at the Brotherhood games have been swelled somewhat, I find as a rule they have given the count out straight.... Spalding and the triumvirate are giving away more complimentaries this season probably than all the other teams in the country put together. And not satisfied with that are swelling the count on the attendance double and sometimes triple.

Mindful of the well-attended Phillies games, Murnane engaged in an editorial that named names during its pointed criticism of NL players and fans:

> Sometimes I think the public care little for an honest man. For instance, look at how Philadelphia turns out to see a lot of deserters like Thompson, Myers & Co.—men who sold out their fellow-players for a paltry few dollars and didn't even get enough to put up a new house like our Cambridge favorite, John Clarkson. Most of the honest players could forgive a brainless

chap like Glasscock, but for men who expect to live among an honest community to sell out as several did last winter, and then receive the support of the public, I don't know who to blame the most, the traitors or the unthinking public.

Pittsburgh, on the other hand, earned his praise for supporting the Burghers who "struck for principle," highlighting once again the issue of honesty in the labor context.[40]

SL's Pittsburgh correspondent, however, did not escape the *Globe* writer's wrath for the analysis of the Boston captain in her previous report. Even as he defended the "King," Murnane's comment proved that he was keeping a close watch on the female journalist's efforts:

> And that puts me in mind of Ella Black, by the way, whose letters I read with a great deal of pleasure. I see that this lady criticized Captain Kelly for making several changes during a game in that city. The Boston captain was obliged to make the change on account of the sickness of Mr. Irwin. As a handler of a ball team and for being well-posted on the fine points of play Kelly has no superior. And I would respectfully suggest to Miss Ella that she let team work as a study alone until she has had more experience as a player.[41]

And so, in the midst of the Brotherhood War, a journalistic firefight erupted.

By the middle of the season, the focal points of all three writers had shifted. As exemplified by Chadwick's description of the Fourth of July contests, the game on field had become an opportunity to support his argument that the future of baseball was hanging in the balance. Considering baseball's business aspects became the basis for a scoop and a call for compromise that validated Black's ongoing case for her legitimacy as a journalist. For Murnane, his fellow journalists became targets to advance the PL cause and defend his personal heroes. If a contemporary critic had the temerity to suggest to any of these writers that they were working in the toy department, the wrath of Henry Chadwick the Editorialist, Ella Black the Modern Woman, and T. H. Murnane the Booster would have soon followed, as their mid-season reports attested.

Week 13—July 12-18: Calling Down the Burghers, Comp Conspiracies, and Print Predictions

With total attendance for both leagues topping one million during week 13, compared to just over 830,000 for the year before, both sides would have been able to take credit for growing the sport—or creating a compelling fiction—if they had not been at war with each other. Movement in the pennant races might have helped bring fans to the ballparks. Ewing's PL Giants pushed their way into the top half of the league, moving one game ahead of the Quakers, while the Phillies held first place by a half-game over the Bridegrooms and were two ahead of the surging Beaneaters in the NL. R. W. Wright, *SL*'s Cleveland correspondent, joined the ranks of writers predicting a compromise that would combine the PL and the AA to end the baseball war after the 1890 season. Black and Murnane supported their individual causes with predictions of their own (Chadwick taking another week off), with Black looking at the return of the local teams and Murnane examining the NL comps policies.[42]

In sharp contrast to Boston, where both teams were high in the standings, the mood in Pittsburgh was much less bright. After playing well at home against the teams from the East, Hanlon's Burghers were winless on the road that week, losing three to Ward's Wonders, and dropping the first two to the PL Giants. Echoing the opinion of local fans who were "inclined to think the men have too much of a good time while away," Black continued to throw suspicion on the off-field habits by adding her observation that the numbers in the error column routinely climbed when the Burghers were away. The female sportswriter predicted "a very chilly reception" when the team returned because "[t]here can be no question that Hanlon's men are not playing the ball they are capable of, and the public here know it full well."[43]

Still, a "chilly" reception is better than no reception at all, which was what the Alleghenys were facing due to the transfer of their games with Philadelphia to the better paying city. Continuing to cite the mismanagement of the club, Black demonstrated her baseball acumen when she recognized how the Alleghenys were "rapidly approaching the great record made by the Louisville team of 1889, when 111 was the grand total of games lost." Noting that "Sir Guy" Hecker was only in charge of the players on the field, she asserted that the only solution was to give "full and undisputed control" to "a new and competent manager." The Pittsburgh correspondent recommended Horace Phillips, who had managed the Alleghenys to a second-place finish in 1884, when the team was still part of the AA. While local fans might have agreed with her point, they likely remembered that Phillips had to be relieved of his managerial duties in early August of 1889 when he developed a sudden and dramatic mental illness that brought him to claim that "as the sole owner of all the baseball clubs of the country, he proposed to make many innovations in the national game and have it conducted upon a more liberal basis." Ironically, Phillips's supposed delusions anticipated the advent of the PL in a number of regards.[44]

While answering the volley fired by Murnane the week before, Black made another prediction. Under the subhead of "FOR MR. MURNANE," she singled out "Mr. Tim" and defended her position on the management capabilities of "Mr. M. J. Kelly." Refusing to back down to the more experienced writer, the Pittsburgh correspondent claimed it had been a mistake for Kelly to let Dick Johnston go because it left him short in the outfield. After allowing that Kelly was a good player and captain, Black blamed the press for what she deemed was undeserved fame: "His actions on the ball field in this city have never characterized him as being anything more than a ball player of very ordinary merit. Because he talked back to the "bleachers" and because at one time a Chicago correspondent saw fit to boom Kelly and his parrot, he acquired a fame he did not deserve." Showing a resistance to the growing celebrity culture generated by journalists who "boomed" (or promoted) unworthy figures—and perhaps a personal dislike of Kelly's "plebian" tactics for playing to the lower-class patrons in the cheap seats, Black was able to base her argument on her own observations, even if she bowed to "the superior knowledge" of Murnane. Nonetheless, she claimed that "Mr. M. J. Kelly shows he is no manager by the way he runs the Boston Club, and the sooner a first-class manager is engaged by the stockholders the better chance they will have of securing a pennant, but such an article they will never see in Boston while Mr. Kelly is the manager." For all her confidence as a female sportswriter working in an overwhelmingly male profession, "Cassandra" Black missed on that prediction, yet even Murnane would eventually come to agree with her that the Red Stockings won the pennant that year despite Kelly's contributions.[45]

Having little criticism for the excellent product on the field in Boston during week 13, Murnane advanced the PL cause by editorializing against the management of the local NL team. Citing the time when the triumvirs of Boston earned the displeasure of the public "by refusing to admit even the mothers of some of the well-known League players" without charge, the *Globe* writer noted the contemporary irony that "com-

3. Mid-Season

plimentary tickets are as free as water." He put two and two together for his readers and seemed to hint at a "comp conspiracy" when he reported that Beaneaters President Arthur Soden and "Head Magnate" Albert Spalding were in New York at the same time in the middle of July and that "it was after this visit that the free ticket business was taken up in earnest by the magnates." Noting how the NL owners were once "looked on as men well up in business affairs," Murnane claimed they had been "thoroughly outwitted" and described their current state with a rather graphic—and somewhat mixed—metaphor: "Outgeneraled at every turn, they have gone mad and are now cutting their own throats, like swimming pigs, as they manage to keep their heads above water." Beyond calling the practices of the NL Boston management into question, he threw "hot shot" at A. G. Spalding, Boston Beaneaters pitcher John Clarkson, and Harry Palmer, Chicago sportswriter and NL sympathizer. Claiming that the directors of the NL teams in Pittsburgh and Cleveland, J. Palmer O'Neill and Gus Schmelz, knew "more about raising whiskers than good ball players," Murnane asserted that the "two teams should be arrested for taking money under false pretences."[46]

With the comp conspiracy and the weak NL teams in mind, Murnane answered Spalding's predictions and played the baseball prophet himself. First, the Boston sportswriter refuted the NL magnate by claiming that the backers of the PL could see that their best course of action was to stand fast and meet the fight being brought to them by the NL. Secondly, he predicted a "dead loss" for the "old patrons" because "the older they grow the less brains they give indications of having under their hats." Turning to the shape of the post-war league, he supported a ten-team format that took "in all the good ball towns in the country": Chicago, Pittsburgh, Cleveland, Cincinnati, and St. Louis in the west and Boston, New York, Philadelphia, Brooklyn, and Baltimore in the east. Finally, he predicted that "such men as Colonel McAlpin and the solid men behind the PL will not frighten off as easily as two or three of the magnates hope for." History proved Murnane partially right and partially wrong. Regarding his second and third predictions, the NL owners would lose money in 1890, as did the backers and the players of the PL, and after the NL and AA took the field in 1891, the NL was the only professional circuit in 1892 with a 12-team format that included the ten teams he listed, plus Washington in the east and Louisville in the west. Unfortunately for the PL, the Boston sportswriter was proved dead wrong on his first and last prophecies, but those truths would not be revealed until October of that year. (See the full text of Murnane's July 19 report in Part 4 of Appendix A.)[47]

Just over halfway through the season, the players, owners, and writers were looking to the future. Following the lead of Henry Chadwick, who could just as easily be called the "Father of Baseball Writing," the game's writers used the future, as well as the past, as points of comparison for the present. Even as they skirmished in print, Black and Murnane played the prognosticator role. The rookie writer limited her attempts to the present season, while the more experienced sportswriter took on the outcome of the war on several levels. Both writers were consistent in the stances they had adopted—Black basing her view on the data before her and Murnane more driven by the outcome and the post-war world he wanted to see.

Week 14—July 19–25: PL "Sluggers" and "Kickers," "Comps" Investigation, and Print Predictions

As the 1890 season settled into its second half, commentators, Clarence Dow of the *Boston Globe* included, remained in doubt about the reported ticket sales. Attendance was up in Chicago, perhaps due to the aggressive comps policy employed there by Spalding. Fewer than ten NL games had been played at Recreation Park, but Pittsburgh's overall average was up by almost 800 due to strong support of the PL team or "papering" of Exhibition Park (or both). The pennant races contributed to better turnouts in the stronger baseball cities. In the PL, Chicago moved ahead of New York and Philadelphia into third place behind Boston and Brooklyn, who were separated by just one game in the win column. Despite being a 25-cent city, Philadelphia no doubt added to its NL-best attendance by holding onto first place over Brooklyn, which remained the only city where the PL was being outdrawn by a wide margin by the NL. Drawing just over a quarter million combined, the Phillies led the Quakers by roughly 3,700, while the Bridegrooms were ahead of Ward's Wonders by just over 26,000 fans. Indicating Ward's celebrity status as a player and a labor leader, his team was bringing out twice as many fans on the road, placing the Wonders third in the PL behind the star power of the Boston and New York rosters. An impromptu meeting of Ward, Ewing, Kelly, and Brunell in Boston allowed Murnane to report that these Brotherhood leaders were laughing at any talk of compromise between the AA and the PL. In the midst of this talk—or laughter—Chadwick, Murnane, and Black promoted their pet issues: the effects of the changes in the game, comps policies, and the future of baseball.[48]

With the PL showing no signs of "quitting the field," Chadwick editorialized almost frantically to promote the NL cause. Once more, he "boomed" the quality of the game played by amateur leagues in New York and Philadelphia while decrying the "slugging matches" of the PL games: "Deliver me from lively games with double figure scores on both sides. Bad as pitcher games are I would rather see that extreme than the other end, the slugging home run games, with the so-called "splendid batting," in which there is no real batting skill exhibited." Returning to his program to draw the "best patrons" to the game, the veteran sportswriter was pleased to report that the crowds at Washington Park in Brooklyn were "the best in character" in the Bridegrooms' history due to the fact that Byrne, the club's president, had maintained his tough stance against "the vulgar, rowdy kicking" and "noisy coaching" used by managers in the PL. What's more, the *Spalding's Guide* editor's interview with his boss showed that both maintained William Hulbert's original vision that supported the division between the NL and the AA, with the former "representing the principle of catering to the best class of patrons" and the latter appealing to "the masses" through the scheduling of Sunday games, the sale of liquor and 25-cent admission. Relating that Mr. Spalding was "quite satisfied with the marked improvement shown in the form of an increased patronage of the League teams," Chadwick blamed the "heavy batting scores" of the PL again, while managing to overlook the complimentary ticket issue. He also found a way to turn the racist attitude of the players in the Atlantic Association against the new league:

> The glorious inconsistency of objecting to a gentlemanly colored man in a team, while making no objection to the presence of so many white "toughs," "roughs," and drunkards, who have been allowed for years to bring disgrace on the fraternity, is one of the absurdities of the existing condition of things in the base ball world.

Although the color line had been drawn in professional baseball in 1887, Chadwick's criticism of the "white 'toughs'" who were objecting to the presence of two African American players, Clarence Williams and Frank Grant, on the Harrisburg Ponies, reflected on the "disgraceful" players currently plying their trade in the PL.[49]

Working in his attack mode as PL promoter, Murnane commented on the jump in attendance at NL games with a reference to Alfred Lord Tennyson's 1854 poem "The Charge of the Light Brigade": "Passes to the right of them, passes to the left of them, passes all around them, and within miles of them!" Noting how the NL increase coincided with the milestone date of the Fourth of July, the Boston sportswriter claimed that more free tickets had been given away in his hometown that month than in the entire history of the NL. In contrast to Chadwick's "better class of patrons," Murnane envisioned the stands at the South End Grounds "filled with shrieking, yelling youngsters, many of them hoodlums," and called it "what a fine way to kill your own game." "Regretting" the need to recant his assessment of Spalding as a capable businessman prior to the 1890 season, the Boston sportswriter renewed his attack on NL leaders by suggesting the Beaneaters' director was so desperate that "the newspaper men own him now, body and soul, they can have all the tickets and cigars and merchandise they want." To prove his accusations, Murnane even went so far as to forward a pack of free NL passes to Richter: "You will notice that they are good for any day during the season, rain or shine."[50]

Calling on the help of some of her "gentleman friends," Black put aside the mismanagement of the Alleghenys and the road woes of the Burghers to investigate whether the flood of comps alleged by Murnane was present in the Smoky City. The report from the "Recreation Park Irregulars" came back negative, prompting the Pittsburgh correspondent to refute Murnane's repeated claims and send some "hot shot" in his direction: "There surely must have been a big mistake, or else there has been some wonderful exaggeration, as not even the dullest-minded person living would be foolish enough to believe that the renowned triumvirs of Boston would ever throw tickets around in the manner reported." That Black did not call out "Mr. Tim" by name was perhaps due to the fact that she was already feeling defensive for being singled out over her scoop of the Cincinnati contract story: "I am so unfortunate as to have 'fake' shouted at me, and I believe I am the only one that has been so

3. Mid-Season

unfortunate." Asserting her claim once again, she said she was content to wait for the outcome of the season to see if the "smoke" she detected from all the rumors pointing in that direction turned out to be "a considerable very warm fire." Time would prove her correct, but not before Black had to endure considerable criticism as a purveyor of "sensational stories."[51]

Despite the doubts being cast in her direction, Black nonetheless felt confident enough to make more predictions about the future of the baseball business. Qualifying her remarks with a lead-in of "I may be sadly off my guess," the female sportswriter claimed there would be "a grand change all around":

> At present I think the opening of the season of 1891 will find St. Louis a member of the PL, while Buffalo will be numbered among the missing and there will also be a chance of a club being placed in Cincinnati. As to the NL it can be set down as a dead sure thing that Pittsburgh and Cleveland will be things of the past so far as that body is concerned, and Indianapolis and Detroit [will] be taken back into the League fold. Of course, this surmise of mine is all based on the belief that both Leagues will be in operation again next year. Should anything force the PL to go to the wall, then the NL will once more make up the same circuit it had last year excepting for the change that admitted Brooklyn and Cincinnati.

Black called this guesswork, but it turned out that she was more right than anyone probably wanted to give her credit for at that point or any other during the 1890 season.[52]

By Week 14, putting "fans in the stands" became the primary focus for NL magnates, players turned capitalists, and writers who supported both leagues. At the same time, the quality of the fans was an issue for Chadwick and Black, who wanted to elevate the image of the game. Once again, Black addressed the comp issue from a data-driven perspective, using the resources at her command to conduct a local study. With each passing week, the attendance issue and the future of baseball dominated the discussion even as the pennant races entered the final months of the season.

Week 15—July 26–August 1: The Gumbert Brothers, New Allegheny Management, and More Print Dueling

As much as they could be trusted—which was not much by the end of July—the attendance numbers were holding steady: just over 2,000 fans per game for the PL, and just over 1,500 for the NL. The Eastern teams maintained their dominance of the standings in both leagues, occupying the top four spots in the PL and three of the four in the NL. With the Eastern teams facing off against each other in the next few weeks, the baseball world was watching for the impact of meaningful games. Taking out some space from their business coverage, Black and Murnane scouted promising players. Even though both Brooklyn and Boston clubs were in the thick of the pennant race, Chadwick and Murnane remained in attack mode, cherry picking and critiquing the opposition. Even though her teams were well out of contention, Black resumed her scrutiny of the Alleghenys management.[53]

In the closest instance of brothers taking the field against one another that the 1890 conflict saw, Black and Murnane borrowed a page from Chadwick's playbook to boost the careers of two young players. On Saturday, July 26, Ad Gumbert pitched the Red Stockings to a win over the Burghers at Exhibition Park while his brother Will was leading the Alleghenys to a rare victory over the Beaneaters across the river at Recreation Field, prompting the Pittsburgh correspondent to speculate it was the first instance in major league baseball history of brothers winning games in the same city for rival leagues on the same day. Murnane had praise for Ad that contained one of his favorite culturally coded words when he claimed the pitcher had "the pluck and spirit of a winner": "He is no weakener, that lad, and as game a boy as ever stood in the box." After breaking in with Chicago two years earlier, the 21-year-old was 13–7 at that point in the season, but ten of his wins were against the second division teams. As one of J. Palmer O'Neill's many "discoveries," Will Gumbert was a 24-year-old rookie who pitched only in Pittsburgh so that he could keep his day job. Following the Brotherhood War, Ad became a journeyman, playing with four teams over the next six seasons, while Will pitched in just seven more big league games. Black's supposition about the Gumbert brothers had given Chadwick an opportunity to answer her claim with his one-man nineteenth-century version of the Elias Sports Bureau, but the veteran sportswriter remained silent on the matter.[54]

The sporting press was still making comparisons between the products on the field. "Cato" Chadwick harped once more on the "disadvantages" of the PL hurlers due to the extra 18 inches of pitching distance and the livelier ball. Admonishing his readers to keep those differences

3. Mid-Season

in mind, he compared the records of three PL pitchers—Hoss Radbourn, Tim Keefe, and Pud Galvin,—who had just 43 wins between them, and three NL starters—John Clarkson, Bill Hutchinson, and Mickey Welch—who had amassed a total of 65 wins. Despite the extent of this analysis, the *Spalding's Guide* editor could be accused once again of cherry picking his statistics since a different trio of PL pitchers, Gus Weyhing, Mark Baldwin, and Silver King, had 62 wins in spite of the supposed disadvantages they faced. What's more, Chadwick failed to address the positive effects of the extra distance on the curves thrown by the pitchers while conveniently overlooking the true disadvantage of having to face the stronger PL hitters.[55]

All three writers returned to their favorite aspects of baseball's business side: Chadwick blamed the PL for the war, Black pinned the woes of the Alleghenys on management, and Murnane had the Brotherhood outdrawing their rivals by a seven to one margin on the basis of cash receipts. In a rare moment, Chadwick followed Black's lead and was critical of the large number of personnel changes made in Pittsburgh by J. Palmer O'Neill and company, while Murnane quoted her estimates that as many as 50 men had been under contract with the hapless Alleghenys. Perhaps having heard enough complaints from all sides, the front office of the local NL club named Al Pratt as the new director of the club. Pratt was a Civil War veteran, a former player, a participant in the Union League rebellion of 1884, an NL umpire, and an employee of Albert G. Spalding's sporting goods empire. The Pittsburgh correspondent supported the move by noting how Pratt combined "the executive ability of the manager with the knowledge and practical experiences of the player." Unfortunately for "Uncle Al," the die was cast: the Alleghenys went 5–48 the rest of the way.[56]

Pratt's presence gave Black the opportunity to indulge in the "ancient history reminiscences" of a sports journalist. Claiming that Pratt was "the acknowledged greatest pitcher of his day," the female sportswriter dated herself by remembering his playing days with the Xantha Club, an early Pittsburgh team that played near the present site of Recreation Park:

> It will certainly show I am more than sixteen, or, as a cousin of mine puts it, will make some people think this is my "second time on earth" ... and I can remember when there was a game in which the Xantha Club and Mr. Pratt were going to take part that a crowd of girls used to gather on the

doorsteps and watch for him to pass on his way to the grounds. In those days he was quite good-looking, and how those girls did admire him. Now that crowd is all settled, only a few of them being left here, now, and Mr. Pratt has settled down to a staid, married business man, and can no longer pose in the heroic light of those bygone days.

Because the Xanthas played as early as 1876, Black's choice of euphemism might have been a signal that she was 16 when she first saw handsome Uncle Al pitch, making her about 30–32 years old in 1890.[57]

The print war was still on between Black and Murnane during Week 15. When the Red Stockings were in town, Black remarked, "Once again have I gazed on the massive form of Tim Murnane." After quoting veteran second baseman Joe Quinn to attest to Kelly's effectiveness as a captain, Murnane addressed Ella Black directly to rebut her criticism of the King's managerial skills and his own "papering the house" claims. Citing Kelly's assertion that "no lady ever could have the heart to castigate him even on paper," Murnane revealed that Kelly bet that Black got her information from "the male gender, who generally looks at things through glasses." Unable to restrain himself, Murnane took a shot at Black: "Ah, there, Ella, I'm onto you." With regard to the tickets, he addressed her regular complaints of not being able to conduct interviews: "If you had interviewed me while in Pittsburg I could have shown you a thing or two. I could have sent you a stack of free passes [I] had while in Chicago. Take my word for it, free tickets have been as plenty in the League as flies in summer, and to be had without the asking." The feud, thus stoked by both parties, went on as one of the many fronts that sharpened the coverage of the correspondents covering the Brotherhood War.[58]

With the turn of the calendar, the 1890 season entered its final months, but the struggle between the rival major leagues was far from being decided. The PL had exceeded the expectations of the NL magnates by lasting past the Fourth of July, forcing Spalding and company to "up their game"—and their rhetoric. After it became clear that the upstart league would still be operating beyond Memorial Day, Henry Chadwick followed his employer's lead and adopted a voice very much akin to that of Cato the Elder from the history of ancient Rome to hammer home the NL message that the PL was to blame for all the game's ills and that the future of baseball was dependent on its destruction. On the other side of the conflict, *Boston Globe* writer Tim Murnane was

3. Mid-Season

equally as adamant in his promotion and support of the PL's right to exist as an example of the "old Jeffersonian Doctrine" of self-determination. Writing far from the "center of the war" while covering teams at the bottom of the standings, Ella Black resisted the partisan stances adopted by Chadwick and Murnane as she expressed her disappointment at the performance of both Pittsburgh franchises. At the same time, her candid assessment of the players, the management, and her journalistic colleagues was remarkable given her status as a novice—and female—sportswriter. Her interactions with Chadwick and Murnane are particularly illustrative of the highs and lows she experienced during her journey to prove that women could write baseball.

The second part of the season saw the transition from a focus on the players and the action on the field to the business elements that would ultimately decide the future of the game. This transition belied the assertion that sport was outside the realm of significant cultural importance and demonstrated that sports journalism was often anything but the "toy department of journalism." To be sure, there were moments of blind hero worship, but they were tempered by discussion of deeper issues regarding the future of the game: the behavior of the players on and off the field, and the importance of winning a "better class of patrons." Week by week, the *SL* reports of Chadwick, Black, and Murnane contributed to those discussions as the three correspondents helped write the game into American culture as a site of significant social and economic issues.[59]

As the third act of the drama gave way to the fourth, the three writers adopted different stances. While the level of his "Brooklyn cherry picking" remained the same, the tone of Chadwick's reports became less strident as he felt less of a need to shout for the PL to be reduced to the same pile of rubble as ancient Carthage. Caught up in pennant fever, T. H. Murnane shifted from PL promoter to Boston Red Stockings booster as the team he covered daily played its way toward a pennant. Writing from the middle of the conflict, Ella Black proved she was as prone to change as her colleagues: by the end of the season, it was clear that she was weary of the misguided and misdirected decisions being made by the men in charge of the game. To borrow from the parlance of the time, all three writers were "in it" to the end.

4

Late Season
*Returning to Form and
Feeling the Grind*

When the sensational season entered its final third, the legal battles over Sunday baseball in Syracuse and Rochester, NY, the progress of America's national game in England, and a chance meeting between Cap Anson and Buck Ewing in the billiards room at Chicago's Tremont Hotel were all in the sporting news. The Brotherhood leader denied all rumors that the NL was "going for him," either through Spalding's captain or John Day, the owner of the NL Giants and Ewing's previous employer. Ewing felt the situation looked "decidedly bright" for the PL even though he was not for the league until he gave his word to it. In contrast, the assessments and sentiments of "Pluck," who served as a correspondent for the Tri-State League, illustrated how the effects of the baseball war were felt in the minor league cities of Wheeling, WV, and Youngstown, OH: "There is no disputing the fact that the season of 1890 has been a dismal failure in baseball, and the whole sum and substance of the failure must certainly be laid at the door of the Brotherhood."[1]

After the Fourth of July passed without the wreck of the PL predicted by Albert Spalding, the NL magnates may have privately accepted the very real possibility that the outlaw league would last until the end of the season, but publicly, Albert Spalding was quoted as speaking to the contrary: "I regard the base ball war as practically over, and it is only a matter of time before the Players' League will be a thing of the past." Further, the sporting goods entrepreneur admitted, "We have done some lying ourselves, but nowhere near as strong as the other fellows." Perhaps most significantly, the former player claimed the NL was putting their figures near those of the PL simply to avoid appearing "ridiculous." No matter what attendance numbers were printed or what schoolyard rea-

4. Late Season

soning was behind them, both sides were losing money, prompting the sporting press to spend even more time discussing the business side of the game while covering the pennant races and commenting on each other's writing to a greater degree. The sports journalist's work in all three phases of discussion continued to illustrate their awareness of their own role in the important events that were unfolding in front of them.[2]

The *SL* reports of Chadwick, Black, and Murnane followed the patterns they had established earlier in the season with only a few changes. Exercising his most caustic editorial voice during the month of August, Henry Chadwick discredited PL players and games, blamed PL business practices, and attacked PL scribes. Focusing to a greater degree on the business of baseball once the calendar turned to September, the *Spalding's Guide* editor advanced and detailed his own plan to create a brighter future for the game through the absorption of the PL by the AA. On the other side of the Brotherhood War, T. H. Murnane maintained his promotion of all things PL through interviews with key figures and rebuttals of compromise talk, while continuing his print feud with Ella Black. When the season entered the final month, however, the Boston writer became so absorbed in the pennant race of the Red Stockings that he finished the season with the ultimate identification of the fan's "we" to put himself in the story. Ella Black maintained her stance in the middle of the "war," with balanced coverage of players from both leagues, criticism for bad decisions made by both front offices, and suggestions for writers from both camps. Illustrating the confidence she had developed as a sportswriter, the female correspondent found the voice to express her opinions more readily than before, and the undertones of her views revealed her growing impatience with the leaders and writers from the NL and the PL.

Taken together, the work of all three writers in the closing months of the season reflected the effects of the Brotherhood War. If Murnane gave into the hero worship of a fan as he was drawn into the excitement of a pennant race, his reports were balanced by the steadfast refusal of Chadwick to cover the pennant drives of the two Brooklyn teams as he focused on a more philosophical future for the game. While the stakes of the conflict moved both Chadwick and Murnane to opposite extremes of the partisan spectrum, Black remained the most balanced and objective as a journalist, taking players to task for their intemperance with alcohol, critiquing the personnel experiments of team directors, and disagreeing openly with her fellow writers when she saw fit.

Week 16—August 2-8: Players Above Bribery, Anti-Millennial Business, and Early Compromise Press

While Ward's PL Wonders were pressing Kelly's Boston Red Stockings, the Brooklyn Bridegrooms held a three-game lead on Philadelphia and Boston in the NL, with Cincinnati and Chicago slipping to fourth and fifth. As Albert Spalding prepared to sail for Europe, the NL magnate disparaged the reasons behind the formation of the outlaw league: "The public has come to a realization that the Players' League was started from purely mercenary motives, and not for the purpose of elevating the game." While Spalding's assessment did not speak to the baseball audience's feelings about the NL's efforts to improve the game primarily to make it more profitable at the box office, it was true that the PL's reported average attendance was dropping toward just 2,000. According to Richter, the top story of the week was the talk of a plan to combine the PL and AA, which involved "either amalgamation of, or at least an alliance between, the two organizations." During Week 16, Murnane's interview with Ward and the compromise discussion by Chadwick and Black revealed the larger concerns of the sporting world for the prospects of baseball as a business and the possibility of conciliation between the two leagues.[3]

With Ward's Wonders in town for a showdown series, Murnane took the opportunity to compare the PL frontrunners and interview the Brotherhood leader. After the Red Stockings lost a 6–2 decision in the opener, the player-turned-sportswriter called for more effort from the team and criticized Billy Nash and Harry Stovey who were, respectively, "sick at home with a sore throat" and "no doubt taking things easy down in New Bedford, thinking it was too wet for ball playing." In contrast to the lackluster performance that upset the home crowd, Murnane praised Ward's fielding and batting, and the responsiveness of his team to his leadership and signal calling: "It was amusing to note how each of the 'wonders' would turn to Ward for a nod or a wink as they went to the plate, whether to wait or to hit out. The best of it was that all his men obeyed his orders and sacrificed or hit hard as given orders." Murnane interviewed Ward after the game, allowing the Brotherhood leader to paint the PL as being above reproach by assuring the public that the new league had no intention of bribing players away from the NL and would continue to focus on "putting up the finest article of base ball ever seen in this country" without any thoughts of compromise. Demonstrating keen insight into early advertising, Ward's comment on Spalding's recent interviews took aim at the sporting goods magnate's commercial motives—and thus his credibility as well: "Spalding is anxious to keep his name before the public. You know it answers as an ad for his sporting goods equipment."[4]

Resuming his Roman persona, Chadwick targeted the PL management and journalists who supported the outlaw league. The Brooklyn correspondent replayed (yet again) his argument that the future of baseball was at stake due to the damage done to the game's image as a result of the kicking in PL contests and the harm done by the PL business model to the professional sport's progress toward an ideal "millennium condition." This golden age was delayed by something as simple as a home run hit with the PL's elastic ball because the instance of mere slugging deprived the more cultured patrons of the aesthetic pleasure they derived from superior fielding and scientific hitting. Additionally, the good work of the NL magnates was being undermined by the malicious PL writers, like T. H. Murnane, who had "done more injury to professional base ball playing in six months than as many years of fairer writing can overcome." The only solution, according to Chadwick, was to follow Albert Spalding's desire to strengthen the AA through an amalgamation with the PL—even if it meant placing the newly strengthened Association teams in NL cities. What neither Spalding nor his employee mentioned, of course, was that such a "solution" would amount to a demotion of the Brotherhood cause to the lower culture level of the "beer and whiskey league."[5]

In Pittsburgh, Ella Black was now comfortable enough to offer her opinions about the management decisions made by the floundering Alleghenys and the future of the game in general without apologizing for being a novice or a woman. The numbers supported her declaration that the Fred Osborne experiment was a total failure: the Canadian was 0–5 with an 8.38 ERA as a starter and had committed 18 errors in 35 starts as an outfielder. Advocating for Lee Viau and Hugh Nichol as better options in the pitcher's box after they were released by Cincinnati, Black pointed to the conscientious qualities of Nichol as the best opportunity for replacing the good press that was lost when Billy Sunday was traded to the second-place Phillies. Demonstrating her business acumen, the Pittsburgh correspondent admonished the PL Pirates for giving up on a box office booster like Arlie Latham, the contemporary "clown prince" of baseball. After observing that visiting teams from both leagues were booking rooms in a less expensive hotel to save travel costs, she expressed a desire that the "talk of amalgamation between the PL and the AA will amount to something more than talk." Without such an arrangement, Black argued, "the PL will have a very hard fight to be able to pull through"; in contrast, she believed that scheduling games between the PL and the AA would mean that "the NL will either have to cry for quarter, or else go to the wall." While Black was turning phrases of her own, she entered the world of sport literature when J. F. Donnolly reprinted the following poem by a "lady reader of the SL in Brooklyn":

> Well-a, Ella / Tell-a feller,
> What's the matter really? / Why do men / Of shaky pen
> Thus pursue you freely? / In every line / A fake sublime
> That makes your columns, tell me, / Or is it truth.
> As I think forsooth / Too tersely told to suit, see?[6]

The tone of this "pome" was light; however, the undercurrent called Black's work into question all over again, asking whether she wrote sensational "fakes" or pursued truth, demonstrating the ongoing resistance to her presence in the pages of *SL* into August.

The business and the future of the game served as the primary focus of sportswriters as the season entered its final third, yet all three writers under consideration questioned the play and the players, with Chadwick asking, "What is the cost of a homerun," Murnane asking for better performance from the Red Stockings in general and two players in particular, and Black asking Alleghenys president O'Neill to consider her suggestions for personnel moves. Both Chadwick and Black showed their concern for the health of the game when they discussed the idea of an amalgamation between the AA and the PL, the former seeing the move as being good for the NL and the latter identifying it as the undoing of the older league. As the season moved into the doldrums of

4. Late Season

August, there would be little change from the patterns that had been established, but the volume and the tone would grow louder and stronger in reaction to the stakes of the Brotherhood War.

Week 17—August 9-15: Too Much Player Press, Players Talking Business, and Imagined PL Press

According to the attendance figures printed in the *Boston Globe*, the PL had led the NL in 15 of 17 weeks; Clarence Dow attributed the NL victory during the two weeks following the Fourth of July to "natural and other causes." Based on his observations over the course of the season, Dow professed to have more confidence in the attendance numbers submitted by the PL. To back this, he quoted PL Secretary Brunell's response to Albert Spalding that "We will allow the Associated Press to examine our books if he will do the same. I do not think his club has averaged $100 a game in Chicago this season." Despite admitting that the NL had lost money that season, Spalding remained as defiant as he had been in May: "Nothing but unconditional surrender on the part of the PL people will be listened to by the NL.... To recognize any of the Brotherhood revolutionists by making a compromise would forever do harm to the game." The sporting goods magnate left for Europe after firing this parting shot, so another member of the NL's war committee would do the listening if terms were sought by the PL. All three writers looked to key figures to advance their underlying messages, further illustrating their disparate approaches to the conflict. Black was critical of the way her colleagues reported a gift given to King Kelly, while Ward and Spalding received more press coverage from interviews by Murnane and Chadwick.[7]

The heavy turnover in the roster of the Alleghenys did little to change Ella Black's view of the team as she displayed more of her growing confidence by calling down her fellow journalists' treatment of "star" players. Noting how the roster of the local "old league club" was nowhere near the same team it had been at the start of the season because it had been "gone over and reorganized" so many times, Black reported all the Alleghenys currently needed were "a couple good pitchers and a practical manager"—and a fresh start to wash away the bad taste of 19 wins and 75 losses. After 21-year-old "Whoa Bill" (or "Silver Bill") Phillips won his debut in impressive fashion, the female sportswriter may have thought J. P. O'Neill had found one of those pitchers, but the rookie went on to lose his other nine starts and finish the season with a 7.57 ERA. O'Neill's personnel woes did not diminish. The day after an unsuccessful one-game tryout for Anson's visiting Chicago Colts, the Alleghenys management signed Edward "Pop" Lytle, and the new recruit promptly dropped two fly balls that led to the defeat of the home team. Pop's 16-game major league career featured ten errors in an equal number of starts at second base and the outfield.[8]

In contrast to Black's praise for the steady, consistent play of Cap Anson no matter the size of the audience or the score of the game, the Pittsburgh correspondent expanded her targets from her players and managers to her fellow journalists. Responding to the recent news that King Kelly had been presented with a "house and grounds" by friends and admirers of his work as the manager of the Boston PL team, Black criticized the way in which the news of the gift was "telegraphed all over the country." Extending her earlier appraisal of the "King," she argued that too much undeserved praise for Kelly had a demoralizing effect on Ward, Hanlon, Pfeffer, and other Brotherhood members who had done ten times more to make the PL a success. Returning to the impact and the importance of the sporting press, Black cited the example of Ed "Cannonball" Morris, the "little pitcher" who had recently been released from the Burghers, presumably for public drunkenness—and perhaps drunkenness on the field. At 28, Morris was in his seventh and last year as a professional player, and he had had problems with alcohol in the past. Black cited him as an example of PL members who were taking advantage of the relaxed discipline of the new league. Echoing the concerns of Henry Chadwick, she noted that such behavior would ultimately hurt the league at the box office. (See the full text of Black's August 16 report in Part 5 of Appendix A.)[9]

With the conditions in New York being wet enough to delay the pennant drive of the Red Stockings, Murnane's coverage contained some early examples of actual rainy day interviews with players and team officials in contrast to the fictional pieces written by Charles Dryden in Chicago in the 1890s. Likely aware that Tim Keefe had been in the sporting goods business with Buck Becannon since 1884, the Boston writer reported that the Brotherhood leader was readily available to the press: "as all can find Sir Timothy, who, like A. G. Spalding, is in the business

4. Late Season

and finds it pays to get his name in the papers." Revealing that the president of the New York PL Giants, Colonel McAlpin, had "arrived home from his summer home in the Adirondacks looking as brown as a berry, and as cheerful and willing to talk baseball as the biggest crank," Murnane described McAlpin's assertions that his team stood on financial ground that was "as solid as the rock of Gibraltar" and his belief that victory would be theirs ultimately because of the rights of the players to do business with new backers. Further, the PL leader gave a vote of confidence for his business associates that reflected the social class distinctions between the partners and the players of the new league: "I must say that my connection with the PL has been very pleasant, and I have found some brainy men among the profession and men that can be trusted when it is a case of honor."[10]

Turning to one of those brainy men of honor about the rumors of a union between the PL and the AA, Murnane shared Ward's opinion that it was "rather early" to speak of such an arrangement. The *Globe* writer boosted the new league once more by reporting how it was no surprise the AA was willing to come together with the Brotherhood since the former were "well aware that the PL has taken the place of the NL as the leading base ball association in the business." Extending his attack on the older league, he revealed that Ward thought it was likely that the AA would break away from the National Agreement that fall. Such a move would allow for games between the two leagues in the spring and the fall, which was about the only benefit to the PL in Murnane's mind, showing that he, like Chadwick, saw the AA as a second-class operation.[11]

When Albert Spalding summoned Henry Chadwick to his hotel room at 241 Broadway, the Brooklyn correspondent seized the opportunity to attack sports journalists who supported the PL. Instead of the strategy session he expected, the meeting turned out to be a "jolly" bon voyage party for Spalding and his brother, who were sailing to Europe. After reporting with rare irony that Spalding and Al Reach were "getting stout under the 'great mental strain'" of the conflict, Chadwick took a shot at a PL sportswriter: "Had brother Dickinson seen the quartette of League presidents chatting together that day he would have had a column in the *World* the next day, with a display head, about 'Secret Conference of the NL Magnates!' 'The Desperate Strait They Are in!' 'Their Private Desire for the Compromise!'" After modeling what he took to be the damaging press from the partisans of the outlaw league, Chadwick accepted his employer's excuse that a subordinate was responsible for the NL Chicago club's comp policy and reproduced the NL magnate's "perfectly reliable" attendance numbers to "demonstrate" how Comiskey's PL Pirates had been tripling their attendance figures in early August. Capitalizing on the opening to return to his argument for a better class of patrons, the Brooklyn correspondent used Spalding's report as further proof that the PL's free ticket policy had cheapened the game because it brought "into the grounds the most objectionable of the class of spectators, and drives out the best class of patrons." Second, he offered the sharp decrease in the number of "deadheads" at Bridegrooms' games as an example of how the NL was not "papering the house" and suggested a look at Charley Ebbets' books as proof. Third, Bridegrooms President Byrne served as Chadwick's eyes in Chicago, visiting local saloons and finding that free tickets to PL games were as plentiful as Murnane claimed the NL tickets were in Boston.[12]

The reports from Week 17 demonstrated how PL and NL leaders were willing to bring their message to the public as the "war" entered its final phases. Without access to key figures, Black offered commentary about three key arenas: the impacts of the players' behavior on public opinion, the effectiveness of the management's decisions to sign or release various players, and the impact of the coverage given by her fellow sporting journalists. Spalding called Chadwick in for first-hand "information," while Ward provided Murnane with equally charged "intelligence" intended to maintain or boost the morale of the players. Pennant races were heating up in both leagues; however, sportswriters remained more concerned about the future of the game and the way it was being covered.

Week 18—August 16-22: The 39th Player, Business Compromises, and More Press Criticism

With the combined total attendance—as much as it could be trusted—reaching almost 1.5 million, up over 350,000 fans from 1889, the increase seemed to indicate a growing interest in baseball, growing

4. Late Season

noses of NL magnates and Brotherhood leaders, or both. Boston, Philadelphia, Chicago, and New York of the PL remained the attendance leaders by city, which was reflected in the standings. Ward's Wonders had pulled even with Kelly's Red Stockings in the win column, and their strong play was improving their attendance numbers at home. The PL pennant race and the increased attendance allowed Richter to answer Spalding's claims with "Base ball isn't dead by a long shot." Despite Richter's confidence and Ward's assertion that "There is room for two organizations and both can make money," compromise remained an important topic of discussion for Chadwick and Black, while the Pittsburgh correspondent returned her attention to her fellow journalists.[13]

Moving away from promoting players as celebrities, both Black and Murnane covered how the effects of the dog days led directly to two more short-time players entering the major league rosters. Twenty-two-year-old Frederick W. Truax became the 39th player to don the uniform of the Pittsburgh Alleghenys during the 1890 season. He went one-for-four with a walk and an RBI and made good on his only chance in the outfield. Another Fred, "Count" Fred Doe, stuck around long enough to get into two games—and earn a nickname. In a game where Captain Jay Faatz of the Buffalo Bisons was holding out Connie Mack and Bert Cunningham to give a "surprise party" for John Ward's Wonders, "Count" Doe, a Massachusetts product, was pressed into service by Faatz as an emergency starter. Doe gave up eight runs in a rain-shortened loss to Kelly's Boston Red Stockings. One week later, the Count went into the box against the Red Stockings again, this time to relieve John Tener as a member of the Pittsburgh Burghers. Doe fared better in his second—and final—major league outing, allowing just two runs over four innings in a 16–4 loss. Unlike Truax, who died before the end of the century, Count Doe went on to have a long career in the Eastern League as a player, manager, and owner. Harry Stovey was another apparent victim of the dog days: according to Murnane, he was home with a "bad cold"—again, which likely indicated that he was unable to play for other, less salutary reasons.[14]

Instead of mentioning players by name and contributing to an undeserved celebrity status, Chadwick used statistics to help explain the standings—and attack the PL. First, he compared the win-loss records of the leaders in both leagues to show that the NL had the top four clubs—ahead of all four PL leaders with regard to winning percentage. The results for the comparison of the "tail-enders" were less conclusive since the teams from both leagues were more evenly distributed. While this would have seemed to be a fair comparison of the two leagues on the surface, it could have illustrated the disparity of team strength in the NL compared to greater parity in the PL, a possibility the *Spalding's Guide* editor apparently did not want to consider. Chadwick did provide a more comprehensive picture with expanded standings that added columns for postponed games, games to play, extra-inning games, single-figure victories, double-figure victories, and Chicago victories (which was the veteran writer's term for a shutout).[15]

Turning to the business and the future of the game, Chadwick reiterated his pitch for the supremacy of the NL by devoting a separate column to what he called the "key move" in solving the present dilemma, and that was once again for the AA to absorb the greater part of the PL. Richter's teaser leading into the piece described the idea as "The Nestor Suggests That Jonah Swallow the Whale." As the senior circuit, the NL would remain unchanged in Chadwick's plan, since they had led the way for all of professional baseball by demonstrating how capitalists should run the game. There was not much new in this column, but it was the first time Chadwick had offered his solution in an extended format.[16]

Stepping out of the good father's shadow, Black argued strongly against any union between the two leagues, for several reasons. First, she suggested that the AA was doing "fairly well" and did not need the help. Secondly, she observed that the large number of people who supported the Brotherhood's labor cause would perhaps feel slighted if the PL gave up operation after just one year. Finally, she noted how much Chris Von der Ahe, owner of the St. Louis Browns, had been hurt by the formation of the new league, which took away most of his AA team. Black asserted that he would not—and in fact could not if he wanted to "be classed as a man"—support a union between the two leagues. For Black to go against Chadwick's published opinion marked another significant moment in her development as a journalist because it showed she was finding her own voice as a sportswriter.[17]

Demonstrating the progressive element of her project further, Black sought to reform the errors she observed in the work of her fellow writers. In response to the player-friendly and overly celebratory press given to the Cincinnati Reds, she made use of her own slang to express her nausea from the "regular doses of taffy" being written about "Count" Tony Mullane and "Cyclone" Jesse Duryea. A glance at Ren Mulford's column reveals that his work might have been the cause of the Pittsburgh correspondent's upset stomach. After describing how Tony Mullane recently lost two games due to spotty defense behind him, Mulford went on to defend the Count against the sporting editor of the *Ohio State Journal*: "From Ed Rife's chat I cull this line: 'Tony Mullane has struck the toboggan!' Great Scott! That is on par with the nonsensical obituary notices of the demise of Rhines' power as a phenom." Black was especially incensed that steady, reliable, conscientious players like Hugh Nichol did not receive any positive press and were consequently given their release, while more unreliable players were "kept and petted up" until they thought they owned the city. She went so far as to suggest that the Reds would have been higher in the standings if they didn't have to deal with the inflated egos of the players who had been overrated by the press.[18]

Despite claims by Richter, Ward, and other PL supporters that all was quiet on the PL front, baseball's future was not about to go away as a story. Whether writers like Chadwick used it against the PL or PL supporters like Black offered a number of reasons against the practicality of a union between the AA and the PL, the topic made good enough copy to fill the columns of space available in the various sporting weeklies and major dailies following the double journalism model of the *Boston Globe*. Chadwick's tables and Black's responses to unwarranted coverage and one-start wonders showed that sportswriters did not lose sight of the game on the field while covering weightier matters.

Week 19—August 23–29: Boston Pennant Advice, Brooklyn Business Bashing, and Pittsburgh Rebuttals

At the end of August, pennant fever began to stretch from Boston to the Northwest, where Spokane was leading Seattle, Tacoma, and Portland in the Pacific Northwest League. Richter printed the pro–NL "screed" of "Cincinnati 'Dogberry'" to demonstrate what "sort of ridiculous stuff is being fed to Cincinnati readers who have no better knowledge of the true situation than they can obtain through their local papers, except such as are lucky enough to read THE SPORTING LIFE regularly." Furthermore, *SL* readers and correspondents were informed of Richter's opinion about a promoter's "disgraceful move" to establish a league for women: "Woman has no place in base ball except as patron and enthusiast, and female base ball teams should not be patronized by the public nor encouraged and noticed by the press expect in terms of condemnation." In keeping with his attitude toward most women and the game of baseball, Richter went so far as to call for gentlemen owners to follow Byrne's example to refuse to lease their grounds to such "degrading" entertainment. Showing more signs of succumbing to pennant fever, Murnane began addressing the players more directly. Chadwick remained on the offensive against the PL's effect on the future of baseball, and Black, having proven herself to be an exception in Richter's opinion, illustrated how she'd left the defensive to take her place as a—mostly—full-fledged member of the sportswriting fraternity.[19]

Even though Ward's Wonders had pulled ahead of Kelly's Red Stockings in the win column and Ewing's Giants were just four games back in third place, T. H. Murnane still liked Boston's pennant chances. The player-turned-sportswriter did, however, warn the King's men to watch out for the Giants as good candidates to emulate jockey Edward "Snapper" Garrison and finish first after lagging behind the field for most of the race. Despite the unpredictable qualities of Ward's untested Wonders, Murnane cited Boston's favorable schedule and the championship experience of several key players as reasons for their likely success. Kelly had helped Cap Anson take the flag three times with the Chicago White Stockings from 1880–1882—"when winning the pennant was easy" because the seasons were only 84 games long. Irwin and Radbourn were teammates on Providence's championship team of 1884 when the season contained 112 games, while Brouthers and Richardson hit 12 and 11 homeruns, respectively, as members of the "heavy slugging" Detroit Wolverines in 1887. Still writing from his experience as a former player, Murnane observed that the "public have no idea of the wear and tear a championship season has on a member of one of the leading teams." The Red Stockings proved themselves to be championship material that week by going 5–2 at home against Buffalo, Chicago, and Pittsburgh. Regarding a young player who would participate in a future Boston pennant race, Murnane's "Base Ball Notes" scouted a pitcher for

4. Late Season

the Spiders of the NL: "Cleveland's new pitcher, Young has the making of a good twirler. His associates have named him 'Si,' owing to his country-like ways." Thus, Cy Young was being identified as one of the original Rubes—even before writers settled on a spelling.[20]

If Henry Chadwick was pleased with the performance of the local first-place Brooklyn Bridegrooms and the second-place Brooklyn Wonders, his report at the end of August did not show it. After calling *SL* editor Richter down for his whale simile from the week before, Chadwick linked his rebuttal of the figure of speech to what he took to be the "all press" and "no business model" aspects of Ward and the leaders of the Brotherhood: "You know that the great fish has a remarkably small mouth, while the PL is noted for its great extent of mouth." The *Spalding's Guide* editor went on to reissue almost every one of his rants since he began attacking the PL at every opportunity in early June. Surprisingly, he balanced his attack when he complemented his tentative evaluation of the NL comp policy in a previous report by admonishing the top leagues to engage in a "mutual back-down from the mistaken policy both have attempted to carry out." Perhaps to prove that he had not turned into just a plain "crank," he did have praise for two NL players, Ed Stein of Anson's Chicago Colts and Al McCauley of Wright's Phillies. At just 21 years of age, Stein compiled a 12–6 record in his rookie season and went on to win more than 100 games for Chicago and Brooklyn in an eight-year career, proving that Chadwick had a good eye for young talent half the time. Demonstrating a lack of necessary skill, McCauley made 30 errors at first base, but nonetheless stuck in the NL for the entire 1890 season before going to Washington in the AA for part of the 1891 campaign.[21]

With the Burghers mired in sixth place and the Alleghenys still en route to a record-setting bad finish, Black avoided the pennant race and used her new-found voice to rebut the opinions of her colleagues. First, she came to the defense of the NL after T. T. T., a *SL* correspondent from Baltimore, took the old league to task for raiding teams and players from the AA. Pointing out that Brooklyn and Cincinnati had left the "beer and whiskey league" of their own accord to join the NL and that the AA had been diminished when some of its players were compelled by Brotherhood loyalty to join the PL, the Pittsburgh correspondent adopted a condescending, maternal tone by addressing the Baltimore writer as "My dear boy." Not done yet, she expressed her disapproval of J. Palmer

O'Neill's trade that sent Billy Sunday to Philadelphia and took issue with a local "supposed-to-be well posted" writer who was calling for Fred Carroll, Bill Kuehne, and Pud Galvin to retire from the Burghers, wondering whether the writer could do any better himself. Despite Black's spirited defense, all three players were nearing the ends of their careers. Though the youngest of the pilloried trio at 25, Fred Carroll played just one more season and hit an anemic .219 for the Pittsburgh Pirates in 1891. Kuehne, 31 in 1890, bounced between four teams in the AA and NL for the next two seasons before retiring. The "grand old man" of this trio at age 33 in 1890, Galvin pitched two more seasons in the NL before finishing with a 361–308 record, which led to his induction into the Baseball Hall of Fame in 1965. Further demonstrating confidence in her opinions as a baseball writer, Black disagreed with another local writer who suggested that A. G. Spalding had an interest in the local NL club: "Surely the Chicago magnate has too much good judgment to have made such a purchase as that."[22]

Buoyed by regular contact with a strong team, Murnane revealed his background as a former player as he still suffered from the symptoms of pennant fever. While he was breaking one of the cardinal rules of sportswriting as he cheered from the various press boxes of the PL, the proximity to a pennant drive no doubt reminded him of his championship experience with the 1877 Boston Beaneaters. Chadwick repeated many of the same arguments against the PL, but he also found fault with the NL policies supported by his employer, showing that he might have been growing weary of the conflict. As if she had read similar incriminations of female involvement with baseball, Black's report reflected an even stronger than usual desire to show that a woman could write the game, even if men like the *SL* editor thought it was improper for them to play it professionally.

Week 20—August 30–September 5: Pennant Pressures, "Peter Funk Business," and Press-Induced Lawsuits

As the season entered its last full month, the sensational stories moved toward white heat. Buck Ewing denied reports that he had

4. Late Season

jumped leagues and signed with Day's NL Giants for the 1891 season. After a Washington writer "put two and two together and built himself a nice little Castle in Spain," John Ward wrote to *SL* to put an end to rumors that his Brooklyn Wonders would be moved to the nation's capital. When Philadelphia reporters learned of a secret meeting between the PL and the AA, the event generated at least three more stories about how the AA "magnates were tracked to their lair ... escaped through a tunnel ... and planned to bounce the Wagner brothers" from the PL. In the face of all the fiction being published in the sporting press, Murnane's reports proved that baseball games were still being played—with some of them being disputed. Chadwick backed away briefly from his ancient Roman persona to decry dubious business practices on the part of both leagues, while Black covered the press's influence on impending lawsuits.[23]

The rainouts were starting to add up in Boston, where the PL team was feeling pressure from New York and Brooklyn in the standings and the front office. Ewing's Giants had climbed into second place and were just two games back in the win column. Murnane's rainy day report revealed that Kelly's team was questioning Ward's impartiality in two player-eligibility disputes that he helped settle. Ward had sided with the committee in charge of running the Bisons when Boston protested the "loan" of Larry Twitchell from Cleveland and ruled that the Red Stockings had to replay three games when Gil Hatfield had filled in at shortstop without being officially released by New York. "Kel and the boys" felt that they were getting the worst end of the decisions made by the five umpires who were from the New York area and questioned the value of the double umpire system since "four good men were better than eight bad ones." Overall, the treatment of the Red Stockings by the league office had Murnane asking some hard questions: "Where does Boston come in?" and "Are John M. Ward and Frank Brunell running the league to suit themselves or has Boston any rights that must be respected?" On the field, the Red Stockings responded to these issues like potential champions: playing eight games in seven days, they went 7–1 at home against the second division Pittsburgh Burghers and Cleveland Infants to advance their pennant drive. Perhaps the rain reminded the "boys" of when General "Hi! Hi!" Dixwell had extended his "rich uncle" role by taking them on a side trip to see Niagara Falls in early August.[24]

Availing himself of a number of euphemisms and literary allusions,

Chadwick alternated between offering praise and dispensing criticism for players and management alike. The Brooklyn correspondent took both leagues to task for the "Peter Funk business" they were engaging in with the false attendance numbers. George Miller of Pittsburgh was a regular "Joe Bagstock" for taking a blow to the neck with a ball and continuing to play the game. Estate sale regulars may have recognized "Peter Funk" as slang for an auctioneer's accomplice who poses as a bidder to drive up the price of items, while followers of Charles Dickens' novels may have appreciated the reference to Major Joseph B. Bagstock from *Dombey and Son*. Replaying another of his favorite arguments, the veteran writer countered Richter's description of the "good luck" experienced by the Louisville Colonels in the AA that season:

> What rot this is! For "luck" please read *good management*.... Of course, there are exceptions in such cases as when a team has a number of players disabled by accidents—not by dissipation. But when a club has alleged "hard luck" in the disabling of its players by drunkenness or debauchery set it down to bad management, for that is what it is, and nothing more.

Maintaining his moralist stance, Chadwick named individual players with regard to drunkenness or the absence of that vice. He echoed Richter's praise of Boston Beaneaters outfielder Marty Sullivan for having the "moral language" to "redeem" his errors of the past and condemned the "heap of moral cowards" who preferred "liquor indulgence to making men of themselves." One of the latter was Cannonball Ed Crane, and, as if to extend his moral crusade, Chadwick went to the trouble to construct a table to compare Crane's pitching record with that of John Ewing, with the underlying purpose of calling PL pitchers to account by showing the effects of "visits to saloons at midnight" (See the full text of Chadwick's September 6 report in Part 6 of Appendix A).[25]

Perhaps prompted by Ella Black's regular analysis and repeated criticism in her *SL* column, the troubles of the Pittsburgh Alleghenys were finding their way to the attention of writers in other parts of the country. In the place usually occupied by Clarence Dow's tabulation of the weekly attendance figures, the *Globe* ran a story out of Pittsburgh about the NL club's lack of funds and first-class players. The story led with the feud between the local leaders and the magnate in the league office: "The friends of A. G. Spalding are highly indignant at the alleged statement of Director J. P. O'Neill published in the Eastern papers to the effect that

4. Late Season

Mr. Pratt owes the Pittsburgh NL club $500 for stock." Pratt, who was Spalding's agent in the Smoky City, would not talk to the press, but an "intimate friend" was willing to allude to the "many curious things" that could be known about the club—and would be known if the directors did not get their house in order. That same friend was willing to explain how a bad loan to "Peek-a-Boo" Mack had soured the business relations between Pratt and the Alleghenys management, which had asked Pratt to buy into the club's stock at a reduced rate. Spalding's response to the proposed deal showed how he was more than willing to play hardball with the clubs in his own league: "Mr. Spalding's opinion was to the effect that if the officials of the club had gotten the club into such unpopularity, and that if Mr. Pratt's name would do it any good, he, Mr. Pratt should have the stock free."[26]

The stock issue was only the surface of the continuing saga of the Alleghenys management. According to Black, the dispute was another example of the "sensational stories" that had been published locally—as well as around the country—all summer. The salient story, according to her, was that Pratt had taken out a lawsuit against the Alleghenys stockholders in order "to recover his bill of several hundred dollars for uniforms and equipment he had sold them." As before, she lamented her inability to "go and procure one of the regulation interviews" so that she could ask some of the questions that weren't being posed by the local writers. Then the Pittsburgh correspondent went on to reveal a sensational story of her own about a secret meeting that she learned about from an informant she was "thoroughly acquainted with" who was "intimately connected with some of the old club officials." According to Black's informant, the Allegheny stockholders met and planned to withdraw from the NL if the PL kept their Pittsburgh franchise for the 1891 season, even though J. P. O'Neill was determined to fight on. O'Neill's stance prompted Black to write, "He seems to be a very nice, clever gentleman, but as a friend of mine remarked, 'What he don't know about base ball would fill enough books to start a library.'"[27]

Amid protests, threatened legal action, and sensational stories from both camps, the Brotherhood war was taking a toll on players, management, and the press alike. The trio of *SL* correspondents was not immune to the season's grind. Murnane's report revealed some of the cracks in the PL system even as it demonstrated his growing identification with the team he was covering. Proving that Cato the Elder could be critical of Rome, Chadwick highlighted the mistakes of the NL as well as the PL, while Black engaged in the same kind of rumor mongering she had disparaged in earlier reports. The cracks in their journalism would only grow wider before the end of the season.

Week 21—September 6–12: Pennant Drive Plans, "Unbusiness-like" Assessments, and Questions for Editors

With just three weeks remaining in the season, the pennant race was reduced to a two-city affair: Boston in the PL and Brooklyn in the NL due to the leads held by the Red Stockings and the Bridegrooms. Richter's assessment of the "war" determined that the present situation was "quite to the liking of the capitalists of the various clubs, and there is not the slightest weakness in any quarter." The *SL* editor asserted that there was "little doubt that at last the National League is in the mood for a compromise—upon terms favorable to itself," but an unnamed NL magnate (most likely Phillies owner Al Reach) echoed Spalding's earlier assessment when he told the *Philadelphia Inquirer* that he expected an amalgamation of the AA and the PL would serve as the only compromise acceptable to the NL, which desired "Simply the return of the men they stole from us." Moving away from his role as PL promoter, Murnane monitored Boston's drive for the PL championship, while Chadwick and Black evaluated the local and national scenes with more balanced perspectives.[28]

In Boston, the Red Stockings were planning their push to the pennant. After yet another Saturday rainout that saw nearly 2,000 loyal cranks have their "silver halves" returned to them when the game was called in the second inning, the PL frontrunners traveled to Philadelphia, with several players visiting their hometowns when a Saturday rainout provided them with an extra off-day. Hardie Richardson, Dan Brouthers, and Billy Daley found their way to Gloucester, NJ; Wappingers Falls, NY; and Poughkeepsie, NY, respectively. Murnane left the details to his reader's imagination when he reported that Captain Kelly was "making things lively" at the gathering places near the silk mills of Paterson, N.J., while the rest of the team was reportedly "viewing New Jersey scenery through a Scotch mist," with the last phrase being atmospheric or

4. Late Season

euphemistic—or both. Old Hoss Radbourn and Ad Gumbert agreed to go into the pitcher's box every other game until the championship was decided. After a shortened schedule that saw the Red Stockings take three in a row from Ewing's Giants at home but drop a one-run decision to Ward's Wonders on the road, Murnane claimed that the next six games with the Philadelphia Quakers and the Chicago Pirates would be "for blood" as the Red Stockings looked to secure the pennant. In response to rumors that Mike Kelly might be shipped to Cleveland for the 1891 season, the Boston writer doubted that Al Johnson would secure the King's services. After asserting that the Kelly rumors were "not producing the sensation people would think," Murnane revealed that his attitude toward Boston's captain had cooled when he went on to note that the Red Stockings were balanced enough to win when Kelly was "on the bench or off on a vacation" and that Kelly was "only missed for his batting and base running."[29]

Moving his editorial stance toward a more neutral perspective, Chadwick scrutinized components of both leagues. The veteran sportswriter reported that on September 1, the Brooklyn Bridegrooms had achieved the record of winning three championship games in a single day. No one who was following baseball that season could have been surprised that the first team to lose three games in a day was the Pittsburgh Alleghenys. Noting how O'Neill's team had battled back from a 10–0 deficit in the opener and kept the second game close before dropping the final contest in the triple-header, Chadwick nonetheless asserted that "no more incompetent control of a club" had been exhibited in the NL in years. After this criticism of an NL operation, he resumed his assault on the PL by pronouncing that Kelly had "blundered" as a manager and that Comiskey had been a "sad disappointment." Then Chadwick offered rare praise for Ward's management of his talent-starved PL club against "long odds" and reversed his position on the NL-backed idea of amalgamation:

> The best class of patrons of the professional clubs are as much opposed to the existence of one great controlling professional league—or base ball trust—as they are to the longer existence of the unbusiness-like methods of the PL. The power to govern the professional base ball world must be placed in the hands of what one may call the Senate and House of Representatives of the professional republic, and these can be most fitly represented by the National League and the American Association, each possessing co-equal

powers of governmental control, and yet have both run on an independent footing as regards its individual club government.

As before, when speaking for the "best class of patrons," Chadwick railed against the PL business model and reaffirmed the dominance of the NL, but the tone in this passage was less shrill and urgent than it had been earlier when he harped on the same points and declared that any hope of baseball reaching a "millennial era" lay in the destruction of the PL. The Brooklyn correspondent's attack was countered two days later when Clarence Dow published Secretary Julian Hart's assurance that he was "willing to allow an expert to examine the attendance figures on his books and compare them with the announced figures" to prove that the Boston Red Stockings' lead over "everybody" with 197,346 paying fans was accurate and above board.[30]

Turning away from the Alleghenys losing their 100th game of the season, Ella Black reported that Comiskey's supposed "wreck" of a club had taken two of three from the Burghers in Pittsburgh. She was not critical of his "picked nine," but she did not offer a ringing testimonial for the player-manager either: she opined that the success of the 1890 St. Louis Browns in the AA served as evidence that Comiskey had benefitted from a strong front office instead of being a superior "manager and handler of men." The Pittsburgh correspondent had good reason to be short with her fellow journalists and the local management. Her take on the Kelly-to-Cleveland rumor was to express shock that any man would have enough "cheek" to write such a "fanciful fake," as well as that any editor "should allow such a yarn to pass through his hands and get into the paper." Claiming Al Johnson couldn't run enough trolleys to afford Kelly's salary, she doubted that the City by the Lake would "be likely to give him real estate and other little testimonials of esteem," similar to the house and grounds given to him by the "blue-blooded aristocrats of Boston town." Citing the proper treatment she received when she met Henry Chadwick in June, Black returned to her refutation of "Baltimore Tease's burlesque argument" that a woman could not understand baseball well enough to serve as a correspondent to *SL* by discovering that sacrifice hitting and 20 players with a pitching decision were the sources of the Allegheny's poor record. The Burghers perpetuated the woes of their local rivals when they went ahead and played a game on a rainy day after agreeing to go along with J. P. O'Neill's suggestion that both teams cancel their games.[31]

4. Late Season

In the waning weeks of the season, Murnane provided his readers with more of an inside look at the daily lives of the Red Stockings as well as their stretch drive mindset. When Black addressed the Kelly-to-Cleveland story, she disputed such rumors from the perspective of a writer who was still trying to prove her legitimacy, while Murnane could afford to approach the subject with a sense of humor. Chadwick's and Black's assessments of Comiskey's shortcomings as a manager—as well as Chadwick's praise of Ward—were both neutral observations, indicating a move toward the middle as the Brooklyn correspondent showed he was not too old to follow the lead of *SL*'s "capital journalistic find" from Pittsburgh.

Week 22—September 13–19: Small Pittsburgh Victories, Business Acquisitions, and Journalism Historian

On September 20, the Tremont House in Chicago was filled with ball players making pennant pushes in both leagues, and the talk in the lobbies surrounded the late-season rumors that were circulating around the premier circuits. The Boston Red Stockings and the Brooklyn Bridegrooms, who would have been looking at the good possibility of playing against each other if a last-second peace agreement could have been reached, were working to cement their first-place leads in their respective leagues. The Red Stockings had already clinched the season series over every other PL team, so when they took the first two games from Comiskey's Pirates on the road, Kelly's men secured bragging rights over the entire league—even though Kelly was away from the team on another of his "vacations." Using more early baseball slang to describe how the Red Stockings put "up a game full of dash and 'get there,'" Murnane reported that the club was elated because "Chicago was the one team in the West the boys feared the most." Across town, Byrne's Bridegrooms secured a true "Chicago victory" when they shut out Anson's charging Colts, who were just two games behind Brooklyn after going 4–2–1 over the previous week. With two losing seasons long-since assured, Black commented on what few positives she could find from her seat in Pittsburgh, and Murnane returned to promoting the PL since the pennant was secured, leaving Chadwick to play journalism critic and baseball historian.[32]

With both of their teams out of town to finish the season and no opportunity for either of them to move up in the standings, Pittsburgh fans could do little but celebrate whatever small victories came their way and look to 1891. Black took pride in the fact that the Pittsburgh clubs won three games on Saturday, September 13, when Hecker's Alleghenys surprised the Reds and Hanlon's Burghers took two from hapless Buffalo. The female sportswriter looked forward to the prospect of the Burghers spoiling the chances of Ewing's Giants to overtake Ward's Wonders for second place; since the Alleghenys and NL Giants were firmly established in eighth and sixth places, respectively, there was no mention of Hecker's men having any say in how anyone finished. The only thing that the Alleghenys had to play for was to avoid breaking Louisville's "disgraceful record" of 27–111 the previous year in the AA. Because the team was sitting at 21–104, Black noted, "It will take harder work than any the team has yet done to escape this." Perhaps in keeping with the general mood in the Smoky City, she lamented the lack of pitching on Pittsburgh teams across the years and further regretted that Yank Robinson would likely not return the following season because injury and illness had prevented him from playing enough to show his capabilities. In 1891, Robinson did play 97 games with King Kelly's Cincinnati Porkers (also known as "Kelly's Killers") in the AA, but did little to distinguish himself, batting .178, well below his .229 pace in Pittsburgh, and committing 13 more errors at second base. *SL* readers who were familiar with Robinson's 1889 "one-man strike" against Browns owner Von der Ahe may have detected the subtext: that the sportswriter was disappointed at the potential loss of a player who was willing to "assert his independence," rather than the exit of a utility player on the downside of his career. (In Robinson's defense, he died of consumption at age 34 in 1894, so perhaps his 1890 performance was hampered by the early stages of the disease.)[33]

Beyond the pennant, the major story that week surrounded the potential sales of NL franchises to the PL. Al Johnson, a backer of the Cleveland Infants, and PL Secretary Brunell were in St. Louis "with the money to complete the deal," according to Murnane. Aaron Stern was selling the Reds for $40,000 because "the league magnates never consulted him and held secret meetings all summer." The deal came as no surprise to the Reds, according to the Boston writer, who couldn't resist adding a plug for the Brotherhood: "The Cincinnati players knew of the deal some time ago, and all but Latham and one or two others were pleased to get into the crack base ball league of the century." Following up on this report the next day, he observed that "President Byrne of the Brooklyn club of the NL is much worked up tonight over the report that Cincinnati and Brooklyn will go over to the PL." Byrne had not been consulted on the matter, but Ferdinand Abell, who was one of the "lesser triumvirate" that owned the club and the owner of a professional gambling establishment, was reportedly "willing to sell out," leaving Byrne to wonder whether he should try to re-sign players for the next season. Brunell was due back from St. Louis on Tuesday, when Murnane hoped to know if a deal had been reached—or if the NL magnates had topped the deal offered by the PL.[34]

Recognizing the improvement that needed to be made to his profession, Chadwick took on the "sensational school" of baseball journalists and resumed his adopted role of baseball historian. Murnane's reports about the potential sales of the NL teams in Cincinnati and Brooklyn postdate Chadwick's letter, but the Brooklyn correspondent would have counted the Boston writer among the "fake story purveyors" who published rumors in the name of increasing circulations and sales. Chadwick further proved his aptitude as a soothsayer with the following sporting metaphor:

> Ever since the PL was evolved and the new League was started the rival magnates and their special organ players have been engaged in a big game of poker, with pens in the place of cards with which to play their respective little games, and the party which bluffs the best "takes the pot." While all these fakes are in progress with the object of keeping up the unhealthy excitement, arbitrators who have their wits at command, are busily and quietly at work laying their plans for the ending of the base ball war in the near future. A settlement of the dispute must come, and it will come before the end of November.

As it turned out, Soothsayer Chadwick was right on most counts—with the exception that Albert Goodwill Spalding was the best "bluffer" of them all.[35]

Returning to his Nestor role, Chadwick added the historical perspective of earlier baseball labor disputes without resorting to his usual harangue that catalogued the abject failures of the PL. Taking his 1890 readers back to the beginnings of professional baseball, his thumbnail sketch included how "the rottenness of the old Professional National Association in the early seventies" led to "the time of the honesty of the existing National League in the eighties" with the hiccup of "the revolt of the contract-breakers, which brought into existence the Old Union Association," which, in turn, led to the "enactment of the National Agreement." While conveniently glossing over the "bulldozing" and other questionable practices of the 1880s, he used an even, matter-of-fact voice to blame—again—the current crisis on "the greed of exorbitantly paid star players, whose self-aggrandizement was the prime incentive of the revolt of 1889." Despite arguing that the "revolutionary eras" had "temporarily demoralized" the game, Chadwick expressed a belief they would ultimately have the benefits of improving the "legislative workings of the professional organizations." Tapping into baseball's link to the Horatio Alger myth, he defended the game's potential for upward mobility, arguing there was no "earthly reason" why players couldn't "wisely" save up their salary "in trying to become a magnate in a stock company club."[36]

As the end of the season approached, Ella Black found little new to report and resorted to covering the small things the Burghers could do to influence the standings while holding out hope that the Alleghenys would avoid bringing disgrace to the Smoky City. Her wishes and the desired victories—small or otherwise—would not be fulfilled. With the pennant all but secured by the Red Stockings, Murnane was able to take a breath and resume his role as PL promoter with his report on the sale of the Reds. The sight of the season's end allowed Chadwick to return to Nestor the soothsayer and historian more often; he used many of the same arguments, but with less of the agitated voice of a Roman senator who saw danger in the offing. Significantly, the *Spalding's Guide* editor predicted his employer's skill in the poker games that were about to take place in October and November. Perhaps buoyed by the arrival of crisp autumn weather and the sight of the finish line, sportswriters turned reflective as the significant season of 1890 ground to a close.

Week 23—September 20-26: "We" Are the Red Stockings, PL Business Surprise, and Covering the "Old Rut of Slugging"

At the beginning of the penultimate week of the season, the Boston Red Stockings and the Brooklyn Bridegrooms each had a "cinch" on the

4. Late Season

championships of their respective leagues, so the discussion focused on the future of baseball in America. When Clarence Dow interviewed director Conant, the Beaneaters leader estimated that the two leagues would evenly split the half million dollars lost over the course of the season, with his fourth-place team being just $25,000 in the red due to posting the league's best attendance for a 50-cent city. After vowing to offer no quarter to the PL, Conant would not be convinced that there was enough room in the country for two leagues and promised there would be no compromise because he and the rest of the triumvirs would "continue the fight until one of the leagues is dead." Instead of asking Charles Byrne about his championship-winning season, Murnane investigated the rumors that some of his players had already signed with the rival league and received a defiant, yet defensive response: "If any of them care to desert that is their lookout." As the final pitch of the season approached, Murnane and Black summarized the events of the "war" and looked to the future, while Chadwick returned to more of his usual self by calling for rules changes.[37]

Writing his *SL* report from Cleveland while on the road with the Red Stockings, Murnane wrapped up the 1890 season and looked forward to the next one. After Boston won its first championship in seven years, he showed his strong identification with the team at the end of the campaign through his use of the first person: "Our success in Chicago…. We wanted all three games. We would not have murmured if we had won but one." Along with noting how several teams were already looking to strengthen their rosters for the following year—which included a number of NL players who were prepared to jump to the rival league, he admonished the senior circuit for underestimating the new league and addressed the magnates directly: " Gentlemen, take my advice and turn your attention towards your own bodies and endeavor to bring that about by which the game will be restored to that popularity among your own patrons, which it deservedly had, but which now has been sadly shattered." Writing with the same tone of the gracious winner, Murnane boomed the "magnificent struggle" made by John Ward over the course of the season and included him among the team leaders searching for ways to strengthen their teams.[38]

Like Murnane, Black split her column between putting a wrap on the present season and looking toward the future. Reporting "the burlesque on the national game that was perpetrated" by the NL Giants in

Pittsburgh on September 23, she noted that Jesse Burkett, who was a rookie that year, and Amos Rusie, who was in his second season at age 19, walked five straight batters to force in two runs. The image provided by Black's description of the reaction revealed how Alleghenys fans had to take their excitement wherever they could find it: "By the time the small but select audience of some three hundred and odd people were yelling like madmen and fiends combined, and the enthusiasm had even infected the few feminines in the grand stand and they were helping the uproar along by waving their hankerchiefs [sic]." After the game, which was loss number 109 for the home team, Black claimed that her brother and cousin, who had served as her escorts, could hardly speak above a whisper three days later when she was writing her letter to *SL*. Clearly, the Alleghenys would have benefitted from even just the minimum of 72 fans who would have attended with the Young Ladies of the Diamond. Of course, they would have needed wins to bring Black and her fellow fans and their gentlemen escorts to Recreation Park, and they would have needed home dates that weren't shifted to better-paying cities, but both were in short supply for the NL club in 1890.[39]

When the New York PL Giants were in town, Black used one of her proxy interviewers to gather the latest intelligence from Buck Ewing, who asserted that the PL was "all right" and that "there was a large-sized surprise in store for everyone in base ball." Linking this surprise to the recent rumors about the Cincinnati club, she went on to assert that Ewing was instrumental in the efforts to transfer the local franchise to his hometown because his wife did not like New York City.[40]

Henry Chadwick divided his report between calling for rule changes and challenging the claims of his fellow baseball journalists. Alerting—or warning—his readers of his plan to examine a different rule each week until the rules committee meeting in November, he was ready to throw out the livelier ball used by the PL, but wanted to test the longer pitching distance with the NL ball in order to promote a more scientific game and reduce the "old rut of slugging for home runs and making fungo hits to the outfield." To advance this improvement in the game, the man who invented the box score wanted to toss out extra-base hits in favor of "runs batted in by safe hits" and "sacrifice hits." He further supported this assertion by once again recognizing what he took to be the class differences in the fans and speaking for both classes:

> The patrons of the game have begun to realize the true inwardness of scientific batting, as shown in the securing of single bases by well-timed *place hits, safe taps* of swiftly pitched balls to short outfield, and skillful efforts in *sacrifice hitting* and *bunting,* every such hit forwarding a run or sending a run in. Of course, to occupants of the bleaching boards, as a rule, the great attraction is the long hit over the fence for a home run, which is made at the cost of a 120 yards sprint and at the loss of all chances for skillful fielding [italics in the original].

Taking his lead from the "better" or "best" or "true" patrons of the game, or the ones with the capacity to appreciate its finer points, not the ones who wanted to swill beer at the ballpark on Sunday, Chadwick thus admonished his "journalistic confreres" to cover "scientific batting" and the other fine points of the game instead of promoting "heavy hitting" and the more sensational elements.[41]

Although the furor over comps and the attendance figures had died down, neither side was willing to admit defeat or grant quarter to the opposition. Murnane's interview with Bridegrooms president Byrne and his scolding of the NL magnates to look to their own affairs reflected the attitude of assumed PL victory. After taking her readers out to the ballpark to help them savor the last few games, Black utilized the small number of journalistic devices open to her to produce significant copy through a proxy interview with a key PL leader. Chadwick's return to the more sedate voice of Nestor the advisor/historian and his focus on the need to address various rule changes marked an end to the earlier urgency and an assumed victory for the NL. Both sides could see the end of the fight, but the war was far from over.

Week 24—September 27–October 4: Season's End

Having already clinched the pennant, the Boston Red Stockings went 3–4 in the last week of the season while playing road games in Cleveland, Buffalo, and Pittsburgh. They closed the season with three games in Pittsburgh against Foxy Ned Hanlon's Burghers. Finding Bill Daley's deliveries to be "pie" in the first game of a doubleheader, the Burghers collected ten runs on 12 hits to win the penultimate contest of the season. Murnane reported that the Red Stockings were "handicapped for want of a left-fielder" because Hardie Richardson had to play shortstop due to the absence of Arthur Irwin and King Kelly. Answering the "telegrams from home" that asked the Red Stockings to "get the last game if possible," Ad Gumbert held the Pittsburgh nine to three runs on six hits, allowing the Boston team to end "the season as 'twas begun, with a victory." With the appreciation of a former player, Murnane closed his coverage of the championship season by granting Richardson the fielding and hitting honors for both games, noting how he accepted 11 of 12 chances while filling in at shortstop and collected five hits—including a double and a triple—in nine times at bat.[42]

When he expanded his reporter role once more to that of promoter, Murnane's final reports took on an unintended irony. Sunday's triumphant lead, "With today's sun went out the first championship season of the PL," would have been bittersweet at best to members of the Brotherhood who might have run across it just a few months later. Parts of his short update scribbled in haste the next day would have been equally hard to swallow by the end of the year. After announcing that the "Champs" were coming home, the Boston writer provided his readers with the team's accommodations (the Westminster Hotel), their schedule (exhibition game in Paterson, NJ, on Monday and travel to Springfield, MA on Tuesday for another game), injuries (catcher Morgan Murphy and third baseman Billy Nash), and reported that Captain Kelly was expected to rejoin the team for the game in his hometown. Correctly predicting that the Red Stockings would receive a "hearty" reception in Boston, he borrowed key words from Henry Chadwick when he claimed, "they have worked faithfully and played ball scientifically." Murnane's other declaration would not fare so well in hindsight: "The members of the team are highly elated over the Cincinnati deal, and express the belief that next year will find the PL the strongest organization, financially and in playing ability, ever seen in this country." While the PL may have indeed possessed the talent in 1890, its backing was still shaky enough to bring about its demise in the next two months.[43]

Recognizing the end of the season as the time to check the accuracy of predictions and settle the score of the contests on and off the field, Murnane launched his most vitriolic attack on Henry Chadwick, taking the veteran sportswriter to task at length. Responding to the Brooklyn correspondent's spleen-filled rampage against the PL over the previous months, Murnane objected to Chadwick's age, partisan stance, apparent absence of facts, and presumption to know Boston attendance figures

4. Late Season

without being present at the games. Then the attacks became even more personal: Murnane accused Chadwick of spreading rumors about drinking and rowdyism in the PL and refuted his allegations of bad behavior on the fields of the new league. Perhaps most damning of all, Murnane questioned Chadwick's independence as a journalist: "What else could have been expected of the compiler of the League Guide and under League pay?"[44]

As the attack went on, it became clear that Chadwick and Murnane had a history that dated back to the year before when the *Globe* writer was covering the championship between the New York Giants of the NL and the Brooklyn Bridegrooms of the AA. Apparently Murnane had the temerity to praise the play of the Giants during a game in Brooklyn, prompting the veteran sports journalist to "glare and privately insult" Murnane. Still stinging from this treatment almost a year later, he addressed Chadwick directly: "You tried your tongue and pen on me, old fellow, but I was on the right side then as I am now." Then he correctly predicted that fewer readers would be influenced by Chad's "screeds" in the following season and came back to the *Spalding's Guide* editor after taking some other NL supporters to task for their inaccurate predictions and attendance assessments. Beyond their differences regarding the rights of players and the future of the game, it was clear that Murnane had some unresolved issues with the Father of Baseball.[45]

For his part, Chadwick appeared once more to have put aside the shrill tone of his editorial persona to view the season's end with the more stately perspective that had earned him the titles and nicknames he enjoyed. Proving once again to be above the partisanship of the hometown fan, the Brooklyn correspondent only mentioned the NL champion Bridegrooms to note how they were the "tail-ender" of the league one week into the season and to refute Murnane's claim from the week before that members of Byrne's team were looking to jump to the PL:

> If there is any one professional club in any of the leagues in which players desire to get a position it is in the Brooklyn NL Club. Not a player who was wanted in the team for 1890 left it to join the Players' League clubs a year ago; and if they did not go then, what earthly inducement can that League offer the Brooklyn players now?

While Chadwick would no doubt have claimed to be working from facts, his more discerning readers may have detected the strains of local pride running underneath his declaration as he described what he took to be one of the NL's top clubs, illustrating that he was not 100 percent free from the sports journalism sin of rooting from the press box.[46]

Chadwick did not give up his attack on the PL entirely. With concealed glee, he pointed out how Comiskey's "picked nine" experienced a reversal of fortunes when the Chicago Pirates went from first place in the PL on May 10 to fifth place four months later. The *Spalding's Guide* editor took one more opportunity to advance his argument that the double umpire system had been a failure in the PL because of "the great license given to kicking by the player-director-managers and captains" and to remind his readers of how the same system had succeeded "in important NL games" where it was "conclusively shown to be the only correct plan yet tested." Speaking once more in the voice of wise Nestor, Chadwick averred that PL backer Colonel Talcott had learned a great deal about the true nature of baseball players: "Had he my experience of the majority of the playing fraternity he would long ago have known what he knows now, viz.:—that gratitude for favors shown is not a conspicuous trait of professional players' character, while vulgar conceit is." By the end of November, the PL would learn the true nature of Talcott.[47]

As the final days of the season approached, Chadwick turned to the impending peace process. Returning to his phrasemaking role, the veteran sportswriter described an informal October 8 meeting in poetic and almost religious terms: "The light which is to usher in the dawn of coming peace in the professional base ball world has appeared in the east." With regard to the sale of the Reds, he was more reticent than Murnane, calling the arrangement merely "proposed" in contrast to the completed deal assumed by the PL backer. More significantly, Chadwick's persistent support of William Hulbert's moral vision of the NL was revealed in the tone of his report that he had learned "the vote among the PL clubs in favor of the Association rule of Sunday games, free beer and twenty-five cent admission fee for 1891 is about five to one in favor of its adoption." Noting that the "club capitalists" of the New York PL team were the dissenting vote, Chadwick apparently reversed his position once more when he made another pitch for "amalgamation" by suggesting that the PL backers in favor could "help to reorganize the AA." Though he was willing to throw up his hands and admit, "Stranger things have happened," Chadwick's plan still represented a step back for the PL to a less discerning—and profitable—audience.[48]

4. Late Season

Similar to nearly any point during the last months of the season, there was little good baseball news to report in Pittsburgh. Reflecting on the long campaign, Black examined the various performances of the local teams, as well as her performance as a baseball writer. The female journalist adopted her critical, analytical tone while recapping how the bad luck of the Alleghenys was largely due to mismanagement. After one "only a woman" moment at the beginning of her review, Black spent very little time "speaking for her sex" and turned instead to evaluating talent for the next season, starting with the woeful Alleghenys:

> It must certainly be admitted, unless I am even worse a judge than the average woman is supposed to be, that the team is fully able to play a first-class game with any other club in the NL if the management would only endeavor to correct the weak spots that are now in it. The principal ones just now are at first base, at short stop, and in the pitcher's box.

The signings in early October made by J. Palmer O'Neill did little to shore up those gaps. George "Doggie" Miller, whose other nicknames included "Foghorn" and "Calliope," played the bulk of his 138 games at third base and made a total of 82 errors in 1890. Playing all over the infield for Pittsburgh in 1891, Doggie committed 80 errors in 135 games. As a solution in the pitcher's box, the re-signing of John "Phenomenal" Smith cast further doubt on O'Neill's judgment. Going 1–3 in five games with the Alleghenys after bringing a 8–12 record from the Philadelphia Phillies, Smith failed to live up to his nickname in 1891, finishing his eight-year career with a 1–1 record and a 4.26 ERA in three games with the Phillies. Black had high hopes that Billy Gumbert would be back and was confident he would one day earn more than $15 a game and "draw a larger salary from a professional club than ever his brother Ad has received." Billy did not pitch in 1891, but did go 3–2 in six games for the Pirates in 1892 with a sparkling 1.36 ERA.[49]

The questions about Pittsburgh's ability to support two major league teams lingered at the end of the season. J. Palmer O'Neill admitted to losing money—an admission that was perhaps forced by the overwhelming evidence of the poor home attendance figures of the Alleghenys, given as 16,064 for 39 games in the *Boston Globe*. The Burghers, on the other hand, claimed to have broken even, an assertion that was not entirely supported by their attendance figures, 117,123 for 64 games. Black challenged that claim in print but went on to rebut Murnane's assessment by asserting that her hometown possessed the capacity to function as a battleground city if both leagues took the field in the spring of 1891: "There is no doubt about it that this city will support two clubs and do it well. The only thing the enthusiasts here want is good playing, and if that is to be had they will most certainly patronize the games." Ella Black's hometown pride thus came through at the end of the season. The Pittsburgh correspondent returned once more to covering the feminine side of the baseball equation when she expressed her sorrow for Horace Phillips' relapse, noting how his wife "was a lovely little woman" and suggested that perhaps a future Alleghenys manager would benefit from being so "nice and attentive" as to make himself "very popular with the ladies."[50]

Black's final report during the regular season revealed that she did not think of herself as a finished product. Referring to another side conversation with a fellow journalist, she thanked New York *SL* correspondent William H. Harris, who had been a supporter of hers all along, for providing her with instruction on "sacrifice hitting." Showing renewed confidence in her opinion, she disagreed with a fellow writer who "evidently had a very vivid imagination" that let him make the claim that "Ward, Anson, and some others, are not only able to hit the ball whenever they want to, but are able as well to knock it wherever they please." Working from this premise, she used her own imagination to envision some of the "picked nines" of the future: "Is it not a pity that we cannot get up a team of such players as these? For, surely they would never have any trouble to win a pennant."[51]

The close of the 1890 season brought representative changes in the approaches used by each of the sportswriters under examination in this study. Focusing his late-season editorial efforts on discussing the business model that would best suit the future of the game, Henry Chadwick still addressed the players and the state of sport journalism, but these topics were clearly of secondary importance to him. Another significant change was his shift away from his strident, shrill Roman persona, which may have indicated a return of his confidence in the ability of the NL to survive the PL challenge, a reduction in pressure from his employer, A. G. Spalding, or both. While T. H. Murnane was more balanced in his coverage throughout the closing months, the tenor of his reports reflected the degree to which he became caught up in the pennant race and the eventual championship earned by "his" Boston Red Stockings.

4. Late Season

Lacking (apparently) Chadwick's investment in the game of more than three decades and Murnane's experience as a former player, Ella Black remained balanced in her coverage of the three key issues. If anything, she moved away from overt references to the projects she undertook as a female sportswriter; at the same time, her reports demonstrated her confidence in her work while finding her voice after more than half a year of weekly missives from the Smoky City. The conclusion of the championship season did not bring an end to their reports, however: there would be a pennant to celebrate, a business argument to settle, and the future of sports journalism to decide.

5

Post-Season

Reporting on the Scene and Watching from the Sidelines

Once the "Last Games of a Year of Warfare on the Diamond" were played, only the pennant winners for each league were decided; the future of baseball remained undetermined. Brooklyn and Louisville looked to battle for the Dauvray Cup, but supporters of the Brotherhood opined that the series would produce only "So-Called World's Champions" due to the absence of the PL pennant winners. With "The End of the Costly War Now In Sight," local "cranks" put the losses by both Cleveland teams at a minimum of $60,000 as officials in battleground cities tallied similar red numbers. Francis Richter dropped the page count of *SL* from 16 to 12 pages, and the coverage of the players and the games was reduced accordingly. While the "Base Ball Magnates" were "Talking Compromise" and otherwise "Dickering," the negotiations between the NL and the PL became the top story in October and November. Even though sportswriters devoted much of their post-season reports to the resolution of the long conflict, they remained aware of each other's work and the development of their profession.[1]

Beyond Richter's "Brief Review" of the "Financial Failure" and "Relative Merits" of the PL's "First Championship Season," the post-season reports of *SL* correspondents reflected the diminished importance of the players and the games at that point in the baseball calendar. Writers from the championship cities of Boston (PL), Brooklyn (NL), and Louisville (AA) covered pennant celebrations, exhibition tours, and Dauvray Cup games. Other writers interviewed local players and wrapped, recapped, and commented on the season while monitoring the celebrations and negotiations locally and in other battleground cities.

5. Post-Season

Ward, Ewing, Kelly, and key Brotherhood leaders remained in the press, but the focus of their coverage shifted away from their performance on the field to the decisions being made about the future of the game.[2]

During the post-season months of October and November, the sporting press was keenly interested in the question of which business model would emerge from the conflict between the NL and the PL. In particular, the discussion focused on three possibilities for peace in the baseball war: 1) an amalgamation of the PL and the AA; 2) a compromise between the NL and the PL; or 3) a consolidation between the two leagues. The impacts of each option on the business of the game were also explored at length in the sporting weeklies and daily newspapers in the battleground cities. Supporters of the PL continued to advocate for the rights of the players to determine the shape of their employment, while others adopted an anti-player stance that reaffirmed the capitalistic governance of the NL owners. Writers from dual-team cities covered the negotiations between their local NL and PL franchises, while other writers were sent to New York City to report on the negotiations taking place there. In November, reporters were also sent to the annual meetings of the PL in Pittsburgh and the NL in New York City.

The image of the game was of secondary importance to the settlement of the conflict between the NL and the PL, yet Murnane, Chadwick, and Black addressed it at the end of the season. After covering the exhibition tour and the pennant celebration of the Red Stockings, Murnane worked to put the Boston team and the Players' League in the best light. In addition to evaluating the players on both sides of the issue, conducting just his second player interview of the year, and attempting to bury the PL, Chadwick turned in his final performances as Cato the Elder and looked ahead to the future of the game. Wrapping up the disappointing season in Pittsburgh and closing the books on the dubious business practices of both local teams while harking back to two of her initial goals, Black used her final *SL* reports to establish her place as a female sports journalist and improve the image of the players to help win over the best class of audience for the game. Perhaps not surprisingly, Black and Murnane showed considerable growth as a result of covering the 1890 season, while Chadwick remained largely set in the approach developed over almost four decades of covering the game.

I. The Game on the Field—Murnane's Post-Season Tour, Chadwick's Use of the Players, and Black's Championship Challenges

Of the three writers under study, only Murnane covered the players regularly in the post-season due to Boston's pennant and his good working relationship with the Brotherhood men. Conducting his second player interview of the year, Chadwick talked with Buck Ewing of the PL, but it was another chance meeting, like the one with Ward in March. Without direct access to the players, Black reviewed the moves of the local managers. While each was different in tone, Murnane's and Black's post-season coverage was mostly reportorial in nature, while Chadwick worked to extend his previous arguments.

Covering the victory tour of the Red Stockings for the *Globe*, T. H. Murnane traveled with the PL champions as they played their way home with a series of exhibition games against the PL Giants in Paterson, NJ, Springfield, Worcester, and Boston, MA (and then back to Paterson). Upon reaching their hometown, the champions were feted in a daylong celebration. PL President McAlpin presented the pennant to Captain Kelly before the exhibition game held on Saturday, October 11. While the attendance fell somewhat short of the 19,000 who paid to see the Fast Day Game in April, more than 3,000 fans braved a chilly rain to see the pennant raised at the Congress Street Grounds. The PL champions took the three exhibition games played before the two teams reached Boston, but the "Gothamites" stole the thunder of Kelly's boys by winning the five-inning game that was shortened due to the weather. Writing with the magnanimous grace of the victor, Murnane credited the New York win to the "steady, heady game" pitched by Hank O'Day, who held the Red Stockings to a pair of runs on five hits, and the fact the "Giants played their positions to win." According to the player-turned-sportswriter, the game's features included King Kelly starting a "pretty" double play on a bunt with the bases loaded and Dan Brouthers' "daring" sliding and batting. Despite his stated aversion to exhibition games like the controversial Elmira contest in June, Murnane treated all the games he covered in October with the same level of detail and style, demonstrating that he was willing to move past his bias to be in the spirit of the moment. Perhaps he was hanging onto the last few write-ups in

5. Post-Season

anticipation of the long, dark off-season ahead. (See the full text of Murnane's October 4 report in Part 7 of Appendix A.)[3]

Invoking the "local boy made good" trope often found in baseball writing, Murnane covered Mike Kelly's return to the site of his first amateur game in his hometown of Paterson, NJ. Three thousand people turned out on October 17 to watch the PL champions take on their New York rivals one last time on a cold, blustery day, and nearly half again as many people watched "from windows of adjoining houses, from the tops of sheds and trees, as well as the tops of teams pulled up alongside of the fence." The grass hadn't been cut and the temperature was too cold for hard running, but the players were able to put on a hitting exhibition into the howling wind. The two teams combined for 31 hits and a total of 51 bases; unfortunately for the man of the hour, "Only Kel" was held hitless in five trips on his day. Ever the PL promoter, Murnane boosted the players and their cause by reporting that the tour had been "a big financial success." Kelly's homecoming game was the last of 32 meetings between the Red Stockings and the Giants in 1890; Boston won 12 of the 19 regular season contests and 7 of the 13 exhibition games.[4]

Not far from the silk factories of Paterson, NJ, Henry Chadwick extended his season-long argument against the PL by using his role as baseball historian to compare the "faithless" players of 1890 to those of the 1884 labor conflict. Pulling no punches, the veteran sportswriter broke out some fancy prose and a pack of prepositions in the process: "The taint of the rascalities of the period of the existence of the old Union Association of contract-breakers and revolvers has pervaded the professional atmosphere all this season; especially rank has been the odor of it from the Eastward." As a cautionary tale of how "baseball heroes of yesterday are of but little account today," he offered the example of George Washington Bradley, who finished his career on the "Outlaw" Cincinnati Reds. The games to decide the world's championship were being played in Brooklyn in October, yet the readers of SL would not have known anything about the series from Chadwick's reports other than a brief mention of how the "Little Corporal," or Bridegrooms manager Bill McGunnigle, held "a mortgage" on the championship.[5]

Parallel to his encounter with John Ward in April, a chance meeting with Buck Ewing at Nick Engle's Home Plate allowed Chadwick to submit his second player interview of the year and advance his argument by showing how a PL leader agreed with his views about what was best for baseball. When Ewing "openly acknowledged" that "there was but one way to control a player, and that was *through the medium of his pocket*" (italics in the original), the *Spalding's Guide* editor heard that the player was "in full accord" with his views about the failure of the cooperative system used by the PL. After Ewing advocated "the fining of every player of a team who fails, by his bad habits, to keep himself in thorough playing condition for the work in the field he is called upon to perform during the championship season," Chadwick took it to mean that Ewing, as a player, wanted "to see a reorganized and improved professional club government take the place of such socialistic schemes." Toward the end of finding a settlement between the NL and PL, Chadwick told the player that he "hoped he would succeed in bringing about a union of interest between Messrs. Day and Talcott, which Buck is striving for." A week later, he repeated his argument when he praised Ewing for having the "manliness to offset his action in aiding the revolt of 1889 by a commendable effort to make some sort of show in grateful acknowledgement of his indebtedness to Mr. John B. Day for the years of kind consideration shown him." Further, Chadwick commended Ewing's "great amount of moral courage to bravely acknowledge an error of judgment" in supporting the PL a year earlier. Of note here was that Chadwick's "kind consideration" conveniently omitted the reserve rule and the Brush Classification System, two of the management tools at the heart of the Brotherhood's decision to form their own league. Other NL supporters saw Ewing as a "spy for the Brotherhood" when he turned up at one of their November meetings. Then, as now, the extent of Ewing's involvement was open to speculation, but it was clear that his "peace efforts" were not universally approved by members of the PL. What's more, receiving the praise of the *Spalding's Guide* editor may not have worked in Ewing's favor given that the writer had done little during the 1890 season to improve his popularity with the players.[6]

After ignoring elements of the "rebel" league for most of the season, Chadwick quoted other PL players and officials, but only when it appeared they were ready to agree with his views. He could not resist reprinting John Ward's remarks about the current "danger" threatening the game as a result of the Brotherhood War and the notion that the public had become "disgusted" by the fight. Secretary Brunell's approval of "'the demand of the press and public for a cessation of hostilities, which has done so much harm to the game'" warranted reprinting as

5. Post-Season

examples of how two key PL figures were "beginning to see things from a new light apparently." Adopting his fatherly stance once more, Chadwick dispensed a bit of parental wisdom and engaged in homespun adage-making aimed at Ward, Brunell, and the rest of the misguided players and their backers: "They will all come to their senses in due time. The nerves of the pocket have been rudely jarred this past season, and the shocked parties don't relish it." At the same time, he proved that he wasn't above floating rumors and sensational "fakes" of his own when he repeated the claim of Ward's official scorer that the Brotherhood leader planned to manage the Bridegrooms in 1891. Covering himself by asking Byrne, the owner of the NL franchise, to corroborate the scorer's second-hand story, Chadwick was thus able to make his own contribution to consolidation fever under the guise of good journalism.[7]

As the "peace process" between the two major leagues dragged into November, Chadwick renewed his attack on the Brotherhood and took some shots at their capitalist backers as well. Reprising Spalding's earlier comment about the mercenary quality of the PL, the veteran sportswriter claimed to be surprised that the backers were not able to see that the players were "solely 'out for the stuff'" as the only motivation for their revolt against the owners. Then Chadwick went on to criticize the demeanor of the players as a class:

> By and bye, when the *morale* of the fraternity is improved by the introduction of a more educated and intelligent class of players, in the place of the roughs and drunkards who at present are far too numerous for the good name of the players in general, there may be an opening for less arbitrary methods, but at present the strong arm is the only available means of enforcing discipline in the ranks [italics in the original].

Resuming his attack two weeks later, he admonished "the professional ball players who spent their salaries in dissipation at the brothels, the saloons, and all the gambling houses this past season—as too many of the fraternity habitually do." After predicting an especially hard Shakespearian "winter of discontent" for the players who revolted, he warned that the faithless, ungrateful reprobates would be especially hard-pressed due to their intemperate habits. Once more, Chadwick proved his independence from the "player class" and demonstrated that he was willing to make himself unpopular with it in the service of improving baseball's image with the patrons whose acceptance could put the game on a more secure footing within American culture.[8]

Reporting from Pittsburgh without apology, hesitation, or reference to being "only a woman," Ella Black covered "Foxy" Ned Hanlon's signings for the 1891 season with the confidence of a veteran writer. Looking for some pitching help to shore up Harry Staley and Al Maul, who had been his stalwarts in 1890, Hanlon went west to sign Martin Duke and was planning to re-sign Ed Beecher to play left field. Recalling Beecher's arrival in the Smoky City to debut at age 27 in 1887, Black described the outfielder as an early incarnation of the Busher, a figure that would become a staple in early twentieth century baseball fiction:

> On the morning of his arrival, I saw him walking down Fifth avenue with Manager Phillips, a friend telling me who he was, and he certainly was nothing like a ball player in appearance. His resemblance, however, to a country youth, who had put on his Sunday suit and come to town for a holiday, was very striking.

Despite this approval from the now self-assured female sportswriter, neither of Hanlon's recruits appeared for Pittsburgh, and even if they had, it is doubtful they would have helped the team: Duke played in only four games for Washington in the AA in 1891, going 0–3 with a 7.43 ERA; Beecher played for Washington and Philadelphia in the AA, hitting just .235 in 71 games split between the two teams. Hanlon had better luck at the end of the month when he signed Connie Mack and Lou Bierbauer away from the Buffalo Bisons and the Brooklyn Wonders, respectively. Some observers felt the Pittsburgh manager had overstepped with these signings, which led to the Pittsburgh franchise being nicknamed "the Pirates" in 1891. Black applauded Hanlon's actions and revealed some impatience toward his critics in the press: "…because he happens to be shrewd and knows how to look after the interest of his club, is no reason he should be made to suffer, to suit people who are too lazy and stupid to know what is best for their club." Gone was the meek, hesitant tone of the rookie scribe whose work first appeared nine months earlier; in its place were the opinions of a full-fledged sportswriter.[9]

Continuing in that same vein on October 31, the Pittsburgh correspondent commented on the "nerve" of Brooklyn and Louisville to play for a "world's championship" while leaving out the winners of the Players' League. After the series between the NL and AA representatives ended in a tie, the two clubs agreed to meet in the spring of 1891 to decide the

5. Post-Season

winner. Following the line of her argument, Black went so far as to suggest that Mike "King" Kelly challenge the winner of the series—and then claim the title when they refused to play his Boston Red Stockings. Some *SL* readers might have found this suggestion to be medieval and others might have felt the rules she "read up" on had more to do with boxing, but PL supporters, including T. H. Murnane, might very well have agreed with her assessment that that year's title of "World's Champion" would be a "very empty honor, and one that carries with it but very little to be proud of." In any case, it should have been clear to Black's doubters that she was not afraid to advance her positions on the players and opinions about the policies of the game alongside those of her fellow sporting journalists.[10]

II. The Business—October's Scheming Magnates and November's Traitors

Away from the ball field, the future of the game was decided in two phases: in a series of conference meetings in October between representatives of the two premier leagues and the AA, and during the annual meetings for the PL and NL that took place in early November. Talk of compromise or consolidation had been in the press as early as July; however, there was very little consensus on either side. On one level, "compromise" meant "surrender" to many of the Brotherhood members; moreover, it was unacceptable to NL adherents because it meant an alliance between the PL and the AA, which amounted to an affirmation of the right of the PL to exist—as well as the right of the players to take matters into their own hands at the expense of the capitalist magnates. For others, the arrangement would mean an unwise blending of a product intended for the "better class of patrons" (the PL) with a lower class audience (the AA fans who spent but 25 cents on tickets to attend Sunday games and drink alcohol in the parks). Yet another group objected due to the weak, unmanly sound of the term itself. "Consolidation," or the combination of NL and PL franchises sharing a city, was equally thorny because the two sides had to come to an agreement on how the assets should be divided and the percentage of ownership given to each side in the new arrangement. It was less desirable from the NL perspective because it meant the players would meet at the table with the owners as equals, with the players holding the best cards. Thus, the issue went past rhetoric and economics and became political. Regarding the business of baseball, Murnane spent much of October and November in New York to report on the aftermath of the Brotherhood War, while Chadwick and Black covered the negotiations indirectly as "Cheap John" and "Cheap Jane" journalists who watched from a distance.[11]

When conference committees from the NL and PL met informally on October 9, T. H. Murnane was still traveling with the Red Stockings and the Giants on their exhibition tour. It was in this meeting that Spalding set the tone for the negotiations between the two leagues over the next month and a half when he unnerved the inexperienced PL backers by bluffing that the NL had not lost nearly as much money as was admitted to by the PL backers. Since our source for this story is Spalding's own memoir, its credibility must be questioned.[12]

Henry Chadwick's early October reports make it clear that he was not invited to attend the meetings, forcing him to monitor the proceedings from Brooklyn the best he could. The stated purpose of the official October 10 meeting between the big two and the slightly smaller one was to discuss the ramifications of the Cincinnati sale, but Chadwick saw the offer by the NL as being an important first step in getting the combatants to communicate with each other. A week later, he repeated the need for the NL to agree to meet with the PL representatives to avoid having "the whole odium of a continuance of the base ball war" thrown onto the image of the senior circuit. In the same column, Chadwick praised the strength of the PL by writing that the league was "financially backed up to a degree entirely unexpected by the NL." In order to facilitate the peace process, the veteran sportswriter went on to acknowledge for the first time that the PL had achieved "quasi success" and suggested that the NL "will be obliged to realize the fact that the rival League is in the market to stay." These statements were hardly the sentiments of a victorious party, which may have explained Chadwick's ongoing absence from the negotiations.[13]

As reports of the various meetings were released in the weeks that followed, the baseball world sought clues for which league had the upper hand. On October 10, Black observed that the capitalists backing the new league appeared to be calling the shots, leaving her worried that the players would find themselves in the same condition as they were

5. Post-Season

before they started their labor movement. In her analysis, better public perception that the PL experiment was "being run by the players and for the players" would have created more sympathy and financial support. "By the players" and "for the players" put the PL two-thirds of the way to the "Jeffersonian Doctrine" identified by Murnane in April, but Black recognized that the experiment would not have the same impact if the public believed that the players had merely substituted a new set of millionaires for Spalding and the other NL magnates. Continuing to illustrate confidence in her opinions regarding business matters, she went so far as to call for the PL to be run by the players with their backers as silent partners.[14]

On October 18, that confidence was back when the Pittsburgh correspondent used a wry, ironic tone to report that the PL organization had the upper hand over Nimick and O'Neill of the NL. Black's lead reflected the smug perspective of the local PL officials—as well as her frustration with the extent and results of the season-long conflict:

> Well, well, who would have thought that such a thing would ever have come to pass as what has happened within the last few days. Only to think, that the people who less than one year ago were breathing all sorts of threats of blood and gore against each other, should now be lying down together after the fashion of the proverbial lion and lamb and be endeavoring to effect a compromise that will suit both parties and allow them to do away with the warfare that has so completely wrecked the base ball business during the past year.

The PL organization in Pittsburgh was clearly the lion in her analogy as Black mentioned twice how Nimick and O'Neill were "literally down on their knees begging for a compromise" and noted how "the PL people do not want any of the old club's men except George Miller." This stance by the PL led the reporter to believe that there would be no consolidation in her hometown since both clubs lost money, but she felt the Burghers had gotten the best of the fight on the strength of the club, the attractiveness of Exhibition Park, and public opinion. At the same time, Black warned the local officials to heed the possibility that "the NL would some day be again the great favorite in the eyes of the fickle public that it once was."[15]

In New York, the activities of the backers of the PL Giants were as prominent as in Pittsburgh. When the group met on October 17 to "straighten out" the deficit faced by the club, Murnane reported that

"Messrs. McAlpin, Talcott, Van Cott and Robinson" were not talking to the press, though Robinson did say that "if there was a consolidation[,] a majority of the stock would be placed in a trust for 10 years to prevent any freezing out process." Murnane reported on the disposition of Edwin Talcott and speculated on his position with regard to the end of the conflict:

> Mr. Talcott was deeply agitated over the report that several of the league players were not satisfied with the work of the committee that met the NL last week. The tone of his remarks implied that the two New York clubs would consolidate and force a settlement. They might or might not be successful.

The players would have been happier with the work of the committee if they had at least one representative at the meeting. John Ward was in New York at the time, but chose not to participate. According to the Boston reporter, supporters of the PL saw this decision as "a disastrous mistake, for it gave the NLrs a chance to cry, 'The players are not in it; I told you so,' a cry that at once created a dissatisfaction, and brought about the present state of affairs." Perhaps Ward was aware of the original stipulation that no player would be allowed to take part in the conferences, as well as the attitude of John B. Day, owner of the NL Giants, to hold to that stipulation absolutely. In Murnane's opinion, one man would determine the fate of the PL: "Upon the shoulders of President McAlpin the burden now rests."[16]

Returning to his more reasonable "Nestor" role, Chadwick advised both leagues to seek peace by calling attention to the overall cost of the "war"—after polishing up some old chestnuts and doing a little phrase-making of his own. Once again, he enumerated the failures of the PL, which included the double umpire system, the "elastic" ball, and the "impossible joint stock organization of the league." In a passage directed to *SL* editor and PL supporter Frances Richter, Chadwick decried how the "sentimental experiment" of the new league had cost "at a fair estimate" the NL magnates and the PL backers $500,000 in contrast to the players, who were operating under the motto of "*we can't lose any way*" (italics in the original). This assessment may have applied to the players in the NL, but it also left out the considerable sums invested by John Ward, Connie Mack, and a number of other players in the new league, which amounted to their life savings in some cases.[17]

5. Post-Season

By the end of October, however, Chadwick was back on the offensive as he renewed his attacks in a wide array of business and non-business dealings of the PL. The *Spalding's Guide* editor went so far as to blame the new league for the lackluster attendance of the World's Championship series between the Brooklyn Bridegrooms and the Louisville Colonels of the AA:

> The players' revolt made the fall exhibition season a lamentable failure this year, and it knocked the world's championship series out in a half a dozen rounds. Put it down as a fact that the record of the world's series for 1890 will go on the books as a drawn contest and a financial failure, the first on record, and the last, I hope.

Other accounts cited the poor weather as a primary factor for the minimal attendance, but Chadwick seldom missed an opportunity to blame the Brotherhood of Players for the ills experienced by the game in 1890. On the eve of the fateful meeting in which the players were expelled from the table, he wrote the following eulogy for the new league that barely contained his glee at seeing his year-long project fulfilled:

> The "PL," as a title, is now a misnomer. The conference committee gave its death-blow at their first meeting, and no doubt its funeral will take place after the meeting at noon today. It was conceived under the influence of a mistaken sentiment; it represents a plan practically inoperative, and the theory of its construction has been proven to be a fallacy, while the costly nature of its experimental trial has opened the eyes of its financial supporters to the innate weakness. Let it rest like the old Union Association, as one of the costly experiences of professional base ball history.

Returning to this issue a week later, Chadwick blamed both the indifference of his fellow Brooklynites and the fact the series was discontinued until the following spring on the presence of the PL. Saving some of his best phrasemaking for the end of the long season, Chadwick was more than willing to send the PL into its long goodnight and consign it to the dustbin of other historic failures.[18]

The local scene in Pittsburgh promised even less chance for compromise on October 21 when Black used her report to vent more of her frustration at the peace process and the men behind it. Noting how the PL management was demanding 70 percent of any combination of the two teams despite being a losing venture (but not to the same degree as the woeful Alleghenys), she revealed more than her opinion when she asserted that she would crush the NL if she were in the PL position:

I am, I suppose, like most of my sex, very stubborn, and I have always felt that if I was a man and got into a fight with any one (not that I approve of fighting at all) I would push it just as far as I was able to, and if I could defeat my opponent I would not leave him a single chance or hope of recovering. Now, I regard this base ball war in just that same way.

Such an aggressive stance was unusual for her, and perhaps indicated that she was frustrated with the negotiations between the two leagues. Black even speculated that the willingness of the PL club to negotiate at all was a sign of weakness because they were not confident of complete victory. Using her report to advance a peace accord of her own, she suggested that the two clubs appoint a neutral board of appraisers to evaluate each team's assets and decide the proportions each would own in a consolidated club.[19]

Sensing the shift in the prevailing winds near the end of October, Murnane wrote that New York City was "still full of scheming magnates" after he attended a five-hour meeting between Al Johnson and Albert Spalding at the Hoffman Hotel. The player-turned-sportswriter was apparently keeping score because he opined "the Cleveland man got the best of it." Contrary to what he told John Ward in December at the Manhattan Athletic Club, Spalding's view on the compromise vs. consolidation issue was that the players should not be taken into account in either case. Johnson previewed Ward's sentiments at the end of the year when he averred that the audience's opinion of how the players were treated should be considered: "'If the public can believe that the players have been treated fairly, why, then you can get back the old interest in the game, and not until then.'" Ever the PL partisan, Murnane reminded his readers that "A. G. Spalding's great object in getting the two leagues together is to give him a chance to handle the base ball supplies. I have learned from a pretty reliable source that his business this season was but half of what it was last year." Although he was certain that Spalding wanted to see the players "get the small end of the bargain," Murnane recognized at that point in his development as a journalist that the "scheming magnate" was capable of realizing that he needed "to win the good will of all the lovers of the national game."[20]

Murnane might have added "scheming backers" to his list of baseball men in New York who needed to be watched. President Addison of the Chicago PL club was in the city on Saturday and then went to visit league President McAlpin at his home in Ossining, NY. From the *Globe* writer's perspective, both men were not to be trusted: "Addison is the man the others are afraid will sell out, as McAlpin and his New York partners are still working to keep the agitation for compromise going." Murnane didn't pull any punches when he borrowed a term from a fellow PL partisan to describe what he took as the league president's duplicity: "Col. McAlpin, while blowing his trumpet about the glorious institution of the players, is quietly giving them the 'razzle-dazzle,' as George Dickinson would say." Edwin Talcott, who was a backer of the PL Giants along with McAlpin, was another target for Murnane's suspicions. One of the Philadelphia backers assured the Boston writer that Talcott promised "New York would [do] nothing dishonorable." Despite this assurance, Murnane told his readers that "Talcott is very clever at bluffing" and went on to blame the New York backer for the predicament the PL found itself in at the end of October: "The week winds up with the PL in the most uncomfortable frame of mind since it started in business, and all brought about by Talcott of the New York club." Instead of backing the PL blindly as he had done for most of the season, Murnane demonstrated his growth as a journalist by being critical of the Brotherhood backers when he saw fit to do so.[21]

Writing on Halloween, Ella Black used her report to vent more of her frustration with the peace process. Moving past the wry, dry, reflective tone she used earlier in the month to describe the folly of the men doing the negotiating, she resorted to angry name-calling to admonish those responsible for the lack of progress in reaching a solution:

> It is a great puzzle to me why full grown supposed-to-be sensible men should go on in such a deliberate, obstinate, pig-headed manner just like a lot of little children might do, and even the children would behave far better because it would not be long until they would be trying to "make up" with each other, but nothing of the sort is to be seen in this instance. I am more surprised than I can express to see so many bright, intelligent men as there is at present gathered on either side of this case showing so much childishness in the way they act, and really, to tell the honest truth, nearly all behaving as though there was not a single grain of common sense to be found in the combined brains of all the crowd.

Beyond her irritated tone, *SL* readers who were paying attention would have seen the breakdowns in her usual style and command of grammar as she went so far as to admit the difficulties she was having while trying to express her reactions. As always, there was no threat of her losing access to the owners and the players, so she could call things as she saw them to a greater degree than either Chadwick or Murnane. Beyond her usual candor, Black was starting to sound like someone who was getting ready to wash her hands of the whole business.[22]

Chadwick used his November 1 report to summarize the peace process to that point and provide more commentary on the recalcitrant players. After chastising the Brotherhood for not trusting their backers and expressing surprise that the backers didn't see the out-and-out greed of their partners, he solved the "compromise" vs. "consolidation" issue by using both terms, suggesting that the four teams in the area had found a "basis of compromise" that would allow them to find a "joint consolidation of their financial interests." Examining the role of the players in the peace process caused Chadwick once again to see them as coming up short:

> All the sentimental sympathy which was elicited in behalf of the "poor base ball slaves" last spring has vanished into thin air. If anything were wanting to open the eyes of the public to the true intent of the players' revolt, it was given by the action of the players in their effort to block the movement for peace. They then and there exposed their hands, and the public saw into their little game as plain as day.

This lack of sympathy for the players was further shown on the eve of the NL meetings in Chadwick's call for the NL to bury their upstart rivals: "If things turn out as I hope they will, it will see the finishing blow given to the players' revolt of 1890, followed by the funeral of the PL, and the end of the fratricidal war, inaugurated by the high salaried players, under the leadership of Ward." While this opinion would not win him any friends from the Brotherhood, it was consistent with the attitude the Brooklyn correspondent held at the beginning of the season.[23]

Writing on the eve of the annual meetings of the PL and the NL that would begin on November 11 and 12, respectively, Murnane recognized the coming week as "the most important one in the history of the national game." The *Globe* writer maintained his criticism of McAlpin and Talcott and added Wendell Goodwin of the Brooklyn PL club to his backers-to-be-watched list, saying that all three had "shown themselves utterly unworthy of the confidence of the players and their friends by meeting agents of the NL in secret and planning to turn them over to the men they had left but one short year ago." The "New York syndicate"

5. Post-Season

of McAlpin and Talcott was willing to put up half of the $30,000 Addison wanted from Spalding for his Chicago franchise, but, according to Murnane, "Spalding thought he had Addison in a bad corner, and told him that he intended to drive him out of the business." This development provided some hope for the PL, along with the point brought up by President Prince of the Boston club, who reminded all the clubs that they had signed a ten-year agreement and might be legally responsible for any ruin they brought to the league by leaving it early.[24]

While the negotiations were underway, John M. Ward was present in New York City and at the table for some of the meetings. Murnane described him as "very quiet" during the first part of this period but caught up with him in early November. Ward pointed to how the NL papers were "working hard to separate Mr. Talcott and the brotherhood players," a project Murnane himself might have contributed to with his comments about the Giants' backer. Ward's main concern was that the public knew it was not the players but "the men who went in to back them that have talked compromise." Beyond protecting the image of the Brotherhood, Ward felt it would have been more practical to have players at the table to bring about a better solution:

> If there was any compromise talk, why not have the men that understood the move on hand? It's rather amusing to hear these New York capitalists talk about saving the game. If they were anxious for our club in their city, why not take John R. Day in as half partner and remain in the PL? This would have settled all the ill-feeling in New York and allowed the club to remain in the strongest league in every sense.

After being locked out of the conference meetings at the end of October, Ward, Ewing, and other Brotherhood players began considering the possibility of running a six- or four-team circuit. By contrast, other players, most notably Mike Kelly, were not to be found in the thick of the discussions: "Capt. Kelly is taking life easy down on his Hingham farm, fishing, gunning and taking long walks over the country roads in the daytime and tickling the ivories on his own private table by electric lights by night."[25]

Murnane was in New York once again (or still) when the NL meetings started. The Boston writer returned to describing Spalding as the "brains of the old league in this great fight" and described the mood as high-spirited due to the rumors that the Pittsburgh clubs might consolidate along with the New York and Brooklyn clubs: "The league men are in high glee tonight over the news from Pittsburgh and feel as though they bluffed both the Pittsburgh and New York backers with a pair of deuces." Murnane further demonstrated his recognition of how sensationalism in the baseball press affected public opinion of the game: "It is believed here that New York will need all the care possible to keep it in line as a good base ball city, and the partisan papers will have hard work to make up for the harm they have done the game by allowing young and inexperienced hands to take charge of the department." As a 38-year-old journalist with five years of experience, his list of "young" New York sporting editors may have included 30-year-old PL backer George Dickinson of the *World*, 32-year-old NL loyalist William I. Harris, formerly of the *Press*, and 33-year-old John Mandigo of the *Sun*. His own partisan perspective and relative youth (when compared to Chadwick) notwithstanding, Murnane's stance here further illustrated his concern with improving the image of his profession and his position as a reporter.[26]

Writing once more from his Brooklyn seat without a hint of being invited to the NL annual meetings, Chadwick softened his stance when he called for the NL magnates to emulate the magnanimity of General Grant at Appomattox when dealing with the defeated players to "ensure the faithful service at the hands of the employee, not by means of arbitrary enactments." Proving once again that he would use 25 words when just five would do, he suggested that Charles Comiskey and Chris Von der Ahe let "by-gones be by-gones as to the past of 1890, and that the 'boss manager' and his once 'great captain' pool their interests" to work together to assemble a team that could once again contend for the AA pennant. The two of them provided a case study for Chadwick's argument about how baseball clubs needed to be operated: only under the "financial control of veteran Chris Von der Ahe" would Comiskey have the "opportunity to recover the prestige, as a manager and captain, which he undoubtedly lost in 1890." The veteran sportswriter added advice that would be echoed by Spalding in December when he met with John Ward: "Let Chris give Comiskey entire control of the working up of a reorganized St. Louis Browns team." Chadwick's extended treatment of this case study illustrated the degree to which he was already looking to the 1891 season, as well as how prominently the concept of the AA fit into his and his employer's visions of baseball's future.[27]

Once the annual meetings for the NL started on November 12, Mur-

5. Post-Season

nane was present in New York to report the NL's jubilant response to the good news that came from the PL meetings in the Smoky City. When Pittsburgh resigned from the PL and the New York PL club indicated it was ready to follow suit, the announcements were met with joy by the NL magnates in New York City even though the rest of the PL did not accept Pittsburgh's resignation. Mike "King" Kelly signed a contract with the Boston Beaneaters after meeting Albert Spalding and Director Conant. Kelly tried to soften the blow to his fellow players by putting the contract into his pocket and saying it was just something for him to hang onto until "he is sure just where he stands," but some of the NL men saw the stunt as "one more of his advertising breaks." J. Palmer O'Neill, as the director of the newly consolidated Pittsburgh club, claimed that John Ward backed down from a $10,000 offer to play baseball in the Smoky City in 1891. Ward was part of the conference committee sent by the PL to meet with the NL magnates gathered in New York, but Murnane reported "that Ward has gone off on a fishing excursion and will not be present" because he knew from experience that he would not be allowed to sit at the table with the money men. After being the target of much bad press over the course of the season, J. Palmer O'Neill enjoyed a number of accolades at the NL meeting: he was called "one of the heroes of the war of 1890" and was the recipient of a blue silk banner adorned with 113 white stars, one for each loss that season by his Alleghenys. Proving that he was able to take a joke as well as anyone, he enumerated the other records that his club had set in the process: most miles traveled, fewest games played on home grounds, played to least number of people, most players signed and released. O'Neill expressed his sense of humor when he shared his hope that the league would be as generous with a rebate to help cover his team's traveling expenses, which he gave as 2,230,000 miles above the travel of any other team. As a professional, Murnane put aside his partisan leanings to report what he observed, even if it meant providing negative press for players and leaders he'd supported earlier or giving attention to NL front office officials he'd criticized.[28]

On the evening of November 13, Murnane wired back the news of the sale of Addison's Chicago franchise to Spalding, which ultimately spelled the beginning of the end of the PL. Delegates from the new league traveled to New York to meet with their counterparts under the stipulation that none of them would leave unless all of them left together, but the damage was done and the die was cast. Once again, John Ward was absent from the proceedings; Murnane reported that he did not return from Pittsburgh, due to "a hunting expedition planned for in the West." The *Globe* reporter resumed his commentary on McAlpin's double dealing and King Kelly's "chewing of the rope at both ends," even as President Prince of the Boston Red Stockings signaled defeat by meeting with Spalding and President Thurman to negotiate for an AA franchise in Boston. Perhaps Charles Comiskey summed up the situation best when he said, "The trouble with the PL is that they are too many confidence men with a little money in the venture." A source who spoke to Murnane under the condition of anonymity evaluated the value of rhetoric, whether sentimental or firebrand, at the end of the day: "It is very well to talk about traitors and all that kind of nonsense but this is business and every one is looking for his own interest."[29]

Just as the PL leaders were leaving Pittsburgh at the end of the first—and last—annual meeting of the league, Ella Black returned from a wedding in Chicago. Regretting the missed opportunity to meet many of the magnates to whom she had been promised an introduction, she nonetheless planned to "postpone this pleasure and put it off to some future time." After reporting on how Comiskey's failed leadership cleared the way for Anson to earn public favor in Chicago with the effective management of his young team, Black turned to the "big surprises" of the PL meeting. Without mentioning that Hanlon had been one of the three players excluded from the October 22 meeting in New York, the Pittsburgh correspondent discussed his apparent capitulation and revealed that she held out little hope for the PL's future:

> I am afraid the whole organization is now in a very bad way, and that it will either make a complete consolidation, play next year as a greatly weakened body with only four or six clubs, or else give up the ghost entirely. What a change from the brilliant start that was made last April. Who would have thought it?

Using her "tell it like it is" style here, Black showed she was willing to let go of her support for the PL to provide her readers with a truer picture of the recent events. Perhaps her objective stance was motivated by her memories of Henry Chadwick's patronizing assessment of her misguided "feminine" sympathies for the outlaw league. In any case, Black's growth as a journalist was clear, even if she missed covering the PL meeting due to family obligations.[30]

5. Post-Season

Once the PL was dead and buried, Chadwick discarded his strident Roman persona for good and returned once again to Nestor, the wise, seasoned advisor. When the dismantling of the PL was nearly complete in the middle of November, the veteran writer extended another olive branch of peace to the PL backers when he praised their generosity in making up the deficits from their own pockets to pay the salaries of the same ungrateful players who had the gumption to want representatives at the negotiating table because they felt the backers were not looking out for their best interests. When discussing his vision of the future of the game, Chadwick had three main points, each of which he touched upon twice. First, he reprinted—or asked Francis Richter to reprint—significant portions of his August 20 column where he called for a two-tiered organization for baseball. In the analogy Chadwick used to describe this scheme, the NL would play the senate to the AA's house of representatives. With its 50-cent admission, Blue Law-observing schedule, and prestige as the more established circuit, the NL would continue to operate as the senior organization for a higher class clientele than the less prestigious, junior organization of the AA with its 25-cent admission, Sunday games, and liquor sales aimed at a lower class of patrons. This is not to say that Chadwick wanted a weak AA; in fact, two weeks later he circled back to his vision with a suggestion to bolster the organization by giving it a stronger name, and predicted its future: "In the *National Association* I shall look for a successor to the old AA, which will avoid the errors and shortcomings of the latter's past history, especially as regards its exceptionally poor record since the season of 1889." Chadwick re-reissued his argument, and then repeated his new name for the AA. If he was trying to make the new moniker for the "beer and whiskey" league stick, he was unsuccessful, but he did correctly predict six of the nine teams that played in the league in 1891.[31]

Remaining in his patriarchal role, Chadwick reviewed the lessons of 1890. One lesson was that no city in America had enough baseball patrons to support two top-flight teams, as illustrated by the NL and the PL going head-to-head in seven of the eight cities. On the other hand, he felt there would be no problem for the NL and the AA to share a home city because the latter's model was "not in opposition to NL club interests." Should the senior circuit and the junior circuit share a city, he suggested that the rivalry would be "beneficial to the financial interests of both organizations." When he returned to this aspect of the baseball business, the Brooklyn correspondent allowed that New York and Philadelphia were both ready to host two teams and that Chicago and Boston might be ready for the same in 1892. As it turned out, the latter two cities jumped the gun and took on Association teams in the following season, which turned out to be the organization's final year. The primary lesson learned from the Brotherhood War, according to Chadwick, was that baseball needed to get back onto a sound business model, as suggested by NL veteran Harry Wright, who called for "two leading organizations and a National Agreement of some kind." The only positives that the Brooklyn correspondent observed from the experience were the longer pitching distance and the double-umpire system, but only after they were tested using NL standards. Thus, baseball's and Chadwick's growth were minimal with regard to the business of the game.[32]

III. The Journalism—Celebrations and Contributions

Because it contained some of his best writing of the year, Murnane's primary post-season contribution to the developing profession of sports journalism was his coverage of the extensive celebration of the Red Stockings' triumphant return to Boston. Chadwick made three contributions to the field that were in keeping with his pet projects, and Black worked to improve the image of the game and herself. Both Murnane and Black demonstrated growth over the course of the significant season, while Chadwick remained largely set in his ways, as illustrated above.

During the second weekend of October, T. H. Murnane and the *Boston Globe* spared no ink in marking the achievement of the Red Stockings in winning the PL pennant. On the day that an exhibition game was played to mark the occasion, the *Globe* printed a pen-and-ink portrait of the team and biographies of each of the players. Murnane treated his readers to a history of the "World's Champions" to demonstrate how Boston had won eight of the 23 championships listed. Other hometown boosterism included the Fast Day game as the "largest crowd at a game": "19,000 paid admission, and as many more were turned away" and the three players from Boston's 1883 championship who were still playing at the highest level, Charlie Buffington, Joe Hornung, and Sam Wise. Returning to old enmities, Murnane could not resist a dig at a fel-

5. Post-Season

low baseball journalist: "Henry Chadwick, often called the father of base ball, predicted an early demise for the sport if admission was charged to witness the game."[33]

Demonstrating some of his most colorful and sparkling prose of the season as a reporter, Murnane's coverage of the championship ceremony featured detailed description, and the superlatives flowed as freely as the champagne, providing his readers with a mental image of the pennant-raising, a sense of the labor struggle, baseball history, and local pride:

> Up the lines the banner rose, and as the wind caught its folds it stood out clear and strong, gracefully snapping in the cold blast of the afternoon breeze toward the ocean.
> To the stanch [sic] admirers of base ball, under the new regime, it suggested the season which had just closed, the most notable, by long odds, in the history of the national game.
> The word "Boston" that stood on the flag in letters that all could read, had a double significance when raised by the hands of the winners with the equally willing assistance of their chief rivals in the base ball business.
> It was truly a union of sentiment.
> No games were more bitterly contested than those between Boston and New York, and yet the vanquished were not only willing to acknowledge a beating, but to do it in the broadest sense of "brotherhood."

Unfortunately for Murnane and organized baseball, the "dawn of an era" that was supposedly heralded by the raising of the banner was as short-lived as the strains of "Where Did You Get That Flag" that were played by Reeves' American Band of Providence, RI.[34]

Beginning with the parade that was similar to the ones held earlier on Fast and Opening Days, Murnane employed a similar stylistic flair while detailing the day's events. The *Globe* sportswriter had an excellent seat in the second carriage between General Dixwell and Harry Schafer of the champion Red Stockings from the National Association of the early 1870s in the van, and Mike "King" Kelly and his Paterson, New Jersey friends in the third car. His position in the procession allowed him to include examples of how "the boys were cheered along the whole route." As a nod to his *BG* employer, Murnane included the entire text of Charles Taylor's speech that accompanied the presentation of the pennant. Among other things, Taylor noted how the banner was "justly earned after many months of hard labor," called the Red Stockings "the grandest aggregation of ball players that this country has ever known," and praised their demeanor on the field to highlight once again the game's need for a better image: "In this campaign you have shown a capacity to govern yourselves which has silenced your critics. Fines were never fewer and rumors even of dissipation have been unknown." Tom Brown and Harry Stovey gave "an exhibition of base running" in an attempt to break Harry Berthong's record for circling the bases, which the Washington National had set in 1868, but the ground was too soft for them to challenge it seriously. The attempt to break the throwing distance record, which was to be undertaken by Ed Crane and Harry Vaughn, was called off due to the chill of the day. Borrowing a strategy from the society page, Murnane concluded his report with a list of the important people who were "noticed" in the crowd.[35]

But the celebration was not over when the five-inning exhibition game ended. That evening a standing-room only crowd gathered at Music Hall in Boston to fete the Red Stockings. Commenting on the hero worship he'd helped create with descriptions of the glamour of the ball diamond, Murnane observed the response of the fans: "A grand treat it was for the hall full of people to see their favorites outside of their regulation uniforms, and get a glimpse of them as they appear in real life." The program included several local performers and some from as far away as New York. De Wolf Hopper and Charlie Reed were scheduled to appear originally, but circumstances kept them away, leading to the "only disappointment of the evening." Even so, Charles Evans and William Hoey performed several pieces from the "Parlor Match," the farcical comedy they made famous, to "take the pennant." Baseball enthusiasts likely appreciated Murnane's image of the Red Stockings' captain: "Kelly never looked so happy as he sat in the front row, surrounded by his little army of ball players." Kel and his crew even took a turn on the stage to the tune of "Hail the Conquering Heroes" to complete the celebration of their feat. When Boston's champions returned home, both the extent of the *Globe*'s coverage and the stylistic element of Murnane's prose illustrated that the editors of a major daily newspaper in the late nineteenth century were willing to look past the trivialities of professional sports and risk the wrath of journalism critics on certain occasions to give extensive attention to men who played baseball for a living.[36]

While avoiding the stigma of being partisan or trivial by making only limited references to the NL Champion Brooklyn Bridegrooms,

5. Post-Season

Henry Chadwick nonetheless offered three primary contributions to the developing profession of sports journalism as the "season of sensational 'fakes'" came to a close. First, he highlighted the business model that was being developed by big city daily newspapers to call for positive changes in baseball coverage. Secondly, he advocated improvements in the rules and the scoring of the game. Thirdly, he continued to work against the negative effects of the gossip and partisanship found in the work of his fellow sporting writers.[37]

After a season that saw an abundance of negative journalism, as well as the advancements of the "double coverage" found in the *Boston Globe* and other big city daily newspapers, Chadwick actively attempted to influence the press coverage and create a more favorable public opinion for the game. Embracing his sport historian role once more, he reminded his readers of how the press was driven by the demands of the audience and of how editors of the "great dailies of the country" had responded to the public interest in sport by filling "the columns of their journals" with "subjects of sporting interest." Ever the patriarch, though, Chadwick admonished his readers—especially anyone with a say in the baseball war—that the recently won coverage, which culminated with the interest generated by the 1889 season, would quickly begin to disappear, and if this decline were left unchecked, the coverage would soon drop off in a runaway fashion: "Once this tobogganing process goes into effect, and the valuable aid of the press countenance is taken away from professional ball playing, it will be good-bye to the era of big bonanzas in base ball stock company history, and bankruptcy will set in with fatal effect." Clearly, Chadwick had been around the game long enough to recognize the importance of the symbiotic relationship that was developing between the press and the game of baseball. To that end, he called for the public to be informed of the end of the war: "The sooner this is known officially the better for the interests of the ensuing campaign of 1891, for the patrons will then begin to turn their attention to a renewal of interest in the movements of the clubs, which is now practically dead." Chadwick was not above asking Richter to reprint articles from a rival Philadelphia paper when it supported his argument for the need of a magnanimous peace between the two leagues and commending it "to the attentive reading of the NL magnates" to better inform their decision making. The paragraph from the *Philadelphia Sunday Times* read like a prayer:

It will not do to harbor resentful feelings in this, the hour of much-needed peace.... Let all those who, led by false leaders, had gone astray return to the fold, and let them be welcomed as men, not as slaves. Let the League correct all the abuses that led to this disastrous outbreak, and in the future steer clear of the semblance of such, and all will be well.

As much as Chadwick may have agreed with the moral sentiments expressed in the paragraph, the treatment of the players in the subsequent season would indicate that not many of the NL magnates completed their reading assignments. Salaries were reduced and the weakened AA was consolidated within the NL in December of 1891.[38]

Chadwick's journalistic activism extended to the rules of the game and the ways in which it was scored. On the eve of the NL's annual meeting, he devoted a significant portion of his report to convincing the magnates to make the time to address rule changes he felt were important to the development of the game. With his concerns heightened by the fact that the announcement of the PL a year earlier had prevented the NL from addressing the needed changes at their 1889 meeting, he was determined to make sure the issues were addressed during that year's meeting in New York. Chadwick's rule committee days were long behind him, yet he demonstrated an enduring desire to shape the game he'd promoted for so long.[39]

As the inventor of the box score, Chadwick retained a vested interest in how those rules generated "data for an analysis of the play in a game likely to afford a fair criterion of a player's skill in batting, fielding and base-running." Referencing the quality of play during the 1890 season—especially the "heavy slugging" that he "saw" in the PL games due to the livelier ball, the veteran sportswriter suggested changes in the way ERA was calculated, as well as new methods of scoring that recognized the teamwork of hitters in cases other than extra-base hits. In the middle of this discussion, he could not resist reminding his readers that he was, after all, the Father of Baseball: "I established earned runs in my scoring record over twenty years ago, and did it for the purpose of obtaining a fair criterion of a pitcher's skill, based on the record of runs earned off his pitching by base hits, and such hits only as are made before he has given the field a chance to put the side out." Chadwick's argument was that the pitcher should not be penalized for runs generated when base runners were able to steal second or third off the catcher—an argument

5. Post-Season

that most pitchers would no doubt agree with. While "heavy slugging" has had its periods of being in vogue and pitchers are still penalized for runs scored off their catchers, Chadwick had more luck with his second scoring issue, the recognition of timely, team-oriented hitting. However, it is most likely that he would argue that the current definition of "sacrifice hits" could do more to reward the hitter who "forwards" runners instead of "slugging " for two- and three-base hits and wasting at-bats on easily catchable "fungos" hit to the outfielders.[40]

Finally, Chadwick's willingness to take his "brother"—and "sister" in the case of Ella Black—scribes to task demonstrated his ongoing awareness of their journalistic work. As part of his ongoing feud with T. H. Murnane, he asked his readers pointed questions about the response of his rivals:

> Have you observed how the class of scribes who are subsidized in one form or another by the PL kick and squirm when they are hit hard.
> Also how invariably under such circumstances they characteristically resort to wholesale lying, mean subterfuges, and abusive personalities in sending out their missives in support of their fearfully weak cause?

Just in case his *SL* readers were still wondering about the target of this jab, Chadwick's use of "missive" provided a significant clue in this response to Murnane's extended attack from October 4. The Brooklyn correspondent likely had the same "class of scribes" in mind when he blamed writers for trying to keep the baseball war going "in the face of public opinion." Returning to the analogy he used at the beginning of the conflict, Chadwick illustrated once more how little he'd developed stylistically when he couldn't resist "downing" the PL partisans with one more Civil War analogy: "It reminds one of the course of the disappointed rebels who failed to realize the fact that the rebellion had died at Appomattox."[41]

Ella Black's post-season take on baseball journalism included her last efforts to improve images—both her own and that of the players. When she called for recognition about her Cincinnati scoop, it was clear that she was still battling for her reputation as a female journalist, as well as the reputation of Pittsburgh journalism in general. Singing her own praise for the Cincinnati scoop in consecutive weeks, she began by noting the significance of the story to the baseball world: "In the SPORTING LIFE dated July 12, I had the pleasure of making public one *genuine item of news* that had never been published before that time" (italics in the original). The passage revealed her pride in her work, and that feeling was strong enough that she called on one of her fellow baseball writers to acknowledge her achievement: "Mr. Ren Mulford, Jr., was kind enough to laugh at my story and intimate that I was trying to keep up Pittsburg's reputation as a starting point for base ball 'fakes,' by claiming there was nothing in what I said." A week later, Black promoted her status as a female journalist when she called attention to her achievement a second time: "I am more than proud to think that for once a woman was able to get a 'scoop' on the masculine members of the profession." Running underneath these expressions of pride, however, is the realization that she was too often forced to accept the role of a "Cheap Jane" journalist who did little more than comment on someone else's published reports—when she didn't have access to an inside informant or wasn't able to be in the right streetcar or theater line to overhear key information being imparted by loud-talking NL club officials.[42]

When John M. Ward visited Pittsburgh in early October as part of an exhibition tour he made with his Wonders, Black had been "counting" on meeting him to acquire some first-hand material for her report. However, she missed the opportunity due to the carelessness of a mutual friend, who was supposed to introduce her to the leader of the PL. Black had claimed to have met Ward "several times" in her March 19 *SL* report, and her readers with long memories must have wondered at the reason for the change in her story at the end of the season. The Pittsburgh correspondent missed her call with regard to the leader of the Brotherhood on November 22 when she lamented how John Ward was likely done with the game. Ward went on to play four more seasons, so perhaps Black was projecting her weariness onto the young captain.[43]

Both her pride at the "one genuine" story she reported and her desire to interview John Ward show that Ella Black wanted to be a full-fledged reporter, but something about her circumstances prevented her from following Nellie Bly's example to a greater degree. It seems likely that she came from a good enough family that she could not—or would not—step into the twilight realm of a reporter and rub elbows with the hoi polloi as Bly did. She had her credentials from *SL*, but she was not able, for some reason, to take them to the ballpark and walk up to one of the players or the management and say, "I am a journalist with *SL*, and I'd like to ask you about..." So she made do with what was available

5. Post-Season

to her: her ability to read and read between the lines—what was printed in *SL* and other papers, her long memory since being initiated "into the mysteries of baseball" in the early 1880s, her collection of reference materials, her notes, and her own eyes based on the games she attended—always sitting in the stands instead of the press box, with the possible exception of the game she watched with Chadwick in June.

The image of the game was also on Black's mind in the final two months of her reports for *SL*. She regretted the loss of former mayor McCallin for his ability to draw the "best patrons" to the game through his association with the Burghers:

> I think the club will make a big mistake by allowing Mr. McCallin to leave if it can be helped. He is one of the most popular men in this city, and I know for a fact that last season many people went to the games just because they knew he was at the head of the club, and they were certain everything would be conducted on a fair and honest basis.

Once more, the last line of the quote underscored the image problem faced by baseball in 1890: memories of the gambling issues of the 1870s and the "kicking" and "bulldozing" of the 1880s were strong enough to keep the "best patrons" away from the game unless someone like McCallin was involved.[44]

The disposition and comportment of the players on the field was another issue that needed to be addressed by the people running the game. Black pointed this out again in her last report, when she was not shy about identifying the drinking of the PL players as a source of "the big wreck":

> ONE REASON FOR THE BREAK-UP that I recently heard was that the capitalists got disgusted after putting in their money, to find that many of the players were taking advantage of the extra freedom they had, and instead of trying to do their best, as they would have been forced to do in the National League, were drinking hard and were in no condition to play ball.

While she did not blame the reluctance shown by the league's backers, she admonished them for giving up so easily after just one year without making the effort to enact and enforce stricter rules for the conduct of the players. Her criticism of both parties showed once more that she was concerned about the league and the game and not protecting the players or their backers.[45]

Beyond defending her image and the image of the game, the female sportswriter demonstrated she could laugh at herself. When the Cleveland correspondent for *SL* had "a little amusement" at her expense regarding the consolidation of the Pittsburgh club after she went on record claiming little chance of such a merger, Black responded with a bit of fun as well: "I am no prophetess, or even the daughter of one, but in this case I will admit I was badly fooled." She went on to adopt a more serious tone regarding the hard lesson she learned from the experience: "It has taught me that in the future no dependence is to be placed on what a man or men may do, even if they have agreed to anything, and that they are just as fickle and liable to change of mind as we women are popularly supposed to be." In contrast to the solidarity implied by "we women," Black missed an opportunity to advance her cause by pointing out that she had correctly predicted in the pre-season that the backers of the PL would be less enthusiastic about the baseball business if they incurred heavy losses during the season. (See the full text of Black's November 22 report in Part 8 of Appendix A.)[46]

When Black signed off, her last column did not provide a single hint that she was about to make her exit. Her letter was simply missing from the next issue and the issue after that, never to re-appear. The disappearance of her report brought very little response, as if her colleagues were relieved or gladdened by her absence. Nonetheless, the Pittsburgh correspondent demonstrated to the readers of *SL* that a woman could: 1) write baseball and provide insightful analysis and commentary; 2) break stories and scoop her fellow writers; and 3) possess the stamina to cover the game for an entire season. While it is natural to call Ella Black a pioneer and a feminist, she might have been satisfied to receive praise for doing a good job as a journalist and be accepted as such, with some acknowledgement that a woman could indeed write the game. The body of her work is nonetheless impressive and significant in the larger scheme of baseball journalism, and we are left to wonder what she might have accomplished if she had remained a *SL* correspondent and been given the same opportunities as her "brothers" who had the advantage of "wearing trousers."[47]

Over the course of the long season, Murnane remained a staunch supporter, fighter and a critic to the end of the negotiations and beyond. When the Boston correspondent met with Spalding and Ward in the middle of December, he was perhaps the person at the table who most believed that there was a small chance the PL would take the field in

5. Post-Season

1891. His post-season reports showed that he became more identified the players and their cause than either Chadwick or Black, but he was already halfway to that position at the start of the campaign given his background as a player. Murnane's 1890 work thus provided an early example of how sports journalism would be affected once writers became "imbedded" with teams on a regular basis in the early twentieth century.

The bulk of Chadwick's post-season columns concerned the business of baseball as it appeared in the late autumn of 1890. Mounting the podium to deliver one last editorial as Cato the Elder of the NL empire, he adopted an anti-player stance to attack the fading remnants of the PL to sow the field with salt and make sure no stone was standing upon another stone. At the same time, he covered the peace process as the two major leagues and the "almost major" league of the AA worked toward compromise and/or consolidation. Thirdly, he looked to the future of the game and tried to find a way to be ahead of the curve. Of the three sporting journalists, Chadwick was the only one with an active argument in all three phases of discussion.

From her first appearance as a "novelty in base ball literature," Ella Black established herself as a voice of reason through the criticism and analysis of her reports, and her post-season work was no different. Because she no longer needed to play the role of the ingénue, and having thus found and established her voice, she was not about to relinquish her place in the conversation, even though she felt less compelled to call attention to her gender. In short, she was all business because she had to be, despite the hint of female disgust at male foolishness when she called out the NL and PL officials for acting like "pig-headed children."

Conclusion

Although the 1890 season has been largely undiscussed in any detail until recently, the year of the Brotherhood War remains significant in the development of the cultural status of baseball players and the game itself, the recognition of the game's economic and business impact, and the shaping of sports journalism. While Alexander and Koszarek have examined the year in book-length studies, no one has focused on the writing of the journalists who chronicled the season in weeklies like *Sporting Life* and daily newspapers like the *Boston Globe*. Such a close look is important because it reveals the foundations of today's sports media complex, both in style and how the meaning is created en route to making sport a significant element in American culture. With these points in mind, the conclusion of this study has three goals: 1) to describe the writers and their audiences, 2) to summarize the changes in their styles and significant messages in response to the Brotherhood War, and 3) to describe the lasting impact of the 1890 season.

Working within the pages of *SL*, all three writers were aware of the self-image they were projecting to a national audience. Henry Chadwick needed no more introduction than his name at the top of his correspondence due to his long-time association with baseball and the editorial voice he'd developed in the *Brooklyn Eagle* and *Spalding's Guide*. The veteran writer spoke with the authority of 30-plus years of involvement with the game and the benefit of "being there from the beginning." At the same time, however, he was removed from the day-to-day operations of the NL, which may help explain why he did not cover the business side of the game during the first part of the season. The Brooklyn correspondent watched the games from the press box at Washington Grounds and spoke with the team's owner, but he had little involvement with the players. Thus, as the inventor of the box score and a former member of rules committees, Chadwick wrote for an audience who was interested in evaluating the game through statistics and creating a product that would appeal to the better class of patron, especially capitalists. From the beginning, the veteran writer claimed to be concerned with the game's future.

Like many baseball writers in 1890, T. H. Murnane was interested in bringing middle- and upper-class fans to the ballpark, but as a former player-turned-*Boston Globe* reporter, he wrote from the labor side of the equation and backed the Brotherhood cause without reservation from the beginning. Where Chadwick was writing for an audience that backed the established NL, Murnane took a revolutionary stance that echoed the "Jeffersonian Doctrine" of self-determination. Similar to Chadwick, Murnane was an immigrant (or the son of an immigrant depending on the source), but he spoke with a brogue and played his way out of the industrial cities of central Connecticut. Both writers were loyal to the game, but Murnane's audience was the Brotherhood and other supporters of labor.

From what is known of Ella Black through her body of work in *SL*, she was neither a player nor an immigrant; nonetheless, she was an ardent supporter of the game and had spent a significant portion of her 25–35 years immersed in its "mysteries." Whether she was motivated by Nellie Bly (Elizabeth Cochrane), Ella Wilcox Wheeler, or other female journalists is speculation, but she made it clear that her goal was to prove that women could write baseball even though she couldn't interview players or front office personnel directly. The Pittsburgh correspondent's peers comprised her audience, and she was no doubt trying to reach whatever women possessed the temerity to pick up *SL* in the late American Victorian period. Despite being an avowed supporter of the players and their labor cause, Black worked from the middle of the equation—even as she sought to bring attention to the marginalized feminine perspective.

After Memorial Day passed and the PL remained in business, the style and rhetoric of all three writers shifted away from the excitement of the opening of the season. Chadwick focused more on the players and the future of the game and adopted a shrill, strident persona that was reminiscent of Cato the Elder calling for the destruction of Carthage each time he rose to speak in the Senate of ancient Rome. The veteran writer upped the cost of the kicking and slugging he found in the PL by observing how professional baseball was losing the better patrons to the college games, which were free of such behavior and lively baseballs.

Further, he decried the "picked nines" of the PL to argue that such practices did not lead to strong teams. To Chadwick, all of these things led to a loss of an ideal era for the game—the "Millennial Age" that was receding from view with each passing day the PL was on the field. The *Spalding's Guide* editor appeared to be taking his cues from his employer, who sounded similar notes in interviews he gave at the end of May and early June. Whether or not he was directed to step up his attacks on the PL, Chadwick clearly responded with an intensity that was reflected in his work.

As if responding to Chadwick's offensive, Murnane defended the PL and attacked the NL in the early going. Unlike Chadwick's mostly one-dimensional efforts, the *Globe* writer's offensive was more balanced. The player-turned-sportswriter "boosted" Mike Kelly and "the boys" of the Boston Red Stockings while "downing" the players who turned against the Brotherhood and the fans who supported such unworthy men. The Boston correspondent promoted the business decisions of the PL and attacked the practices of Spalding and the NL, focusing on the "comps" issue in particular. When the Red Stockings received bad press, he defended them just as he entered into a print feud with Ella Black when she had the courage to be critical of Mike Kelly's leadership. Some players were more worthy of praise than others in Murnane's thinking, just as some journalists were not in the position to judge the merits of managers. News items like the complimentary tickets became weapons to use against the business judgment of the rival league's leaders. Murnane's awareness of Chadwick's stance and Black's criticism showed he was well aware of the work of his peers, adding another dimension to the conflict.

Even though she didn't pick a side, Black's mid-season attack was equally balanced and defensive in nature. The Pittsburgh correspondent took issue with Kelly of the PL and Glasscock of the NL. Continuing to employ her creative work-arounds, she scooped J.P. O'Neill of the Alleghenys and wrote about Will Gumbert's preference to keep his day job and pitch for the NL team only when they were in town, providing important insight to the lack of security for baseball players in 1890. Digging deeper as a reporter, she floated syndicate rumors, brought up compromises early, and scooped the secret signings of the Cincinnati players to PL contracts. Beyond demonstrating her skills as a journalist, these stories showed the importance of baseball as a business. While the

Conclusion

start of the nine-year monopoly held by the NL was two seasons away, Black's signing scoop proved to be correct and her call for compromise was timely and shared. In addition to being in the thick of matters regarding the players and the business aspects of the game, she was interacting with her colleagues both in person and in print. Her visit with Henry Chadwick put to rest the doubts about her identity, giving her one less element to defend, while her print feud with Murnane proved she was not afraid to enter the lists with her male counterparts.[1]

When the season moved to the final months, the approaches and rhetorics of the writers shifted once more. Chadwick focused almost exclusively on the business of the game. He interviewed Spalding, took his word on the comps issue and spent considerable time discussing his plan for the future of baseball. While he worked to bring about the end of the PL—either by combining it with the lesser league of the AA or compromising it out of existence, his shrill, strident Roman voice diminished, as if he, along with Spalding, was confident that the NL would reach the end of the season intact. Except for the occasional "hot shot" aimed at journalists who supported the PL, the focus of his reports at the end of the season was on editorializing about the future of the game. The veteran writer continued cherry-picking facts that would support his argument, illustrating the limits of his rhetoric, or perhaps underestimating the abilities of his audience. In the end, Chadwick was working toward maintaining the status quo, with the NL as the dominant "house" of baseball and the AA as the lesser body catering to the beer- and liquor-swilling crowds who preferred "heavy slugging" to "scientific hitting" while watching baseball on the Sabbath.

Answering Chadwick's editorials and traveling with the Red Stockings as a reporter, Murnane transitioned from PL promoter to Boston supporter in the final months of the season. Through interviews, he gave Ward, Keefe, and other Brotherhood players a voice in the press, even though journalism critics would have questioned the practice that contributed to the celebrity status of players. The *Globe* writer downplayed compromise talk and gloated over the sale of the Cincinnati club as another sign of the NL's imminent demise. Just as he liked the chances of the Red Stockings to win the pennant, the former player was confident that the business practices of the PL in Boston were above reproach. While continuing his print feud with Ella Black into August, Murnane committed the ultimate act of identification in early September when he used the first person plural to link himself to the team he was covering. Objectivity was still emerging as a journalistic standard, so he cannot be faulted for crossing that line; furthermore, the event demonstrated the extent of his support for the team as a former player.²

Black's stance at the end of the season reflected her confidence after writing baseball for more than half a year. She evaluated players, took other players to task for their intemperate habits, and evaluated management, both locally and nationally, without apology or hesitation. With regard to the game's business side, she openly blamed the local NL management for the team's historically poor season and opposed any union of the two leagues due to the negative feeling it would generate among the supporters of the PL's labor cause. When Boston "blue bloods" gave Mike Kelly a "house and grounds" as a token of their esteem for leading the Red Stockings to apparent victory, Black remonstrated with her peers for trumpeting the news in the press without considering the effect on Ward and other Brotherhood leaders who had worked much harder for the cause without being so handsomely rewarded. What her readers heard from Pittsburgh was a mature voice and they saw the work of a questing mind as she examined the issues without the sometimes pedantic and fawning partisanship of Chadwick and Murnane.

Once more, the styles and rhetorics of the writers changed as the season moved into its final phase. Chadwick evaluated the players from both leagues, looking at the grateful (including Brotherhood leader Buck Ewing), the rascals, and the dissipated (who were mostly in the PL to his thinking). Offering his readers a few more glimpses of his Roman persona, the veteran sportswriter alternated between burying the PL and calling for NL leaders to follow Grant's example at Appomattox. Without being invited to the negotiations and league meetings underway in nearby Manhattan, the Brooklyn correspondent reported them as well as he could and remained an outspoken would-be architect for the game's future. Aware of the press' impact, he called for activist journalism—thus scooping Randolph Hearst by a few years—of the proper kind: one that would support the capitalists as the proper directors of baseball. By the end of the season, Chadwick found his voice again, but he was not asked back to *SL*, as correctly predicted by Murnane. Whether Richter tired of the veteran writer's cherry-picking, his shrill Cato the Elder voice, or the overall repetitiveness of his reports from the City of Churches was not clear.³

Conclusion

Still relishing his association with the champions of the PL, Murnane covered their post-season exhibition tour with the PL Giants and was on hand for the triumphant return to Boston for a parade, pennant-raising ceremony, one final game, and a night of celebration at a local music hall. These events saw some of Murnane's best and most colorful writing of the year, perhaps not surprisingly. Once the meetings in New York started going against the PL, however, Murnane was quick to set aside the celebratory spirit to examine the problems he saw from both sides of the conflict. He decried the shoddy reporting of his fellow journalists and took Chadwick to task in particular. As he saw the PL unraveling in front of him, the former player became increasingly critical of the New York and Brooklyn backers—the same men he had earlier described as stalwart and fearless—as they sought separate peaces from their NL counterparts. Working both as a reporter and an editorial voice, Murnane closed the 1890 season with the ultimate disappointment of the meeting between the dispirited John Ward and the scheming magnate Albert Spalding at the Manhattan Athletic Club. The fight was still in the sportswriter, but it's likely that he knew the war was over.

With no champions to cover in Pittsburgh, Ella Black wrapped and recapped the season using the critical voice she'd developed throughout the year, sparing neither side when rebukes were necessary. She closed the books on the local front offices, once more sparing neither side when they'd made poor decisions. When the local negotiations failed, she showed an aggressive side early and soon became impatient with the man-boys who were squabbling over the game's future. Proving once more that she was not shy about her own accomplishments that season, she touted what she felt to be her best contributions to the coverage of the events while noting once more the restrictions placed upon her as a woman. Beyond her impatience with the male negotiators, her last reports provided no hints that she was about to disappear from the pages of *SL* and sports journalism forever.

Despite its relative obscurity, the 1890 season lives on in today's attitudes toward the players, the recognition of baseball as a significant economic contributor, and as a factor in the development of sports journalism. When the Brotherhood formed its own league and its leaders became part-owners, the public saw the players in a new light. John Ward, Tim Keefe, Buck Ewing, and others earned press attention as businessmen instead of merely men playing a child's game for a living. Mike

Kelly, already an early star and celebrity within the game's circles, earned enough popularity to make him a forerunner of Babe Ruth. Though the game was still on less than sturdy footing, the attention given to the labor conflict put baseball into the equation as an important element in the American economy. The Brotherhood War galvanized the owners, who closed ranks to make sure their control of the game would not be challenged again by the players. This resolve outlasted the successful challenge of the American League in 1901, brushed off the Federal League in 1914–1915 and the Black Sox Scandal of 1919, and extended to 1975 when the Reserve Clause was finally broken. The owners learned an early lesson regarding the power of the press, and soon reporters were traveling with the team in exchange for coverage that advanced the game, following the example set by Murnane and his work with the Red Stockings.

Clearly, the roots of our modern sports media complex were planted in 1890 when baseball journalism became political out of necessity. The *SL* reports of Henry Chadwick, T.H. Murnane and Ella Black demonstrated their concerns about the power struggles of the Brotherhood War; at the same time however, they were interested in the personalities of the players and the quality of their own writing as journalists. The sustained examination of their work in the present study compared and contrasted the dominant position of Henry Chadwick with the revolutionary stance of T.H. Murnane and the voice of Ella Black as she endeavored to speak for marginalized female journalists and break new ground as a sportswriter. The analysis of the dominance, resistance, and validation found in the texts of their reports illustrated the process of meaning making practices at a critical juncture in the development of larger forces at work—and play—in American culture.[4]

Appendix A

Full Texts of Significant Columns from the 1890 Season

Part 1: April 26, 1890, SL, p. 10, by Ella Black

THE FIRST GAME

As Viewed by One of the Weaker Sex—
About a St. Louis Man—A Significant
Remark—The New League's Success—
Twenty-five cent NL Games
in the Near Future.

PITTSBURG, April 25—Editor SL—I have always heard of the wonderful gallantry of the Westerners of the sterner sex, but I have about come to the conclusion that either they have been greatly misrepresented or else they must, as represented by your St. Louis correspondent, Mr. Pritchard, think a woman incapable of having any brains. His imagination that I am sailing under false colors is rather amusing to those who know me, but is apt to create a false impression among strangers. I only wish Mr. P. was in Pittsburg for a time until I could have the pleasure of meeting him and letting him see how greatly he is mistaken. By the way, though, I expect to be in the East sometime within the next month, and after I have seen you, Mr. Editor, you will be able to assure him I am only a poor lone female. Why is it that a woman has such hard work to get credit for anything she may do? I never claimed to be particularly brilliant, but after trying to do my best, I hate to see my efforts belittled as Mr. Pritchard did last week by trying to make out that a woman is not able to write news. I only wish that I had the priviliges of a man, then I would give the St. Louisian an idea of how much superior to *some men* a woman could be. Kindly words such as have been given me by Messrs. Harris and Chadwick are highly appreciated, but—oh, no, it cannot be the rotund Mr. Pritchard is actually growing jealous of a woman.[1]

The Opening Day Parades.

Well the season has been opened at last and it is safe to say that the Brotherhood, as represented by the PL, has so far left the NL far in the rear. There was a wonderful contrast here in the opening day parades of the two bodies. The old League turn-out consisted of a band of music, the players of the Allegheny and Cleveland clubs and the reporters who were compelled to attend the game. The new club had two bands, with the players and a long line of carriages, filled with well-known citizens who favor the move that has been made. The first parade in passing through the streets got no reception at all. There was neither cheers nor hisses.[2] On the other side there was a continuous roar of applause for the Players' parade from the time it made a start from the Hotel Anderson until it passed into the new grounds. I saw both the turn-outs and know whereof I speak. It was very evident the new League only needs to play anything like a fair game to capture the lion's share of the patronage; still it must be acknowledged that the old club, in this city at least, has made by far the best showing. The difference in feeling over the parades was carried out in the attendance at the rival games.

Although I was only at the new club's grounds still I heard of the other one. I know positively that there was not more than 1000 persons there. I have attended games at Recreation Park too often not to know what a poor showing such a crowd would make on those grounds, and I can imagine that both players and spectators felt rather lonely, but oh, how different it was at the new Exposition grounds.[3] There, when the game began, the grand stand and bleaching boards were both filled so that it was almost impossible for any late comer to get a seat. What an enthusiastic crowd it was, too. Every good play of both teams was applauded to the echo, both in practice and during the game. As each player stepped to the plate he was greeted with a round of cheers that could have been heard across the river. Best of all there was a big attendance of the weaker sex and they were by no means slow with their applause, but cheered and shouted almost as much as the men. Of course, Arlie Latham came in for a liberal share of the plaudits, and truly he was a whole show in himself. Still I think the public makes a mistake in paying him so much attention, for, while as a player he is very good, his character as a man is such as should meet with the disapproval of every honest-minded man and woman. If he was not made so much of it is just possible he would be the better for it.[4]

The First Games.

What a disappointment that first game was! For years past the local club has always won the opening contest, but the PL failed to keep up the record and were badly left. I never was more surprised in all my life than I was to see the showing our boys made. Why, actually, they played worse than a crowd of children would have done, and before the game was half over every person present was thoroughly disgusted and quite a number left. It was not a game where one side won through its superior play, but it was simply an exhibition of the most outrageous errors I have ever seen. Then, Galvin, who can usually be relied on to hold his opponents well in hand, was hit at will and added to the general discomfiture. It may have been there was too many flowers, or too many ladies looking on, or too big a crowd, or—well, it was too much something, for certainly the home team was by no means in the game at any time from the start to finish. The visitors by their excellent play made the poor work of the local men all the more noticeable. Although both sides were credited with an unusually large number of errors, many of them were to be excused on account of the condition of the grounds. These are so bad now that it will be several weeks before they are in shape for good playing.[5]

I was surprised to hear of the first game the NL played; from what I was told it must have been one that any veteran team would be proud of. Certainly the young men proved themselves to be a credit to Manager Hecker's careful training. It is wonderful how easy a person can be fooled. After Saturday's games I thought I would make a change and go to see the club that had done the best work, so on Monday I occupied my old-time seat at Recreation Park. That was where I was fooled, for instead of seeing a perfect contest, such as had been played on Saturday, I witnessed more errors than had been made in the Players' opening game. The colts played like amateurs, and only managed to win through their ability to hit and the many errors of Mr. Schmelz's men. At the new grounds the home team not only won, but a perfect and almost errorless game was played. But I'll not get fooled again. I took in the third Pittsburg-Chicago game, and in my humble opinion the best thing the local men can do is to endeavor to avoid having to face Mr. King whenever it is possible to do so. He is a harder puzzle for them to solve than was the famous 15-14-13 article. When his pitching is reinforced by the hitting the Chicago people are capable of, it is hard work to defeat them. Still, the local Brotherhood men have made an excellent showing so far, when their early lack of practice is taken into consideration. I am certain they will take a good position in the race for the pennant, and stand higher than they ever did in the days when they were NLrs.[6]

JOHN WARD'S TROUBLE.

I cannot tell how sorry I am for the trouble that has arisen between John Ward and his wife. From what I know of them both I am sure there has been a misunderstanding somewhere that time will unravel and bring them together again. No better, truer wife lives than Mrs. Ward, and no man could have been more devoted and loving to a wife than her husband was. I never met Mrs. Ward but once personally, and that was under circumstances that caused me to always retain the kindest feelings for her. I once happened to be taking a railroad trip and in the same sleeping car with me was Mrs. Ward. She was pointed out to me by the conductor. I happened to get very sick and for several hours was about as miserable as a woman could well be. Mrs. Ward noticed this and at once came to me, and until the following morning did everything she could for my comfort. My own mother could not have been more kind or gentle with me than she was, and it was something I have never forgotten. Now I know that no woman who would act as she did could ever have done any wrong, and from what I know of her husband I think he is also entitled to be classed as a gentleman. It is for this that I think the whole affair has been caused by a mistake that will some day be explained. I am more than sorry, though to see some persons trying to make a bad thing worse—outsiders who should keep their hands off what is a private matter and no concern of theirs. Oftimes such meddling as this is the cause of additional harm.[7]

Part 1: April 26, 1890—Ella Black

THE FITTING CROWDS.

There is one thing sure, if the NL games in other cities are not being attended any better than the ones here, it will not be long until some sort of a change will have to be made. One day this week while waiting at the box office of one of the local theatres to purchase some matinee tickets, I noticed standing close by me a couple of gentlemen who are connected with the Pittsburg NL Club. They were talking earnestly as I came by, and without any intention on my part to listen to what they were saying, I just caught this much:

"We cannot stand this sort of thing much longer," said one.

"Oh, that will be all right," was the answer, "when we put it down to twenty-five cents, the crowds will come well enough."

This was all I heard, as I moved on towards the window, but it struck me as being rather significant. Everything here goes towards bearing out the rumor that a reduction in price to the NL games will shortly be made. The local officials have always claimed they never made any money in former seasons. If that is the case the losses this year promise to be something awful. Although at this writing the club has played four games I understand the total attendance for the four is less than two thousand. While the management admitted before the opening that they expected the new club to outdraw the old one, I do not believe they calculated on the difference being as great as it has been. I am sure some decided steps will be taken shortly in an attempt to better matters, and the first one will doubtless be the twenty-five-cents admission feature.[8]

ABOUT THE PLAYERS.

Mr. Beckley's jumping seems to have helped him to get "his eye on the ball," as they say, for he has been making some nice three-baggers during the Chicago series.[9] Visner has not done anything particularly brilliant as yet, while Corcoran has been a disappointment at the bat, although he is a nice fielder.[10] Carroll is catching better than I have ever seen him do before.[11] Galvin does not seem to be doing as well as in former years.[12] Staley has done better so far than any of the other pitchers, while Secretary Tener had a very warm reception on Tuesday when he was batted all over the ground, and would have got it worse only for the splendid support he was given.[13] In the old club, all of the new men are showing themselves to be in splendid form and are doing excellent work.

The one exception so far is Schmitt [sic], the Chicago pitcher, who was an easy mark for the Cleveland men to hit.[14] Dunlap seems to be surprising every one by the way he is playing. The local papers are all talking about the way he coaches, something he never did before, and Manager Hecker is quoted as praising him highly.[15] So far pitcher Daniels seems to be the star of the old club.[16]

Feminine Club Troubles.

It now looks as though the female club that was organized for the purpose of attending the local games was going to break up and become a thing of the past. Although all the girls were on hand at the opening game of the PL, where each one paid her own way, it was quite different on Monday when the club was to meet and all go to the NL game at the expense of the Brotherhood girls. The NLrs and their escorts were all on hand, but strange to say all the others failed to appear, and instead word was received from each one saying she was sick or had to go away or some sort of an excuse. This left the others in a pretty fix for they had invited the gentlemen to go with them, and some of the girls did not have a cent. However, they managed among them to raise enough to see them through all right. Now they are all vowing they will have nothing more to do with the other girls, and as that would leave nothing but NLrs there would be no fun in the club, and so, I suppose, it is about run down. I must say I cannot blame the NL girls, for it was a very mean trick to play on them.[17]

Edward Keating, the local second baseman released last week by the McKeesport Club, sends me the following reply, which he hopes will be printed. It is as appended:

"That article in your column of THE SL of last issue rattles me somewhat. What right has that man Torreyson to criticize my batting? Why, he only saw a bat in my hand about three times. For every time Torreyson says I am no batter I can have a hundred to say I am a good one, also a good all-round ball player, and of course the majority rules. Now, that was only a very lame excuse, because I had the quiet tip that they were negotiating with this man Shoupe for my position before I had a ball in my hand, and, another thing, I was signed to play second base and catch, and I had no clothes to catch a pitcher, not even for five minutes.

Part 1: April 26, 1890—Ella Black

"What Torreyson doesn't know about base ball would fill a large book.

"Hoping you will do me justice in THE SL concerning this and thanking you for your previous favors, I remain, EDW. KEATING."[18]

A Little Small Talk.

It used to be that the visiting League clubs always stopped at the Hotel Anderson. Now they are at the Seventh Avenue, and the former house is used by the new league. Judging from what I have seen in passing the hotel the new managers are not as strict as the old ones were.[19]

I have heard a good many people express themselves as being disappointed Williamson did not play in Chicago games. He is a great favorite here, although Bastian plays nicely.[20]

Manager Hecker sits on the bench in uniform, and the enthusiasts are anxious for him to take part in a game.

It will take considerable more work to get the new grounds in first-class condition.[21]

It has been very amusing to watch some of the great, big stalwart players kicking at little Umpire Matthews. He always gets his own way, however.[22]

ELLA BLACK.

Part 1 Notes

1. Black did travel to Brooklyn during the second half of May to visit a sick relative. When she described herself as "only a poor lone female," her readers probably assumed she was single. The conflict between the contemporary male assumptions about women, as signified by Pritchard's doubts and Richter's use of "the weaker sex" in the lead-in, and women like Black who asserted their intelligence and independence, is illustrated in this opening paragraph.

2. The "well-known citizens" were likely the same "better class of patrons" that Chadwick wanted to bring out to the ballparks. The reference to "hisses" could have been a response to Murnane's story about the chance meeting between the Red Stockings and the "deserters" of the Phillies during the pre-season.

3. Recreation Park was the current home of the Pittsburgh Alleghenys, and had been home to local teams since the late 1870s. As the home of the Pittsburgh Burghers, Exhibition Park had been recently completed for the start of the PL season. According to Black, the new park provided a higher grade of seating, extensive cover for the grandstand, and the city's first sod infield (which apparently wasn't completely ready on April 19 as she suggested later in her report).

4. Arlie Latham was in his ninth year as a major league player and was widely recognized as a "clown prince" of baseball. Black's resistance to the public's and the press' adoration of

Appendix A

his antics was part of her project to help the game develop a better image and win a better audience.

5. The box score for the game proved that Black's criticism was well earned. Comiskey's Pirates committed four errors and Hanlon's Burghers doubled that number. Pud Galvin gave up ten runs on ten hits and allowed five stolen bases. If the largest crowd of the "better class of people" was in the stands that day, they were probably not impressed with what they saw, which may help explain the degree of Black's disappointment as the undertones of the paragraph illustrated the depth and experience of Black's perspective.

6. Even though the two teams combined for 15 errors on April 19, Guy Hecker's Alleghenys won a tight 3–2 contest over Gus Schmelz's Cleveland Spiders in the opener played at Recreation Park. When Black attended the second game of the series on April 21 as per the rules of the Young Ladies of the Diamond club, she was treated to an 11–9 error-fest that featured 25 total miscues. Across the river, the sod had been removed from the infield of Exhibition Park, but the paper still had the Pirates and the Burghers combining for 17 errors. Charles "Silver" King started the season 5–1 and went on to win 32 games with a 2.69 ERA for Comiskey's "picked nine." The "15–14–13 article" was likely a reference to a puzzle with 15 numbered tiles in a 4 × 4 arrangement with the goal of returning the tiles to numerical order. Because the Burghers were essentially the same team as the year before, Black's final assertion may have seemed partisan to some of her *SL* readers, including Henry Chadwick.

7. Black explained here how she came to make the acquaintance of Helen Dauvray, but she did not provide a similar explanation of how she came to meet John Ward. Also worthy of note was the absence of a husband to help her when she took ill (adding more support for the theory she was single) and that she did not mention why she happened to be traveling alone. Thus, while the tone of this passage suggested that Black wanted to see good in people, it also demonstrated that she did not favor gossip in the press by her fellow journalists. In contrast to Black's report that Dauvray inspired her husband to start the PL, Ward insisted in August that a slight "imposed upon" his wife by the wife of Albert Spalding was not the genesis of the Brotherhood War (*SL*, August 16, 1890, 5).

8. Adding the "theater ticket line" method to the "streetcar strategy" that allowed Black to obtain her first scoop, she demonstrated once again to be adept at being in the right place at the right time to overhear significant baseball information. This story proved true as well when the Alleghenys cut ticket prices in half in June, but not before the Burghers lowered their ticket prices first.

9. Once he ceased his league-jumping and settled on playing for the Burghers, first baseman Jake "St. Jacob" Beckley went on to hit 22 triples in 1890. In contrast to Black's criticism for his "wavering ways" prior to the season, Burghers manager Ned Hanlon called Beckley "one of the greatest players living" and claimed, "It's only a matter of a short time when Jake will be just as big a star as any player now on the diamond" (*SL*, September 13, 1890). The Veterans Committee of the Hall of Fame agreed with Hanlon in 1971.

10. Right fielder Joe Visner tied with Beckley for most PL triples with 22; rookie shortstop Tommy Corcoran batted only .233, but went on to play 17 more years in the majors.

11. Batting just under .300, Fred Carroll only caught 56 games (playing most of the rest in left field) and committed a total of 56 errors.

12. Near the end of a 14-year career, James "Pud" Galvin went 12–13 with a 4.35 ERA.

13. In his third season, Harry Staley won 21 but lost 25 with a 3.23 ERA; John Tener was a native of Ireland and in his final major league season when he went 3–11 with a 7.31 ERA in 14 games.

14. Chicago native Frederick "Crazy" Schmit went 1–9 in 11 games with a 5.83 ERA as a rookie for the Alleghenys.

15. After being the subject of a protracted contract dispute between the PL and NL, vet-

eran second baseman Fred Dunlap played only 17 games with the Alleghenys that year and did bring managerial experience with him even if he hadn't coached the bases before. At the end of a nine-year major league career, "Sir" Guy Hecker was the player-manager of the Alleghenys in 1890.

16. Despite his strong start, Pete Daniels, who was another native of Ireland and a rookie, went 1–2 in four games with a 7.07 ERA. He was one of 18 players to go "into the box" for the Alleghenys in 1890.

17. Black could be credited for describing the ignominious end of the local fan club without painting her fellow PL supporters in a more flattering light.

18. Keating sent his letter to the wrong Pittsburgh correspondent: McKeesport Manager Torreyson's rationale for releasing Keating was given in *SL*'s "Pittsburg Pencillings" on April 12, 1890: "Keating will not do. He stabs at the ball and pulls away at everything when at the bat"(5). A week later, the McKeesport memo reported that Shoupe played on April 14 after traveling all night and "put up a great game." Keating's release was announced in the same report. Nonetheless, Black was kind enough to include his letter and allow him to plead his case.

19. Worthy of note here is the voluntary separation of the visiting players from the two leagues, as well as Black's observation that the PL managers are not as strict as the NL managers. Likely, the Pittsburgh correspondent was referring to the curfew and drinking issues that would resurface over the course of the season.

20. In the final season of a 13-year career, Ned Williamson played only 73 games with the Chicago Pirates in 1890. After a simple cut on his knee became infected, Williamson had to leave Spalding's 1888–1889 tour and stay back in London, as described in the anecdote given by Ella Black. Williamson played only 47 games in 1889 and never regained his former form as a slugging shortstop (Lamster, 210–11). Charlie Bastian broke in as a member of the Wilmington Quicksteps of the Union Association in 1884. In 1890, Bastian played 80 games for Comiskey's Pirates, primarily at short, but only batted .191 and committed 44 errors.

21. As noted above, reports indicated that the sod was removed from the infield after the first game. The conflicting schedule, however, would allow for the problem to be addressed while the Burghers were out of town from May 5–June 9.

22. A former player with a 15-year career in the NA, NL, and AA, Bobby Matthews was listed as being 5'5" in height.

Part 2: May 10, 1890, SL, p. 12, by T. H. Murnane

MURNANE'S MISSIVE.
Gleanings on the Bostons' Tour—
News-Paper Misrepresentations—Some
Facts About the Pickett Case—A Friendly
Tip to the PL, Etc.

BROOKLYN, May 8.—Editor SL:—Twenty years ago this summer I witnessed my first game of ball on the Capitoline grounds in this city. Harry Wright and Bob Ferguson were the captains of the two celebrated teams of those days, viz., the Cincinnati Red Stockings and the Atlantics, of Brooklyn, and Henry Chadwick was the great authority on the national game.[1] There has been many a change since then, but the three above-named gentlemen are still actively engaged in the game they loved so well and did so much for.

Chadwick Called Down.

I had a call this evening at the Pierrepont House, where I am stopping with the Boston team, from Johnny Ward. John had a Brooklyn *Eagle* in his hand and called my attention to several ball notes presumably from the pen of Mr. Chadwick. One referred to Fred Pfeffer and Comiskey not getting along in harmony, which was the cause of the great second baseman's absence from the team, when the truth of the matter is that Pfeffer was suffering from a severe injury. "This is only a fair sample of the kind of work 'Chad' is doing right along," said Ward, "and like the personal abuse heaped on the parties connected with the PL all winter by the *Sporting Times*, it has done us more good than harm."[2]

I noticed that all of Brother Chadwick's screeds in the *Eagle* started off by complimenting the fair sex present at the games, as if to give out the impression that the best people were attending the games this season at the League grounds. Now, in my experience, I find that ladies' day means the gathering of women at ball parks that neither do the game good or elevate the sport, in fact, just the reverse comes from the free admission business.

I think Ward is right in saying that "Chad" is putting it on too thick about the fair sex who get in on their shape.[3]

Can't Be Driven Off.

There is no mistaking the fact that the Brooklyn team of the PL is here to stay. I was speaking with a wealthy Brooklyn gentleman at the Pierrepont House, and he tells me that the very best people are with Ward and the team. "Messrs. Goodwin, Chauncey, myself and others have gone into the thing to stay," said he, "and I know Colonel McAlpin, of New York, is of the same mind as we are.[4] Do you know how I got interested? Why, it was last fall, when I read about the League going to stop men from going out for themselves and I got indignant and here I am now one of the staunchest friends the boys have. I am with them for a fight to the finish.[5]

Thought He Owned the Town.

I had an impression before coming here that Charley Byrne carried the town in his pocket. You know Byrne is one of the cleverest in the business and can get as much out of his position as any one.[6] I had read "Chadwick's Chat" and screeds from your Brooklyn correspondent until I thought Ward's starting was only a bluff, but I come here and find things altogether different. Ward has not only got one of the best fighting teams, but he has a house for them that is simply immense. The grand stand is far superior to anything I have so far seen on a ball ground. The field is large and in time will be an elegant place to see the game from. You may have an idea of the distance when I tell you that I went from the *World* office in New York to the grounds in less than one hour.[7]

I was not surprised on getting to the new park to find that my old friends Billy Harris, George Stackhouse, and Mr. Mandigo were not in the scorers' pen; no doubt they were doing their day's work over in Manager McGunnigle's stamping grounds.[8] It seems rather hard to think the boys are scattered and I know my travelling companion, Jacob Morse, and myself miss that tilt so sure to come when Boston meets New York. But then it wasn't my fault if the boys chose to go wrong.[9] I warned them in time. Would you believe it some of these gentlemen can't even yet understand why the players have a right to live. I am fully convinced that O. P. Caylor, W. I. Harris, with his boomerang philosophy, and Colonel John I. Rogers, of Philadelphia, did more to make the PL a success than John M. Ward and all his associates.[10]

"Truth crushed to the earth will rise again."[11]

Can you imagine for a moment the fun truth had with the above trio during the last six months?

When I think how thin and worn out those three old friends of mine are from many sleepless nights of plotting the downfall of the PL I feel sad.

This Tip Is Timely.

The PL must remember just one thing, that while the writings of those men who have always been dead against them can not hurt them one iota with their friends, yet the suppressing of one piece of news by their friends of the press must not be expected. So far the PL has run very smoothly. It seems almost as if the hand of Divine Providence was guiding the helm. Look at the obstacles overcome since the first meeting of the new League at the First Avenue Hotel last fall, and yet they start the season with well-equipped teams and hold the winning hand from the very start. I am not sentimental, but I knew last winter that the base ball public would go to see the men they knew of rather than go to see the ones they knew not of.[12]

Al Spalding used excellent judgment when he sent season tickets to the members of the PL Club of his city. Mr. Spalding has a clear head for business, and it will be he and he alone that will bring the League out of the bad mess they got into by conflicting with the PL, and showing how truly weak they were as drawing cards, for had not the games conflicted the friends of the old league could have said—"We are doing the same old business."[13]

Right here, I want to call attention to one more of Mr. Chadwick's paragraphs in the Brooklyn *Eagle*:

"There were only about 3000 people at the two games in Chicago yesterday, as the day was cold."

As the Chicago League attendance was but 125 on that day, it would have been well to have made a note of the attendance at each game. It is paragraphs like the above that creep into the daily papers and are misleading.[14]

PICKETT'S CASE RECALLED.

The decision in the Pickett case was a good thing for base ball and will stop the contract jumping business. While I fully believe that Pickett did what he thought he had a perfect right to do, yet it couldn't have helped the game in the long run.

During the week John Ward received word from Philadelphia saying they could hold Tom Tucker, who was then with the Boston Club playing in that city. Ward sent back word that he had no use for the man, and would not ask him to fill his original contract with Brooklyn.

At the last PL meeting in New York, Chicago, Boston and Brooklyn voted against the Philadelphia Club's claim to Pickett.[15]

Jogging Along the Road.

Ward's Brooklyn team will be in the race this year. They play all the fine points and are never lost when sharp fielding is called for. Ward himself is putting up a much better game than he did last year.

Van Haltren is pitching 25 per cent better than he did for Anson's Chicago Colts. In Daily, Cook and Kinslow Ward has a trio of catchers hard to beat.[16]

The Boston Brotherhood team were [sic] delighted with their reception in the Quaker City. The games, too, were on the same plan of last season, plenty hitting and sharp fielding.

In Griffin and Shindle the Phillies picked up two of the finest ball players in the business.[17]

As the pitchers' box on the Brooklyn grounds is very high, Buffinton should be a puzzle when in this city.[18]

Dave Orr is the happiest man on earth this season—"I have been trying for years," said he, "to get into the leading organization and now feel like a new man." Dave is pounding the ball hard.[19]

Kid Madden was very sick in Brooklyn.[20]

Umpire Gaffney should be given a chance by Secretary Brunell to umpire other than the Brooklyn games. Gaffney is not doing his best work with Ward haunting him. I have seen him now nine times in Boston-Brooklyn games and I must say Ward got almost every decision and a good many that were not close. I am not finding fault with Ward, but I am with a man like Gaffney, who can umpire as well as any man living when at his best.[21]

I think Billy Holbert is going to make a fine umpire on base decisions.[22]

As the Brooklyn Club were presented with grounds and one of the handsomest pavilions in the country for a starter, no wonder they felt good after leaving Boston with $10,000 velvet.[23]

Buck Ewing's men are in hard luck. They are sure to get thawed out after a while, and then look out. They are in the race for one of the first three positions.[24]

Never was the outlook brighter for base ball.

T.H. MURNANE.

Appendix A

Part 2 Notes

1. On June 14, 1870, Harry Wright's Cincinnati Red Stockings, then the first and only openly professional team, met Bob Ferguson's amateur Brooklyn Atlantics and lost, ending their 89-game win streak. According to reports, between 9,000 and 20,000 people paid 50 cents to watch the game, no doubt spurred on by the fact that the Atlantics had given the Reds their last loss almost two years earlier at the Capitoline Grounds (Miklich "Bob Ferguson").

2. Chadwick's work in the *Brooklyn Eagle* typically did not appear with a byline, but his style was readily discernable to anyone familiar with it. The *Sporting Times* was the weekly newspaper purchased by Spalding to serve as the mouthpiece for the NL after *SL* and *The Sporting News* endorsed the PL. John Ward may have been doubly disappointed in Chadwick's partisan journalism after he made the effort to meet with the *Spalding's Guide* editor in March to tell his side of the story.

3. Beyond laying the foundation for a print feud with Ella Black, note how Murnane borrowed Chadwick's elevated rhetoric here to argue against the practice of admitting women to the games for free.

4. Wendell Goodwin, a streetcar financier, Brooklyn banker, George Chauncey, and fellow banker Edward F. Linton (likely the unnamed speaker in Murnane's interview) were the primary investors in Ward's Wonders. Edwin A. McAlpin was a New York real estate developer and tobacco broker (Alexander 28–29).

5. For anyone who had missed his pre-season "screeds," Murnane made it clear here that he was a PL supporter due to the restrictive labor practices of the NL owners.

6. Charles Byrne was the primary owner of the Brooklyn Bridegrooms in the NL. Henry Chadwick esteemed Byrne as the ideal magnate owner.

7. Completed in 1890, the *New York World* building was built by Joseph Pulitzer to house his newspaper. It was located on Park Row, overlooking New York City Hall. Ward's new ballpark was located in the eastern part of Brooklyn near Jamaica Bay. After 1890, Brooklyn's NL team played at Eastern Park, but eventually moved back to Washington Park due to the distance from the city's center and the difficulty reaching it (http://www.covehurst.net/ddyte/brooklyn/eastern_park.html. Retrieved 2014-06-07). Murnane's initial skepticism about Ward's hastily assembled Brooklyn PL team became significant given the degree to which he eventually supported the new league.

8. William H. Harris was the New York correspondent for *SL*; George Stackhouse was a New York City sportswriter with the *New York Tribune*; John Mandigo was a New York City sportswriter. Bill McGunnigle was the manager of the Brooklyn Bridegrooms in 1890; this trio of players backed the NL during the Brotherhood War.

9. Jacob Morse was a sportswriter for the *Boston Herald* who supported the PL.

10. *Sporting Times* editor O. P. Caylor, sportswriter William I. Harris, and John I. Rogers, part owner of the Philadelphia Phillies, were all staunch opponents of the PL.

11. This line was taken from "The Battle Field," a poem by William Cullen Bryant, American poet and *New York Post* editor. The Civil War served as the poem's topic and may have been selected by Murnane to draw a comparison between that conflict and the current "Brotherhood War."

12. After a series of secret meetings that did not sit well with Henry Chadwick and other moralists, the formation of the PL was announced in November of 1889.

13. Murnane's attitude toward Spalding would change by the end of the month—and then change again by the end of the year. Murnane's words proved prophetic in October.

14. Both Chadwick and Murnane were guilty of cherry-picking facts and statistics to support their partisan reports throughout the season.

15. Due to a lack of jurisdiction authority, the court decision did not keep John Pickett

from playing the 1890 season with the Philadelphia Quakers. Tommy Tucker played 132 games for the Boston Beaneaters of the NL in 1890.

16. George Van Haltren was a .500 pitcher at 13-13 with Anson's White Stockings in 1888; he was .600 at 15-10 with Ward's Wonders in 1890, so Murnane's math was slightly off.

17. Mike Griffin played outfield and batted .286 in 115 games for the Quakers in 1890; Billy Shindle played 130 games at shortstop for the Quakers, batted .324 and scored 127 runs. Both players were with the Baltimore Orioles of the AA in 1889.

18. Listed at 6'1" and in his ninth major league season, Charlie Buffinton went 19-15 with a 3.81 ERA for the Quakers.

19. After eight productive seasons with AA teams in the "Beer and Whiskey" league, Big Dave Orr jointed Ward's "leading organization" in 1890 and hit .371, missing the batting title by .002. Soon after the close of the 1890 season, Orr suffered a stroke at age 31 that ended his career.

20. At 22, Michael "Kid" Madden went 3-2 with a 4.79 ERA in seven starts with the Red Stockings. The "Kid" pitched two games against Norwich's (CT) minor league team in August and September, prompting *SL*'s Norwich correspondent to describe him as being "full of ginger" as he "amused the audience by his antics" (*SL*, August 9, 1890, 8). In September, he pitched a game for Mystic, CT, against the Norwich team in a game that featured a crowd that "was the most insulting, the most insolent and rowdyish that the writer ever saw," which was decidedly not the type of crowd that Chadwick and Murnane were looking to bring out to NL and PL games (*SL*, September 6, 1890, 12).

21. Before joining the umpire staff of the PL in 1890, "Honest" John Gaffney, called "King of the Umpires," participated in a "double umpire" experiment at the 1887 World's Championship Series. Murnane would have issues with the PL front office in September when decisions by Ward and Brunell went against the Red Stockings. (http://sabrpedia.org/wiki/John_Gaffney_%28a4ba%29. Retrieved 2014-5-27).

22. After a 12-year career in the NL and AA, William "Billy" Holbert became an umpire for the PL in 1890.

23. Murnane was not shy about naming dollar figures to illustrate the effectiveness of the PL business model.

24. Ewing's PL Giants started the season 4-10, but did go on to finish third as Murnane predicted.

Part 3: June 28, 1890, SL, p. 9, by Henry Chadwick

CHADWICK'S CHAT.
The Costly Result of the War—
A Cessation of the Hostilities Advised—
What the Future Holds in Store—Advantages of
The Double Umpire System—Other Topics.

NEW YORK, June 25.—Editor SL:—In the interests of the professional class of the base ball fraternity—a decidedly minority class, be it remembered—I am glad to note the fact that the era of rabid partisan utterances, which have characterized the writings of the press advocates of the two warring factions during the past winter and spring, has

Appendix A

about come to an end, for the utterances in question were doing the professional organizations costly injury. The war between the NL and its seceding players has led to an era of abusive personalities; of gross misrepresentation of fact; of costly and damaging exposures of the inside working of the professional clubs; of selfish greed on the part of ambitious would-be magnates, and of personal aggrandizement of leading players at the cost of the welfare of the fraternity at large, which, if much longer continued, would have relegated the professional clubs back to the demoralizing period of a dozen years ago. Let us have no more of it. The cost of the strike, and the war between employers and employees which it has led to, has cost the League and its greedy, seceding players thousands of dollars, and the end of the loss has not yet been reached. A bitter rivalry, with its accompaniment of public disgust as well as mistrust, has been engendered, and the advance of the professional class toward a millennium period has been retarded for years to come. And all this costly condition of things is due entirely to the selfish ambitions of a small minority of high-salaried star players, if not to the greed for office and emolument of an unscrupulous leader. This fact the history of every day doings in the professional world is rapidly revealing to the opening eyes of the duped players of the fraternity.[1]

What was the position of the players of the NL at the ending of the season of 1889? They were in command of high salaries—three to six thousand dollars for seven months of service—paid them by thoroughly responsible clubs. They were subject to no harsh laws in their club government, nor to any arbitrary enactments in controlling them, which timely legislation—urged in the interest of club management on the plan of true business principles—would not have removed in the near future.[2] But they ran wild after the *ignus fatus* of an impossible co-operative system in the management of professional clubs, and urged on by leaders looking only to self-aggrandizement they deliberately dropped the substance of the marrow bone of League employment which they had at command, and grasped the shadow of the Brotherhood League, and what has been the result?[3] Let the present demoralized condition of the professional base ball world answer.

What will be the ultimate outcome of the unnecessary strike and its still less needless sequel of the existing war in the League arena? The answer is the bankruptcy of more than half of the professional clubs of the country for one thing, and the greatest fall in salaries in 1891 the fraternity have ever seen. How can it be otherwise? There has been no elimination of admirers of our national game; on the contrary, there are more would be patrons of honorable professional ball playing now than ever before known in the history of professional base ball. But the majority are holding their patronage in abeyance until such time as the fraternity come to their senses. The most striking result of the Players' strike has been the wide opening of the door of the professional arena to the colts of the fraternity, by means of which facilities for the admission to the NL employment have been given to hundreds of promising aspirants for League honors, who but for the strike would not have had such opportunities offered to them for years to come.[4]

A false sentiment has been worked up to misguide players. A practically impossible system of professional club management has been advocated, and is now being tried at great cost for the experiment, and all this has been done to serve the selfish purposes of a small minority of ambitious leaders. Professional clubs, to be financially successful, must be run on true business principles, and these principles are at war with the PL plan of co-operative government of a club team. The capitalists must have exclusive control of their clubs, and the players must be none other than employees of the club. Any other plan renders financial success impossible, and the sooner the seceding players realize this fact the sooner will be the return to successful running of the professional base ball club business.[5]

The season has even thus far been prolific of failure of player umpires. There is not one player in twenty competent to discharge the onerous duties of an umpire. The primary essentials of a good umpire—*thorough impartiality, full control of temper, the courage of his convictions* and *quick perception*, together with an intimate knowledge of the spirit and intent as well as the wording of the code of playing rules—are not possessed by one player out of every fifty.[6]

It is a matter of surprise to me to see various League clubs granting free admission to this, that and the other class—ball players, actors, labor organizations, etc.—while they fail to see the advantage of having special days for the admission of ladies free to the club privileges when accompanied by gentleman escorts. The Brooklyn League Club's plan—adopted years ago—of giving ladies free admission to the grand stand at all times—except of course, on holidays—and to the grounds on one day each week, is a paying policy in every aspect, and it should be a regular rule.[7]

Appendix A

Here is truth in a nutshell:—"A man who plays for his own personal record on a ball field is as weakening to the team as an overdose of physic to a human being." And yet there is scarcely a team in which there are not one or more of the self same class of record players; and the more there are of them the weaker the team is, even if every one of them is a star player in his position.[8]

I see it stated that pitcher Schmidt [sic], of the Pittsburg Club, was fined $50 for indifferent pitching. I think this is a mistaken policy. Make drunkards feel the folly of their dissipation through their pockets all you can, but in regard to alleged indifferent play in any position the offense is very different. There are a dozen causes for poor play on the part of a member of a team entirely outside of the intentional neglect. A pitcher may be badly supported, either by his catcher or his field, and the failure to give him the best support be so disguised as to throw the onus of defeat on the single player. Who is to judge fairly whether Schmidt has pitched with intentional carelessness? Analyze the scores of his games carefully and ascertain how many base hits are made off his pitching, *after* he has given the field chances to retire the side for a blank. Of course, there may be exceptional facts in the case to justify this fine, but as a rule, I think some other cause could be more advantageously taken.[9]

What is the matter with my good friend Mott that he interprets my paragraph about the P.L. ball so? Brother Mott says that I said that "the trial at the Brotherhood grounds of the Spalding and Keefe ball was no test at all, because the pitching distance is greater in the PL than in the National." I never said anything of the kind. I simply quoted Mr. Dickinson's paragraph, in which he described a trial test of the superior elasticity of the P.L. ball over that of the N.L. My addenda did not refer to the test, but to the fact that the eighteen inches difference of distance between the pitcher and the batsman *also* helped the P.L. batting. Of course that had nothing to do with the testing experiment. My esteemed friend has been so badly off his base, however, since the secession movement of the players, that I did not wonder at his getting other things mixed.[10]

The days of breaking up of minor leagues, the disbandment of club teams, and the throwing of hundreds of players on the market, consequent upon the demoralizing condition of things in the professional world have begun. By the time the fall season is reached the poor duped players will be exclaiming with Richard:—"Now is the winter of my discontent," without the sequel of the "glorious summer" King Dick referred to.[11]

Do you notice in the papers the paragraphs about the lack of harmony in this, that and the other professional team in the various leagues? It is all a question of ability, and the lack of it, in the management of the team. When a club manager plays favorites in his game he is bound to have discord in the ranks in consequence.

I want to say a word or two about the double umpire system as shown in its working in the PL arena. The Players' code of rules—Sec. 3 of Rule 50—states that "the duties of said umpires are hereby divided between No. 1 and No. 2, as follows:—First, No. 1 shall decide upon and call all balls, strikes, dead balls, fair hits, foul hits, foul strikes, intentional fouling of balls, and all questions arising at home plate, or as to delays by side at bat, or as to batsmen striking out of turn, and he shall also call 'play' or 'time.' Second, No. 2 shall decide all other questions arising between the contestants in any game, including balks and illegal deliveries." Rule 51, Sec. 1 of the same code states that "each umpire is the sole and absolute judge of all questions of play coming within the scope of his duties as above defined and divided." This is the only rule order under which the double umpire system can be successfully worked. That of allowing one umpire to call strikes in one inning, and the other in another inning, robs the plan of half its advantages, among which are the training of each umpire in one set of duties, the one being made practically familiar with the special duties behind the bat, and the other with those connected with the base-running. The giving the latter umpire the power to decide balks is due to the fact that while standing on the base lines he can judge better the violation of the rule than the umpire behind the bat.[12]

It is entirely needless to state that the abusive kicking which has characterized the contests of the PL clubs—the columns of the Brotherhood organs prove this fact conclusively more than no other evidence at command—since the opening of their season renders it impossible that the system be given a fair trial under such drawbacks. That it is the only plan for successful umpiring there is not the slightest doubt. But perfection itself would fall under the kicking abuse.[13]

Beatin seems to be the besting pitcher of the Cleveland team this season.[14]

Appendix A

A marked feature of the season's batting in the way of scientific team work in handling the ash, has been the success attained in *bunting* the ball skillfully. No point of play in batting needs more judgment than that of "bunting." It is the needed sacrifice hit, as a rule, and when the bat is in the hands of a fast base-runner, a good bunt becomes almost a sure base hit.[15]

You are quite correct in your views as to the effect of the two-games-for-one-admission rule. It is cheapening the game. Charge for each game if it is necessary to have two in one day.[16]

Up to June 20, the N.L. and P.L. clubs had played an aggregate of 373 championship games to an aggregate of 618,689 people, including free admissions. This makes an average attendance of 1658 to a game. Inasmuch as 62,000 people attended six consecutive games of the League championship series last season, and the general average reached nearly 3000 to a game, the falling off in the patronage is remarkable. A noteworthy fact in connection with this is that the exciting contests between Harvard, Yale and Princeton during the championship series in June, 1889 did not average an attendance of 2000 to a game, while this year four games have attracted over 21,000 people—5968 at New York, over 6000 in New Haven and nearly 10,000 at Cambridge. What has been the professional club's loss has been the college club's gain.[17]

I see that my fair friend Miss Ella Black has misunderstood a remark she attributes to me about my originally supposing her to be a masculine base ball writer in disguise. I have never for a moment entertained the ridiculous notion that ladies cannot write. I know they can write, and frequently better than men—certainly so in some specialties. How could any one have such an idea while remembering the writings of such old-time authors as Maria Edgeworth, Miss Mitford, Miss Austin [sic], Miss Burleigh, etc., etc., not to mention the large number of more modern lady writers.[18] My most esteemed friend, Mrs. Helen Dauvray Ward, would make a base ball correspondent who would make all us masculines yield the palm to her. No, no, Miss Ella, my surprise was to find a lady writer so well posted in professional base ball matters; not because she was a lady writer.[19]

Two surprise parties marked the record of last Saturday out West, the one was the defeat of Anson's strongest team by Mutrie's nine, and the victory scored by the tail-enders of the PL over the so-called Giants of New York.

Part 3: June 28, 1890—Henry Chadwick

That was a singular occurrence at Chicago the same day, when the P.L. team of Brooklyn defeated the Comiskey combination by 1 to 0 and that, too, without their making a single base hit off King's pitching.[20]

Here is a paragraph I saw in the Philadelphia *Times*:

"Milt Brodie, of Boston N.L. broke the long distance-throwing record in Boston Monday last, when he threw a base ball 135 yards. The previous record, 123 yards, was made by Hatfield and stood for twenty years."

How was the throw made? Was it in one of the two games played in Boston that day, or in a regular throwing trial?[21]

I am very glad to see Mr. Barr's interesting letter from England that the newly organized base ball League there has adopted rules prohibiting all disputing of the umpire's decisions, and likewise all noisy coaching, two existing abuses in professional ball playing in America which are a disgrace to the fraternity. Mr. Barr has this significant paragraph in his letter in reference to the English League's rule of one club for each city, in which he says:

"There promises to be a lively fight for championship honors, and as there are not two clubs to represent each city to divide the interest, we hope to arouse that local pride which lies dormant in the heart of every good citizen to such a pitch that they will take an active interest in the welfare of their respective clubs."[22]

HENRY CHADWICK.

Part 3 Notes

1. Within this strong example of Chadwick's editorial voice, the *Spalding's Guide* editor mapped out the argument that he would refer to time and again for the rest of the season. Key points included the repeated phrasing for effect, the usual lack of transparency in the baseball business, the delayed "millennium period," and the fact he seemed to be going for John Ward as the Brotherhood's "unscrupulous leader." Ironically Chadwick became one of the primary and loudest partisan voices during the 1890 season. The veteran writer's golden age for the game should not be confused with Francis Richter's nine-part "Millennium Plan" to reorganize the National Agreement, which originally appeared in the *SL* in 1887 and then as a separate publication in 1888.

2. Chadwick overlooked the reserve clause—which had been expanded to the entire team in 1889, the practice of selling players, and the Brush Classification System—the trio of "objectionable" practices that spurred the Brotherhood into forming the PL (Rossi, 32).

3. In spite of misspelling "*fatuus*," Chadwick showed off his Latin for "will-o'-the-wisp"

4. Chadwick's vision of a bleak future was another feature of his Roman voice. He predicted lower salaries in 1891 (which did come to pass), and provided some numbers near

Appendix A

the end of his report that did not compare well with Clarence Dow's figures (see note 17 below).

5. For Chadwick to argue for the capitalist model as the only way baseball could be organized was echoing the stance of Spalding (his employer), while reversing his original response to the formation of the NL in 1876 (Schiff, 145–6).

6. The initial ratio of one in 20 was apparently not strong enough to make his point, so Chadwick changed it to one in 50 at the end of the paragraph. The veteran sportswriter was questioning the ability of the same player-turned-umpires referenced by Murnane at the end of the letter reproduced as Part 3 above.

7. Chadwick seconded Black's argument regarding the economic and audience-building advantages of "ladies day" or refuted Murnane's disapproval of the policy—or both.

8. Chadwick appeared to be critical of all professional teams in this paragraph, yet, by the end, he was likely referencing the "picked nines" of the PL that he objected to regularly over the course of the season.

9. At age 24, Frederick "Crazy" Schmit broke in with the Pittsburgh Alleghenys in 1890 and went 1–9 in 11 games with a 5.83 ERA. Chadwick was clearly willing to punish a player for drunkenness or other forms of dissipation, but stopped short of trying to determine their intent on the field. In keeping with the contemporary turn toward science, it was noteworthy that the inventor of the box score called for the analysis of statistics as the basis for such assessments.

10. Here is another example of sports journalists keeping watch of each other's work, as well as conflict generated by the Brotherhood War of 1890.

11. Chadwick was quoting the opening lines of Shakespeare's tragic history play, *Richard III*, proving there was a literary side to his Cato the Elder stance.

12. John Ward went over the separate duties of the two umpires under the PL system when he met with Chadwick in March; nonetheless, the veteran rules committee member seemed to be underestimating the capacity of "player-umpires" to learn all the rules.

13. Despite being in favor of the NL's approach to the double umpire system, Chadwick made sure to take every opportunity to point out the failures of the PL. What's more, the fact that his point didn't "require stating" would not keep him from doing just that repeatedly over the course of the season.

14. Chadwick's scouting report was accurate here: Ed Beatin went 22–30 with a 3.83 ERA in 54 starts (53 of which he completed) and was credited with half of the wins earned by the seventh-place Cleveland Spiders. In August, Richter reported that Cleveland manager Bob Leadley had fined Beatin $125 over the course of one week: "Evidently there is reason for the brace up" (*SL*, August 23, 1890, 4). Four weeks later, Richter reported that Leadley had re-signed Beatin, so perhaps the fines had their desired effect.

15. Even before what he took to be the preponderance of extra-base hits due to the "lively" PL ball, Chadwick was an advocate for "scientific hitting" over mere "slugging" and was not shy about presuming to speak for the "better class" of patrons who appreciated the aesthetic qualities of the more cerebral style of play.

16. It took a number of years, but the owners eventually did away with true doubleheaders, as Chadwick advised here in one of the rare moments he agreed with *SL* editor Richter in 1890.

17. Although the attendance numbers were already being called into question by the end of June, Chadwick's figures did not agree well with those given by Clarence Dow in the *Boston Globe*. Dow's combined per game average showed an aggregate gain in attendance over the year before. The increase in attendance at the college series was not necessarily due to fans staying away from the "professional game." In short, the Roman senator was picking cherries—again—to attempt to prove his point.

18. Of the four writers listed here, Jane Austen is the most well known today as the author

of *Pride and Prejudice* and other novels about nineteenth century marriage and manners. Maria Edgeworth was an Anglo-Irish writer and author of *Castle Rackrent* (1800), a historical novel about 18th century Irish life and manners. Mary Russell Mitford was a prolific English writer who is best known for *Our Village* (1826). Chadwick might have been thinking of Frances Burney, an English novelist, diarist, and playwright, when he mentioned "Miss Burleigh."

19. Chadwick appeared to be seconding Ella Black's earlier support of Helen Dauvray's baseball acumen. While he made no mention of his friendship with her in the report of his meeting with her husband, John Ward, in April, he also seemed to be seconding Ella Black's endorsement of Ward's wife's literary abilities. If Chadwick was aware that Black was using a pseudonym for her *SL* correspondence, his mode of addressing her in this passage offered no hint (e.g., he doesn't refer to her as "Miss Ella" or "My fair friend 'Ella Black'").

20. The New York Giants of the NL were in sixth place when they defeated Anson's Chicago Colts, 8–7, in Chicago on June 21. The Buffalo Bisons of the PL were in last place when they defeated the sixth-place PL Giants at home on Friday, June 20 (not Saturday).

21. As a 22-year-old rookie outfielder for the Boston Beaneaters in 1890, Walter Scott "Steve" Brodie hit .296 and recorded 19 assists. As the ironman of nineteenth century baseball, Brodie went on to play in 727 consecutive games with the Beaneaters, St. Louis Browns, and Baltimore Orioles from 1891–1896 (Akin, http://sabr.org/bioproj/person/cffefl17. Retrieved 2013-4-18). John Hatfield set throwing records with the 1868 Cincinnati Red Stockings (132 yards; the feat was recorded in Chadwick's own scrapbooks, so it is surprising he didn't correct the erroneous distance given in the Philadelphia paper) and in 1872 with the New York Mutuals of the National Association (133 yards, 1 foot, 7½ inches). He was still listed as the distance throwing champ in his 1909 *SL* obituary, so Brodie's record appears to be unsupported (Preston, http://prestonjg.wordpress.com/2009/12/04/the-history-of-the-record-for-baseballs-longest-thrown-a-tale-that-involves-john-hatfield-honus-wagner-sheldon-lejeune-don-grate-rocky-colavito-and-glen-gorbous-among-others/. Retrieved 2014-5-18.).

22. The National Base Ball League of Great Britain started two weeks later than scheduled because "foot ball season" ran long (*SL*, June 7, 1890, 8). "Kicking" and "noisy coaching" were two of Chadwick's favorite signs of the failure of the PL.

Part 4: July 19, 1890, SL, *p. 7, by T.H. Murnane*

MURNANE'S MISSIVE.
Wholesale Papering of Boston by
The League Club Boldly Charged—The Policies
of the Old Magnates Severely Criticized—
General News Notes.

Boston, July 17.—Editor SL:
—"Are you going to the game to-day?"
"Yes, if you will give me a comp."
"Why, the town is full of them; you can get all the tickets you want to the League games just for the asking."
The Triumvirs got themselves most thoroughly disliked for years

Appendix A

by refusing to admit even the mothers of some of the well-known League players to the games.[1]

What a change. Now the complimentary tickets are as free as water. Think of one man in Lynn having 900 of these "comps" sent to him for distribution.

You can find them by the bunch at the police station houses, at the drug stores and about everywhere that people can be worked to "chin" for the old masters.

The above is not guesswork and I can prove the charge and add to it ten-fold.

It looks like one more desperate move to kill the game, for a time at least, with a hope of getting the chance later on to monopolize the business. I know for a fact that the people who go to the League grounds free one day go to the Brotherhood grounds and pay the next day.[2]

There was a time when the League magnates were looked on as men well up in business affairs, but was there ever a body of men more thoroughly outwitted than they have been during the last six months?

Outgeneraled at every turn, they have gone mad and are now cutting their own throats, like swimming pigs, as they manage to keep their heads above water.

What is bound to be the ultimate outcome of all this bad management? I think I can tell, and my honest opinion is that the backers of the PL can see it as plain as I, viz.: Get together, strengthen up the lines in a way to leave no doubt of their determination to not only live and let live, but fight and fight hard and fast. Stop at no quarter until the men who would ruin a fair business rival are given a lesson they will not soon forget.

Because A. G. Spalding and the Boston men have made two or three hundred thousand dollars off of the base ball business is that any reason they should expect to have the public always with them, whether right or wrong?

I contend that it was the honest ball players that built up the game in this country, and as most of them are now in the PL, it must be a queer world, indeed if they can be defeated.[3]

So my friend Harry Palmer is going to take a two week's rest, and A. G. Spalding is going to Europe. My, who will look out for poor, old Chicago now? "Al" and Harry worked together in good style and their loss will be felt if but for a few weeks.[4]

I understand that John Clarkson is fast making himself disliked by the players in Frank Selee's team. That don't surprise me seeing that old "Getz" and young Nichols is doing so well in the box. I understand also that John is trying to copy Mike Kelly by continually alluding to himself as "The King." John, old man, let me give you a quiet tip, the king is dead, and will be soon buried in oblivion.[5]

The League men have an excellent chance to win the pennant this season unless they take a bad tumble on the next Western trip.[6]

The Pittsburg and Cleveland teams are under the charge of Palmer O'Neill and Gus Schmelz respectively, the man that knows more about raising whiskers than good ball players. Perhaps this remark would apply to J. Palmer, as his crop of Burnsides have been universally admired.[7]

These two teams should be arrested for taking money under false pretenses. Neither team is strong enough for the Atlantic Association, but accomplished one thing, viz., fattened up the winning record of the home team, and this is about all they seem to do with such rank management.[8]

The people kicked on having to pay horse car fare. Admission was free, and the individual who came up from the country and gave up a half-dollar will never forgive himself.[9]

Brother Conant has a number of young ladies working in his gossamer factory. Saturday the girls felt happy. Four "comps" each was their allowance. Uncle Bill is rather a clever fellow, and for some time the boys around town, as well as some of the girls, have enjoyed what is known in sporting circles as a picnic.[10]

President Soden was in New York a few days ago. Spalding was there at the same time. It was after this visit that the free ticket business was taken up in earnest by the magnates.[11]

As Spalding had worked it in Chicago, no doubt Mr. Soden got all the points from his old player, who, by the way, got out of this place with his full salary paid up.[12]

If the League had done business in a fair and open manner I think they would have gained the respect of their old patrons in time, but now I can't see anything but a dead loss before them, and the older they grow the less brains they give indication of having under their hats.[13]

Mat[t] Kilroy returned last Tuesday; he had been nursing a sick wife at his home in Philadelphia.[14]

Gil Hatfield was willing to come to Boston provided he was promised a place on the regular team.[15]

Arthur Irwin is walking around town with a gold-headed cane, but too weak to play.[16]

I would be in favor of a ten-club league if a schedule could be made out. Chicago, Pittsburg, Cleveland, Cincinnati and St. Louis in the West, Boston, New York, Philadelphia, Brooklyn, and Baltimore in the East. The above would take in all the good ball towns in the country. I would not object to Sunday games, as I believe it is no more objectionable to play ball on Sunday than to have theatrical performances. I would run the League on business principles and engage only men who were above suspicion. Time will bring about the above circuit. Until then the game will not yield profits to speak of.[17]

I am sure that such men as Colonel McAlpin and the solid men behind the PL will not frighten off as easy as two or three of the magnates hope for. There is big money in the base ball business, and no one is better aware of this fact than the League magnates themselves. The PL should commence figuring at once for their next year's circuit.[18]

Ad Gumbert is now doing good work in the box; the members of the team all say he is made of the right stuff.[19]

The Buffalos were here the first of the week and put up a nice game. Big Injun Sam Wise says that Billy Harris was wrong, as usual, when he had him kicking about his pay.[20]

Before my next screed the directors of the PL will have met in your city and held a meeting that will presage no good to the "magnates."[21]

T. H. MURNANE.

Part 4 Notes

1. Murnane revealed in his next column that Fred Pfeffer and Arthur Irwin had issues with the triumvirs over their mothers being admitted for free. Wives of the Beaneaters players were admitted for 12 and a half cents; wives of visiting players paid the full 50 cents.
2. Like Chadwick, Murnane appeared to be supporting his argument with anecdotal evidence. Murnane also leveled pointed criticism at the opposition: here the magnates came under heavy fire for their monopolistic practices and denying the players their rights to self-determination under the "old Jeffersonian doctrine."
3. Murnane's editorial here was likely shaped by his past experience with the NL—both as a player and a business rival in 1884. He was one of the players who helped start the professional game with the NA in 1871 and observed first-hand the changes brought by the advent of the NL in 1876.
4. Harry Palmer was a Chicago correspondent for *SL*, a writer for the *Chicago Tribune*, a co-editor of the *Sporting Times*, the sporting weekly Spalding purchased to serve as the

national organ of the NL, and one of the three journalists to accompany Spalding's 1888–1889 world tour.

5. Born in Germany in 1864, Charlie Getzien went 23–17 with an ERA of 3.19 in 40 starts (39 of which he completed) in 1890. Breaking in with the Beaneaters at age 21 that year, Kid Nichols went 27–19 with a 2.23 ERA in 47 starts, all of which he completed. Murnane may be referring to the NL or Albert Spalding in the cryptic last line of the paragraph.

6. The Beaneaters went 9–3 on their second western swing to run their record to 56–32 and move into third place in the NL.

7. "Burnsides" was the original term for "sideburns" after Civil War general Ambrose Burnside made the style popular.

8. The Atlantic Association was a minor league in 1890 with teams from Massachusetts to Maryland. The Beaneaters went 6–1 against Pittsburgh and Cleveland at home in the first half of June.

9. Murnane appeared to be referencing the comps policy with this scenario, implying that someone from the city would have known they could get into the game for free.

10. William Conant was one of the three co-owners—or triumvirs—who owned by Boston Beaneaters, along with Arthur Soden and James Billings. Conant was a manufacturer of hoop skirts—hence Murnane's reference to "gossamer" and later rubber goods (McKenna, http://sabr.org/bioproj/person/a1b2e0d0, Retrieved 2014-5-27).

11. Of the other two triumvirs, Billings was the treasurer and Conant was the secretary of the team. The three bought the team in 1877 and turned it into a profitable business through austerity measures, like the one regarding player wives and mothers (McKenna, http://sabr.org/bioproj/person/a1b2e0d0, Retrieved 2014-5-27).

12. After five years in Boston with the NA, Albert Spalding played for the Beaneaters in the inaugural year of the NL in 1876 before moving to Chicago for a salary of $3,500. This move made Spalding a "contract-jumper" in his playing days, much like the Brotherhood players who signed with the PL.

13. Given the sharp tone of Murnane's comments here, it was clear that he was feeling confident of a PL victory in the Brotherhood War.

14. At age 24, Matt Kilroy went 9–15 with an ERA of 4.26 in 27 starts (only 18 of which he finished) as a pitcher for the Red Stockings in 1890. While profiling Kilroy as a member of the PL champion Red Stockings, Richter noted that the young pitcher's arm was "out of condition" for much of the season, preventing him from "doing justice to himself" (*SL*, November 15, 1890, 3).

15. Gil Hatfield played 71 games for the New York PL Giants in 1890, playing at third base, shortstop, the outfield, and on the mound. In September, the PL office ruled that the Red Stockings would have to replay three games that Hatfield filled in at shortstop because he hadn't received his release from New York.

16. The irony of this statement points to Irwin as one of the "sick" players that Murnane alluded to in an earlier report as being in need of a word from the management. Irwin was earning money from the manufacturing and sales of the fielding gloves he designed, which may have been linked to his fancy cane. Irwin's absence at shortstop is what caused the Red Stockings to use Hatfield there.

17. After the PL dissolved at the end of the 1890 season and the collapse of the AA in 1891, the NL had a 12-team configuration that included the ten cities listed by Murnane with the addition of Washington in the east and Louisville in the west.

18. Murnane's confidence turned out to be unfounded as McAlpin was one of the men who helped scuttle the new league in October.

19. Ad Gumbert was the brother of Will Gumbert, the Pittsburgh Alleghenys pitcher that Ella Black praised in her columns. Ad Gumbert was just 21 in 1890 when he went 23–12 with a 3.96 ERA in 33 starts (27 of which he finished) for the Red Stockings.

20. At age 33, Sam Wise played 119 games at second base for the Buffalo Bisons of the PL. William I. Harris was a New York sportswriter who supported the NL and thus took every opportunity possible to cast a negative light on players of the new league.

21. One of the items that PL directors decided was the forfeit of the Hatfield games, which prompted Red Stockings captain Mike Kelly to say, "'If the other clubs, including John M. Ward's, wants [sic] to beat the Bostons out of the championship, why, fire away, but then I don't think they can do it'" (*SL*, July 26, 1890, 5).

Part 5: August 16, 1890, SL, p. 6, by Ella Black

MISTAKES OF THE PLAYERS
How the Members of the New League Are
Injuring Themselves—Dissipation in Pittsburgh
Morris' Queer Ways—The Outlook Ahead—
Kelly's New Home and What it May Do—
O'Neill's Club Will Stick it out.

PITTSBURG, Pa., Aug. 15.—Editor SL:—If I could only have delayed the writing of my last letter for a couple of days I would have had some rather sensational material on which to discourse. This would have come from the general tearing up that took place in the team of the local PL club. For a long time past it has been very evident, even to the best friends that the club has, that but very few of the men were playing the kind of game that they were capable of. As the result of this the long string of defeats that nowadays the Pittsburg [franchise] records was placed to the credit of the team. It has been very plain for some time that several members of the team were doing about as they pleased, and the defeats referred to was [sic] the consequence. The sequel of it all has been that Ed Morris, the one-time famous pitcher of Columbus and Pittsburg, has been given an unconditional release and at the present time several of the other players are under suspicion of doing too much drinking and are apt to be very heavily fined if the directors find their information has been correct.[1]

A MISTAKE OF THE PLAYERS.

In the above line I have reference to those who belong to the PL. It is an unfortunate thing that many of the members of the new organization seemed to be lingering under the idea that as soon as they left the NL they were allowed to do just as they pleased in every way. It is possible I may be mistaken in this, but so far everything that has taken place bears me out in this assertion. I know that I myself no later than two days before the local papers had an item about some of the PL club members taking too much to drink, saw three of the men on the street one evening, each and every one of them so much intoxicated that it was impossible for them to walk along without knocking into everyone they met. This is why such a fuss was made by some of the local papers and why the board of directors took the action that it did. It was similar conduct, unless I am greatly mistaken, on the part of some of the members of the New York, Boston and Chicago Players' clubs that caused them to meet the long string of defeats they have encountered this season.[2]

This is just where the men are all making their great mistake. No one can deny for a moment that when the PL was first put in operation that it had the sympathy of the public, and had it been properly managed would have been sure to have been very successful. However, since the season opened, I am sorry to say there has been instance after instance wherein the members of various clubs of the PL have taken advantage of the position in which they are placed and have caroused around until they were not able to do justice either to themselves or their clubs. It has not taken the public very long to find this out, and the result has been a falling off in the attendance that has made a most appreciable difference in the size of the receipts.[3]

The new clubs must have a much stricter management in the future than they have had in the past or else they cannot hope to be successful. The public will not pay out its money to see a crowd of intoxicated men on the ball field. It pays to see ball playing, and if the PL cannot give that then the people will either go to the NL games or remain at home. As to the action of the local directors, I have found that I am not the only one who thinks they did just right. I have heard several others say the same thing, and what is more, I know of one gentleman (a regular base ball crank) who said he had become so disgusted with the playing the ball club was doing that he had not gone to a game for a week, but now that the directors showed they had some nerve and would not allow players to rule them he would begin to go once more.[4]

About Ed Morris.

This little pitcher is a man I have never thought very highly of. Ever since the first season that he made a record for himself he has shown

Appendix A

himself to be possessed of such an amount of self-conceit as one seldom meets with. Even after his arm gave out, and when he was unable to do any pitching, he still gave ample sign that his conceit was not gone. So far this season he has done but little real work that would be looked upon as being up to average. He pitched one game (4 to 0) in which he shut out his opponents, a couple of weeks ago. That was all that could have been asked for, but since then he has done nothing at all, and seemingly has been trying to live on the reputation he made that day. Now, since he has been released, I hear the local NL team is going to try to sign him. I hope this is not so for the club has had hard luck enough this season without taking any useless material, such as it would find Morris to be, on its hands. He has always been a grumbler and "kicker," and any team is better off without him.[5]

The Present Outlook.

The talk still goes on about what the prospects are for both the major bodies. The partisans of each side claim their organization is all right and that the other League is bound to go under and give up the ghost in a very short time. The old League people are also making a great deal of fuss now over the talk of several of the leading members of the PL being about to "jump" back to their old clubs. Now, leaving all personal feeling to one side, I am inclined to look at the situation in something after the following way:—The PL, while it to-day has got the best players and most experienced men in its ranks, has not got as solid a financial support as its opponent has. If it has to go along without any more support than it has received so far it will have a very hard time to live another year. On the other hand, though, if it should be true that the AA and other bodies are going to join in with it and play games with its clubs, then I think it will get along all right. As to the NL, the members of that body are undoubtedly in better condition to-day than they were three months ago. It has got to be admitted that they are drawing larger audiences than they were at the start. The young players who are in their ranks are also showing they can play good ball and this has also helped to increase the crowds. Should the old League be able to draw back to its clubs any of the players who are now being talked about, I am afraid that this would come very near to being a death blow to the PL. One reason I have for thinking this is[6]

Part 5: August 16, 1890—Ella Black

WHAT EWING SAID

to a gentleman friend of mine during the last time he (Ewing) was in this city. At that time, during a talk with my friend, Ewing said:—"I would like to see John B. Day get along all right and not have any trouble. He is a popular man, and I believe the New York NL Club will be able to hold its own and pull through all right." Of course, I may be attaching more importance to this remark than it may be worth, but at the same time I cannot help but regard it as being very significant. Why should one of the most noted of the PL members be so very sympathetic towards one of the strongest members of the opposition?[7] It was the memory of the remark of Mr. Ewing that caused me to pay more attention to the rumor that he was going to jump back to the old League than anything else would have done, and now I would not be very much surprised should Ewing and one or two others return to the fold from which they deserted nearly twelve months ago. If this should be done by these men it would do more to hurt the new League than anything else that could be well imagined, and I hope and pray they will remain true to their companions. Another thing, I think that will create

BAD FEELINGS AMONG THE MEMBERS

of the PL is the presentation to Mr. Michael J. Kelly of a house and grounds, about which there has been so much talk of late. Why Kelly should be so highly favored above others is what I fail to comprehend. Of course if his friends wish to make him a present that is a privilege they have, but at the same time it ought to be done in such a way as not to offend any one else. The present could have been given without the public ever hearing anything at all about it. Why I say this is because there are plenty of other men belonging to the PL, John Ward, Hanlon, Pfeffer and many others, who are just as good players as Kelly ever was, and who did ten thousand times more to aid in the work of organizing the PL and getting it into working order, and yet no one has ever heard of any of them being presented with a house and grounds. These men are also fully aware of how they will compare with Kelly, and the fact of such presentation being made to him with so much fuss, having it telegraphed all over the country, etc., cannot very well help but cause some bad feelings to be stirred up among them. They would not be human if they would go back over their own records and make a comparison between what they have done and what Kelly has done, and did not feel very sore that such a preference should be shown for him, when they, the men who have done nearly all the work are compelled to keep in the background. If the truth is ever known about the case, it will some day be found that these men have felt this thing, in just the way I have stated and have tried to get even for it.[8]

NL Club Doings.

President O'Neill's team is still going along in its usual slip-shod manner. The management, though, must be given credit for trying to do the best it can in the way of strengthening the team whenever the chance has offered itself. Indeed, the club has been gone over and reorganized so often that but little sign is left of the team with which the season was opened. It is now a fairly strong one, but the men are all discouraged by the long list of defeats that is to their credit and they cannot put any heart in their work. If the team was now going to start out with a clean prospect ahead of it there would be a very different result than what was made by the team that started the season. It is now quite generally understood, though, that the club will stay and be in the field again next season, and it is with this object in view that the effort is now being made to strengthen the team whenever possible.

The series just completed here with the Chicagoites showed the local men were able to take care of themselves with any club they might meet.[9] The only thing the club needs now to make it equal to any in the country is a couple of good pitchers and a practical manager. I saw the game on Monday last when Phillips, formerly of the Washington, D. C., Atlantic Association Club, pitched his first game for Pittsburg. I may not be a good judge, but certainly I never saw a man who impressed me more favorably than he did. With the right kind of handling he will be one of the greatest discoveries of the year and for once the local club will have had a little luck.[10]

What a wonderful player Anson is. No difference how small the audience may be or how far ahead his own side is, he plays just as hard as though it was a nip and tuck game before the largest crowd of the season.[11]

Only that I am not in favor of talking about the umpire I would like to say something about Anson and his combination pitcher-umpire, Mr. Stein.[12]

Part 5: August 16, 1890—Ella Black

Certainly the local NL team seems doomed to have bad luck. The twelve-inning game on Tuesday last was a beauty all through, only it was hard to see the home team tie the score in the ninth and then lose in the twelfth. The defeat, though, can be largely attributed to Mr. Anson's Youngstown find, Lytle. This young man was played in Monday's game in a Chicago uniform, but he did not suit Anson and was not signed. Then on Tuesday he was given another trial, this time by the Pittsburgs, and, of course, had to begin to play like that team has been doing this year, and so dropped two fly balls that let two runs in. Only for this it would have been a Pittsburg victory.[13]

ELLA BLACK.

Part 5 Notes

1. Not only did Black show her non-partisan side here when she was critical of PL players for not going all out on the field and for drunkenness, she also was not shy about naming names, using Ed Morris as an example and returning to his case in more detail later in her report.
2. This report corroborated one of Chadwick's main complaints about the PL and illustrated his desire to improve the image of the game through better behavior of the players. Ever the PL promoter, Murnane maintained that the PL was largely free of "kicking" and that the players were working harder than ever—until King Kelly's frequent "vacations" from the Red Stockings forced him to be more objective.
3. As Black noted in the pre-season, the PL had the support of the public initially in Pittsburgh due to their labor cause, but that support declined once the production on the field declined, perhaps due to dissipation and a lack of discipline among the players.
4. Black's claim that the increased drunkenness of the players led directly to a decrease in attendance was again similar to Henry Chadwick's take on the situation.
5. For the Burghers in 1890, left-hander Ed "Cannonball" Morris went 8–7 with a 4.86 ERA in 15 starts, completing all of them. These numbers were a far cry from previous seasons when he led the AA in wins, starts, complete games, and shutouts. To balance Black's obvious dislike of Morris as a player and a person, "Circle," Pittsburgh's other *SL* correspondent, had more praise for Cannonball's whitewashing of Ewing's Giants even as he referred to the pitcher's past injury woes: "Ed Morris surprised his friends by pitching one of the best games for several years. As a result New York was given the first shut-out of the year." At the same time, Circle's quote from Morris, "'I can still pitch a little bit,'" contained the undercurrents of the conceit that upset Black (*SL*, August 2, 1890, 11). Morris was the proprietor of a billiard saloon in Allegheny (a city later incorporated into Pittsburgh) and Black related how he ran into some difficulty that reflected the low culture status of baseball players in 1890: "Pitcher Ed Morris appeared in a new role this week when he applied for a liquor license. It was rather rough when the Judge asked him if he ever had any business, and when Morris said, 'I'm a professional ball player,' for the Judge to reply, 'I don't count that. Did you ever work?'" (*SL*, April 5, 1890, 11) Given that such establishments were known to be the haunts of gamblers and other "undesirables," Cannonball's chosen off-season profession may have contributed to Black's dislike for him.
6. Black's analysis here was accurate and insightful given that the PL backers were the

Appendix A

Achilles heel of the operation when representatives from the two leagues met in October and November of 1890. The NL could have been "drawing larger audiences" through their aggressive comp policy and inflation of their attendance numbers, but then both the NL and the PL were guilty of "cooking the books" that season (Alexander, 77–8, Seymour and Mills, 237–8).

7. Despite leaving Day's NL Giants for the PL, Buck Ewing remained on good terms with the New York magnate. Rumors in early August had Ewing meeting with Day at the Fitchburg station during a trip to Boston. Ewing maintained his loyalty to the Brotherhood, but also claimed that no one else could determine his associates (Alexander, 85–6). Once again, it was clear that Black was well positioned to have friends and/or colleagues who could allow her to quote ball players.

8. Beyond pointing out the common courtesy (and common sense) of not making everyone else feel badly while singling out one player, Black highlighted once again the negative influence of the press here in potentially creating negative responses to Kelly's "gift" from the "blue bloods" of Boston, as well as what she took to be the undeserved celebrity of Kelly.

9. Black may have overstated—or understated—her case here. After winning their 19th game on August 11 over Anson's Chicago Colts, the Alleghenys won just four more games for the rest of the season. They did play Anson's team tough when they lost the first game, 6–4, and dropped the last one, 13–12, but many of their subsequent losses were lopsided, supporting Black's claim to the disheartened aspect of the team.

10. Bill, "Whoa Bill" or "Silver Bill" Phillips was the engineer of the 6–4 win on August 11, which ended a ten-game skid (before starting a 23-game one). After going 1-9 with the Alleghenys, Phillips played six seasons for the Reds in the NL over the next 13 years and was a .500 pitcher with an ERA below 4.00.

11. Where Chadwick and Murnane mostly refused to find good things to say about players in the opposing leagues, Black maintained a more balanced stance that allowed her to praise quality play when she observed it, no matter the source.

12. Ed Stein broke in as a 20-year-old with Anson's Chicago Colts in 1890 and went 12–6 in 18 starts (14 completed) with a 3.81 ERA. Black appeared to be adhering to Chadwick's policy of supporting the umpire.

13. Silver Bill Phillips and Edward "Pop" Lytle were likely the 37th and 38th players signed to the Alleghenys roster in 1890, illustrating the turnover and reorganization Black mentioned in her report.

Part 6: September 6, 1890, SL, p. 8, by Henry Chadwick

CHADWICK'S CHAT.
The Improvement in the Cincinnati Team
The False Attendance Figures—Interesting
Statistics About the Two Major
Leagues—General Comment.

NEW YORK, Sept. 3.—Editor SL:—I have never seen such a marked improvement in a League team as that shown by the Cincinnatis since last May. Up to this summer the weakness of the Cincinnati team each season has been the absence of team work at the bat, something as essential to success as team work in fielding. Game after game have I been accustomed to see their batsmen face pitchers with the one idea of slugging for three-baggers and home runs in the regular old muffin style of hitting, which prevailed in the sixties, when runs in a game were counted by the hundreds.[1] The idea of batting runners round by team work play in handling the ash was never thought of. To bunt a ball was regarded as death to a batsman's reputation with the bleaching board occupants, and as for a sacrifice hit to forward a runner, it was a point unknown. All idea of playing a ball for a single safe hit, or of tapping a swiftly pitched ball to short outfield was ignored. It was a homer or nothing with all of their batsmen, Reilly being conspicuous in this muffin style of hitting.[2]

What was my astonishment, therefore, to see John in the Cincinnati games at Washington Park last week try to tap a safe ball to short outfield and to do it well, too.[3] Then, too, to see the team go in for sacrifices hits—seven in one game was recorded, each forwarding runners and most of them sending in runs. A prettier game than their team put up on the occasion of the last game of the series has not been seen at Washington Park this year. There was a life and vim to their play at the bat, in the field, and in base-running which was as superior to anything the Cincinnati team have ever before exhibited as light from darkness. Surely Loftus must have brought about this great change of base, and I feel sure Latham has had a hand in it.[4]

By the way, I wish to commend Latham's method of encouraging his men as their captain. He always has a good word for a fine play, and a word of encouraging excuse for errors. This is the way to captain a team; not to growl and snarl at a player when an error is made thereby making things worse all the time. Some captains have this absurd idea that they are not fulfilling their mission unless they are finding fault either with a player's fielding, batting or base-running errors, or with the umpiring. The man who adopts this plan is totally unfit to captain a team.[5]

Lovett did a pretty piece of pitching work in the box in the last Cleveland game at Washington Park, which displayed his nerve and strategic skill very prominently. It was in the ninth inning, when by two good hits and a sacrifice runners had earned second and third bases with but one man out. West came to the bat and he had had two strikes

Appendix A

called on him when he got his base on balls on a close decision. With but one man out and all the bases filled, and only two runs to get to tie the score, the position became critical, and one trying to the abilities of a pitcher. But Lovett was equal to the emergency; the fifth striker was caught out on a foul, and the sixth at right field in trying to hit safely, and the three runners were left and the home team came in victors by 2 to 0.[6]

It was in this game, by the way, that Foutz and Virtue did splendid work as first basemen, both having the hardest kind of widely thrown balls to attend to. The Clevelands have an acquisition in Virtue. I have seen no work superior to that he did in the three Cleveland games in Brooklyn all this season.[7]

Why is it that the two Leagues still keep up the false count business? That is about as silly a thing as they have done of late. No one is taken in by it. Mr. Talcott says that there is but one League Club that has given out the legitimate figures and that is the Brooklyn Club. Do stop this Peter Funk business. It is a disgrace to every club which indulges in it. I am surprised that Messrs. Day and Spalding have been led into following the PL's bad example in this respect.[8]

I saw that genial scribe, Ren Mulford, at Washington Park last week and he told me that Brunell was in the grand stand, so I went up to see him, and, to my surprise, found him as quiet and reticent as a man who has a world of care on his shoulders or who has just realized the fact of his having made the mistake of his life. Sitting next to him was Col. McAlpin and Brother Dickinson, who introduced me to Ewing's boss— I beg pardon, I should say to Ewing's brother director. I had not time to talk with them, and so soon descended to the press box below. Mr. Byrne was not aware of their presence until they had been seated, or the usual courtesies, of course, would have been extended. Dickinson, in rather bad taste, made a paragraph the next day about having paid their way in. Mr. Byrne would not have allowed it had he known of their coming in time. That is not his way of doing business. Mr. Al Johnson, too, was there, but I did not see him. The fact is, Frank's blue looks frightened me off. Poor Frank, how changed he is since the old League days. "Care sits heavily on his weary brow."[9]

I read this in your "notes" of last week "Martin Sullivan is as straight as a string this season." I presume that means that his habits are temperate and not those of 1889. The player is a wise man who sees his folly

Part 6: September 6, 1890—Henry Chadwick

in time and has the moral language to redeem the errors of the past. But what a heap of moral cowards there are in the ranks this season who prefer liquor indulgence to making men of themselves.[10]

A remarkable feature of the make-up of the Brooklyn team this season is that all four of their pitchers, Lovett, Caruthers, Terry and Foutz are all fine fielders, Terry and Caruthers exceeding in the outfield, and Foutz and Lovett in infield play.[11]

What a tough customer in the way of a strong physique George Miller, of the Pittsburg NL team, is. He received a blow from a ball on the side of his neck at New York on Saturday, which would have disabled any ordinary player. But George is like "Joe Bagstock," he's devilish tough, sir, and as plucky a player as there is in the League.[12]

One of your notes last week says:—"The Louisville Club has certainly been playing in good luck all season." What rot this is! For "luck" please read *good management*. That is what Louisville has been playing under all season. When I read, too, about a club's having "hard luck" I generally set it down to the credit of bad management. Of course, there are exceptions in such cases as when a team has a number of players disabled by accidents—not by dissipation. But when a club has alleged "hard luck" in the disabling of its players by drunkenness or debauchery set it down to bad management, for that is what it is, and nothing else. This good and bad "luck" in teams is the result of good and bad management in nearly every instance.

So the Athletics have released Hughes, eh? What could they expect from a player released from another club on account of dissipation?[13]

The experiment of putting an Association team in Brooklyn just to gratify the personal spite against Brooklyn's team cost the Association magnates a loss of $12,000, they backing Kennedy's club. Brooklyn is an out and out League city, as this season's experience fully proves.[14]

The September campaign of the PL clubs begins with Boston, Brooklyn, and New York as the three leaders, their percentages of victories up to Aug. 30 inclusive, showing Boston in the van with .613; Brooklyn second, with .595; and New York third, with .575. Boston's record, however, does not include three games won from Buffalo, which were thrown out, while the equally illegal victories against the Buffaloes, in which Twitchell pitched, are counted.[15] The individual records of the Boston club to Sept. 1 shows the following victories and defeats, counting all the games actually won:

Appendix A

BOS vs.	CLE	CHI	PIT	BUF	PHI	NYY	BKN	Totals
Victories	7	9	9	12	8	9	11	65
Defeats	6	8	3	5	5	8	6	41
Totals	13	17	12	17	13	17	17	106

Brooklyn's individual record to the same date is as follows:

BKN vs.	NYY	BOS	CHI	CLE	BUF	PIT	PHI	Totals
Victories	5	6	8	11	11	12	13	66
Defeats	8	11	6	6	5	5	4	45
Totals	13	17	14	17	16	17	17	111

The New York Club's individual record to the same date is as follows:

NYY vs.	PHI	BOS	BKN	CHI	BUF	CLE	PIT	Totals
Victories	5	8	8	9	9	10	12	61
Defeats	11	9	5	7	2	6	5	45
Totals	16	17	13	16	11	16	17	106

These tables present some very interesting figures for study, especially in regard to judging of the probable outcome of the September campaign. It will be seen that Ward's team has already won four of their seven series, while Kelly's team has won but two and Ewing's but one.[16]

Looking over the PL club pitching records up to Sept. 1 I find the following interesting figures in regard to the victories and defeats pitched in by John Ewing and Crane in the New York team:

J. Ewing.	BOS	BKN	PHI	CHI	PIT	CLE	BUF	Totals
Victories	2	2	1	3	1	3	2	14
Defeats	1	2	2	0	0	2	0	7
Totals	3	4	3	3	1	5	2	21
Crane								
Victories	1	1	1	1	1	1	3	9
Defeats	4	2	3	4	4	1	1	19
Totals	5	3	4	5	5	2	4	28

This shows a percentage of victories pitched in of .667 for John Ewing, against .321 for Crane. Evidently visits to saloons at midnight does not help a pitcher's record much.[17]

From the tables of the NL and PL averages published in our issue of last week, I glean the following interesting figures of the fielding done by the infield and outfield players who take the lead in the fielding averages. I select those only who have played in fifty games and over.

Part 6: September 6, 1890—Henry Chadwick

	National League				Players' League		
	Ga's	Av.	Pos.		Ga's	Av.
Bennett, BOS	75	.957	c.	Ewing, NYY	67	.958
Tucker, BOS	101	.992	1b.	Connor, NYY	96	.981
Myers, PHI	88	.952	2b.	Quinn, BOS	103	.916
McGarr, BOS	87	.923	3b.	Tebeau, CLE	81	.879
Coorey, CHI	104	.925	ss.	Rowe, BUF	87	.908
Sullivan, BOS	101	.959	lf.	Richardson, BOS	100	.988
Holiday, CIN	102	.950	cf.	Griffin, PHI	71	.867
Burns, BKN	98	.946	rf.	O'Roarke, NYY	69	.926

The pitcher's fielding averages do not appear in THE SL record. The Boston Club has the most players in the NL record of leaders in the eight positions, and the New York Club in that of the PL.

I notice in the NL fielding averages of the Brooklyn team that Daly's percentage as catcher is .953, Bushong's .951, and Clark's but .844. At first base Foutz is seventh, with .972; at second base Collins is second, with .945; at third Pinckney is second, with .918; at short field Smith is fourth, at .965; at left field Terry is second, with .953; at centre field O'Brien first, with 1,000, and at right field Burns is second, with .946. Mullane is first there with .963, but he only played in seventeen games to Burns' ninety-eight.[18]

HENRY CHADWICK.

Part 6 Notes

1 Chadwick accompanied the Washington Nationals on their 1867 tour of the Midwest to witness some of the lopsided games—including a 90–10 drubbing of the Columbus Capitals—first-hand. A then unknown pitcher by the name of Albert Spalding and his Forest City team of Rockford, Illinois, handed the traveling clerks, led by George Wright, their only loss (Schiff, 111).

2. Both Chadwick's stance on "scientific" batting and the class element of his bias toward "the bleaching board occupants" are evident in this passage.

3. Chadwick's praise here of Reilly was significant because "Long John" was a notorious free-swinger. Near the end of a ten-year major league career, Reilly hit .300 and led the NL with 26 triples, one of which he described to the St. Louis *SL* correspondent in 1890:

> The occupants of the grand stand and bleachers were wild with rage, and I was notified to hit the ball or die. The next ball was a straight, fast one, and I caught it fair and square on the end of my bat, and it sailed on a line over the centre fielder's head, and when the hog hide was returned to the diamond I was standing on third with a heart as light as a ball players' pocket-book in January [*SL*, December 6, 1890, 7].

While the jury may have been out on whether Reilly actually spoke with such metaphorical flourishes, his assessment of a player's finances was accurate (Ball, web).

Appendix A

4. At the start of the 1890 season, Tom Loftus and Gus Schmelz switched teams, but only Loftus was blessed with inheriting a veteran lineup. After Loftus led the Cleveland Spiders to a sixth-place finish in 1889, Schmelz inherited a decimated team in 1890 and was fired after a 21–55 start. Chadwick's praise notwithstanding, Loftus led the Reds to a fourth-place finish after the team contended for much of the campaign.

5. Chadwick's praise here was a bit premature since the Reds went into a slump after the arrival of Arlie Latham, the "Clown Prince of Baseball," from the Chicago Pirates in early August (Alexander, 80–81).

6. Tom Lovett went 30–11 with a 2.78 ERA in 41 starts (39 of which he completed) for the Bridegrooms in 1890. Lovett injured a finger in early August but returned to "the harness" a few days later, exhibiting some of the newfound toughness observed by Brooklyn *SL* correspondent J. P. Donnolly: He came to us a star of great promise and was pounded to smithereens in the first round, and failed to recover from the shock during the year. He has thought it all over and got back his self-possession, and with a steadier nerve and a few more kinks in his delivery should do all proud (April 12, 9).

7. In 113 games played at first base for the Bridegrooms in 1890, Dave Foutz committed only 28 errors in 1,259 total chances. Jake Virtue played 62 games at first base for the Cleveland Spiders in 1890, accepted 666 total chances and committed only 12 errors. Virtue was signed in the middle of July after the Detroit team folded and Peek-a-Boo Veach was released because he failed to show "the moral courage to let whiskey alone," according to Cleveland *SL* correspondent R. W. Wright (July 19, 1890, 5). To further demonstrate J. P. O'Neill's questionable judgment, he signed Veach to an Allegheny contract, but released him after eight games even though Peek-a-Boo was hitting .300.

8. E. B. Talcott was the Director of the PL Giants. Chadwick maintained all summer that Byrne's books for the Bridegrooms were above reproach. In contemporary slang, a "Peter Funk" was an auctioneer's accomplice who sat in the audience and drove the bidding up to increase sales.

9. Chadwick's interpretation of this chance meeting appeared to be more of his anti-PL work; nonetheless, Colonel Edwin McAlpin, New York PL Giants backer and thus Buck Ewing's "brother director" under the league's organizational structure, was one of the first to sue for peace in October, which might explain the glum disposition of PL Secretary Frank Brunell. Partisanship-wise, the sportswriters in the scene canceled each other out: Ren Mulford wrote for the *Cincinnati Enquirer*, was an *SL* correspondent for that city, and an NL supporter, while George Dickinson of the *New York World* was a PL backer and thus a frequent foil in Chadwick's reports. Charles Byrne was one of the owners of the Brooklyn Bridegrooms and Chadwick's model for the ideal magnate. Extending his penchant for quoting Shakespeare, Chadwick was perhaps reaching for a line from *Henry IV, Part Two*: "Uneasy lies the head that wears the crown" (Act III, scene 1, line 31) to amplify and elevate his assessment of the PL's situation.

10. After averaging just 72 games with Chicago and Indianapolis the previous two seasons, Martin Sullivan played 121 games for Boston in 1890. On August 30, Richter's notes indicated that Sullivan was leading the Beaneaters in hitting; the *SL* editor went on to editorialize that the "fine work" by Anson's old outfielder showed "what he was capable of when he takes good care of himself" (*SL*, 4). The commentary by Chadwick and Richter served as another example of baseball journalists attempting to improve—and ultimately shape—the game's image.

11. Bob Caruthers and Adonis Terry split their starts between the pitcher's box and the outfield, where they committed eight errors each; both players batted over .265 with a number of extra-base hits, making them contributors offensively as well. Chadwick overstated his case with the other two players since Tom Lovett started only one game in the outfield and Dave Foutz started only five games as a pitcher.

Part 7: October 4, 1890—T.H. Murnane

12. Starting at every position except pitcher and first base for the Alleghenys in 1890, George "Doggie" Miller played in all 138 games—113 of which were defeats. Doggie claimed that "the continued defeat hasn't affected the appetite of even one Pittsburgh player," which prompted Richter to quip, "Certainly not; the luckless backers are the ones to lose their appetite" (SL, September 20, 1890, 4); Joe Bagstock was a stock sidekick to the main character from *Dombey and Son* by Charles Dickens (1848).
13. In contrast to the praise Chadwick had for Marty Sullivan, he was equally ready to condemn a player for dissipation. The 1890 numbers for Michael "Mickey" Hughes were indicative of someone with a drinking problem: he finished only one of his eight starts with the Brooklyn Bridegrooms and went 4-4 with an ERA of 5.16. He completed none of the five games he started for the Athletics and won only one with a 5.44 ERA. Hughes was released by Byrne in the middle of July for "insubordination and intoxication," but he was apparently a favorite of the female fans since Richter reported that he "was welcomed home by a bevy of young ladies who waited two hours in a snow storm for the steamer to arrive" (SL, July 19, 1890, 5; SL, April 5, 1890, 10).
14. With an average attendance of about 750 for 50 home games, the Brooklyn Gladiators disbanded on August 26 with a record of 26-72 (Alexander, 84). Again, despite Chadwick's protests that he was non-partisan, the Bridegrooms were clearly the team he admired most.
15. In 1890, Larry Twitchell played 56 games with the Cleveland Infants before being "loaned out" in the middle of July in an attempt by the PL to strengthen the Buffalo Bisons (*BG* September 7, 1890, 3; Alexander, 78-9).
16. Despite a valiant effort by Ward's "plucky" Wonders, Kelly's Red Stockings held on to win the PL pennant. By the end of the season, Boston's PL team won the season series from each team in the league, showing that Chadwick's analysis was premature. The tables that follow demonstrate the veteran sportswriter's love of statistics.
17. The table comparing two PL pitchers was unique since Chadwick usually compared the NL and PL to hold up the former as the superior league. As Buck Ewing's younger brother, John Ewing received some criticism when he got off to a slow start, but finished with a respectable 18-12 record for his brother's PL Giants. Not to be confused with Ed "Cannonball" Morris of the Pittsburgh Burghers, Ed "Cannonball" Crane finished with a record of 16-19 for the PL Giants, so the "talking to" he got from the good father in this report might have helped him stay away from the saloons.
18. In a rare use of statistics that did not reveal obvious cherry-picking on Chadwick's part, hints of NL pride—over anti-King Kelly and anti-Ward sentiment—were present. The examination of the Bridegrooms roster position by position added strength to the argument of anyone who observed that Chadwick favored Byrnes' team.

Part 7: October 4, 1890, SL, p. 3, by T.H. Murnane

MURNANE'S MISSIVE
Father Chadwick Called to Task—
Accused of Treating PL Men and
Measures—Unfairly—The Cincinnati Deal, Etc.

BUFFALO, Oct. 1.—Editor SL. Anything more rabid than Henry Chadwick's last effusion in THE SL would be hard to find. For a newspaper man, who claims to be fair he is about as far from the mark as I

Appendix A

know. The older he gets the worse he gets. Now, Chadwick is an out and out, dyed-in-the-wool League man. He writes against facts continually, and, not a week passes that he does not put his foot into it. Now, if Chadwick does not believe that the PL club in Boston drew almost 200,000 people in Boston this season, or half that number, as he says, I'll tell him that I know for a fact that the figures are true, and will stake my reputation for truth and veracity and fairness against his. What does he know about the attendance in Boston, any more than I know anything about the attendance on the Brooklyn League grounds? But I do know something about the attendance in Boston, and I do know that on no grounds has there been a greater fidelity to the real figures than in Boston. I have attended almost every game, and I have a glimmer of a suspicion that I know more about the matter than one many miles away. We don't have to go to Brooklyn to establish the truth as to attendance. I can back up what I say by something more than mere wind.[1]

THE "FATHER OF BASE BALL" SCORED.

This man Chadwick has put himself to no little trouble again and again to spread rumors about drinking in the PL, about lack of discipline, wrangling, etc. Now, my dear friend, the PL has not witnessed such scenes as have been seen on any League or Association field this year. No PL man has insulted spectators by leaving a field before a game was over. There have been greater squabbles on League fields over the umpiring than in the PL. What else could have been expected of the compiler of the League Guide and under League pay? Criticism is always allowable when fair. But when Mr. Chadwick descends to barefaced untruths, I say hold your horses. A word with you. Mr. Chadwick can still do good work in base ball, but when he attempts to write anything about the PL he makes a monumental failure. He was as bad last year when the world's series was being contested between Brooklyn and New York. If any one mentioned a word in favor of New York in the Brooklyn grounds Chadwick would glare and privately insult him. You tried your tongue and pen on me, old fellow, but I was on the right side then as I am now. Chadwick threw cold water on Ward last spring and has now crust to eat in consequence. Base ball is played on the ball field, not on paper, my fine fellow, and John Ward has been gaining ground in your bailiwick in great style despite your screeds. Mark my prediction, your nets won't draw in '91 what they did in the past season and your utterances will be as unavailing then as now.[2]

What has become of Nick Young's predictions? That the new League would have the best of it at first, would they, and then the old League?[3] It has not been so. The PL has outdrawn the NL in every stage more than three to one in Boston. Manager Selee and Captain Smith are two more Young men that are talking through their hats, and since the gate receipts don't warrant their salary they have to expend more or less wind energy to merit their recompense. Windy Joe Hornung is another of their class. He wants to be retained in '91, and tries to make out that the League nine in New York has outdrawn the Players.[4] Why, the Players have outdrawn the Leaguers in New York fully five to one. They have more sense in Chicago than in Boston and New York. The League people there know they have been beaten and are wise enough to keep quiet about it. I remember that every time the Players have a big crowd in Boston Chad. would write a stirring paragraph. But how was it when the League would "fake" its crowds? I have visited the League grounds in Boston and have known figures over 2500 given out when there were not 1500 people on the grounds.[5]

Everybody knows how Charlie Snyder was treated. At the end of a championship season ('78), when the Boston Club was said to be behind, he agreed to play an exhibition season of one month for nothing, if they would pay his board. When the time came the club refused to keep the promise and he quit them.[6]

But enough about Chadwick. By the time your paper is for sale this week we will know all about that Cincinnati deal. Al Johnson and Frank Brunell will be on hand bright and early next Saturday to meet with President Stern at Cincinnati with the money to pay for the club, and, if I am not mistaken, the deal will be fixed up before they go to dinner that day.[7]

The League will be forced to put up big money this season to keep their best players.

Have you noticed the fine work John Clarkson is doing for our Boston Leaguers. Poor Frank Selee and wretched Ed Stevens. They have my sympathy.[8]

T. H. MURNANE.

Part 7 Notes

1. Murnane's assertions about Boston PL attendance figures were backed up by the willingness of the team's secretary, Julian B. Hart, to allow his books to be examined by the As-

Appendix A

sociated Press. After the end of the season, PL Secretary Frank Brunell claimed that the Boston club was the only team in the league to make money (Di Salvatore, 320).

2. There was no hint of the animosity in Chadwick's description of his meeting with Murnane at George Wright's house after the Fast Day Game in April, but from this passage it is clear that Murnane bore a grudge against Chadwick for the treatment he'd received in the press box during the 1889 Dauvray Cup series. Murnane's prediction regarding Chadwick's "nets" proved to be true in that Richter stopped publishing his "chats" at the end of 1890.

3. While supporting the NL line that the PL would fade by the Fourth of July, President Nick Young further predicted that the NL would not change their schedule (*SL*, May 3, 1890, 5) and claimed that the league would not take the Brotherhood Players back upon the inevitable collapse of the PL due to the development of new players at half the salary, according to R. M. Larner's "Washington Whispers" report (*SL*, July 26, 1890, 14).

4. During the pre-season, Murnane had nicer things to say about Frank Selee as the first-year manager of the Boston Beaneaters, calling him a "hustler." Charles "Pop" Smith was not a favorite, however, drawing the comment that he was "now hitting hard at the wind" to describe Pop's progress toward a .229 season at the plate (*SL*, May 31, 1890, 5). Joe Hornung hit just .238, begged out of the last game of the NL Giants due to illness and was not back for 1891, ending a 12-year career. Thus, his efforts to earn another contract by boosting the NL were not successful (*SL*, October 11, 1890, 5).

5. As noted above, attendance figures were unreliable for both leagues in 1890. Despite his experience as a player and a sportswriter, Murnane's estimates of the attendance at the NL games in Boston have to be questioned as much as the figures given by the "undercover agents" planted in PL parks by A. G. Spalding to give out fake attendance figures to the newspapers (Stevens, 129).

6. 35-year-old Charles "Pop" Snyder was cut from the Cleveland Infants after appearing in just 13 games in 1890 and applied to become a PL umpire. If Murnane was not exaggerating his story in an attempt to discredit the Beaneaters management, then Snyder was most likely the victim of the money-saving practices put in place by Arthur Soden and the other members of the triumvirate after they took over the ownership of the Boston franchise in the NL in 1877 (McKenna, http://sabr.org/bioproj/person/a1b2e0d0, Retrieved 2014-5-27).

7. Murnane had good reason to adopt a triumphant tone here: the sale of the Cincinnati team to a group of 11 PL backers in early October left the NL depleted to a six-team league due to the insolvency of the Pittsburgh franchise (Alexander, 102–3).

8. As one of the chief "deserters" of the Brotherhood, few players received more bad press from Murnane and other PL supporters than John Clarkson. In his worst season since being sold to the Beaneaters in 1888 by A. G. Spalding, the future Hall of Famer won just 25 of his 44 starts (43 of which he completed). In late September, Richter reminded his readers that Clarkson had been unable to pitch early in the season, had pitched badly for a stretch, and then pitched worse: "He pitched so badly in the game against Philadelphia at Boston last Friday that the crowd yelled continually for Getzien. Could anything be more humiliating to a player who stood in his position last year?" (*SL*, September 25, 1890, 5). If the game on September 20 was an example of Clarkson's late-season pitching, he went 11 innings and lost 2-1 to the seventh place Cleveland Spiders, with the winning run scoring on a dropped third strike. Perhaps there were games where he pitched poorly, but it was clear that Clarkson was a player that PL supporters "loved to hate." NL supporter Ed Stevens was a sportswriter for the *Boston Herald* and a *SL* correspondent who wrote about Boston sports under the pseudonym "Mugwump" Frank Selee was the manager of the Beaneaters who brought Clarkson back for another season in 1891.

Part 8: November 22, 1890, SL, p. 7, by Ella Black

THE BIG WRECK

Caused by a Lack of Nerve—Maybe the
Players Have Themselves to Blame—
Hard For John Ward—What Will Pittsburg
Get?—A Chance For Some Good
Men—Players Will Miss Advance Money.

PITTSBURG, Pa., Nov. 21.—Editor SL:—At this writing it seems difficult to tell just what the outcome of the negotiations now in progress between the Players' and National leagues will be. I cannot help but think that matters are looking a little brighter for the former body than they did a week ago. The selection of Mr. Prince, of Boston, as president of the body was certainly a very wise one, as he appears to have put more nerve into the weakening members than they had before, and the stand he has taken may yet bring the League out of its present trouble. It must be admitted that many of the capitalists have shown themselves to be possessed of little or no courage, and the only pity is that they were not all like Mr. Prince or the Wagner brothers.[1] While there is still a faint chance of the organization going on for another season, it is such a slight one that but little hope is to be found in it. The puzzling feature to me is, why is it that every body that has ever tried to oppose the NL has never been successful in the effort? The Union Association was completely wiped out; the AA was also forced into the background, and now the PL is about to disappear from the scene. The latter looked as though it was certain of success when it first started, with the cream of players in the profession and big capital behind it. All this has gone, though, and next season matters will doubtless return to their old-time condition.[2]

One Reason for the Break-Up

that I recently heard was that the capitalists got disgusted after putting in their money, to find that many of the players were taking advantage of the extra freedom they had, and instead of trying to do their best, as they would have been forced to do in the NL, were drinking hard and were in no condition to play ball. This caused the backers to give up and retire from the business. If this was the case no one can

Appendix A

blame them very much for quitting, but at the same time it seems to me they might have held out for at least one year longer, and at the meeting last week they could have made some stricter rules for the control of the men during the playing season, and made them feel they had to attend to business just the same as when they were working with the old League. If this had been done and the fight been kept up for a year longer I think the PL would have been masters of the situation.[3] As it is now the organization hauled down its colors and made an ignominious surrender just at the moment when it had the battle won, and gave in to a defeated enemy. It will now be many a long year again before another revolt will be made, as this experience is one that will be long remembered by both players and capitalists.[4] I am sorry to see the PL go out of existence, but if it has to be, why then everyone should join in and try to make the best out of the organization that will be in power next season.

What Will Be The Result?

is a question that I am certain many of the PL members are anxiously asking themselves just now, as they think of the way they left their old clubs a year ago to join hands with the new body that had such a brilliant prospect ahead of it at that time. It will be rather hard on many of these men to have to go back to their old employers and ask for work. One thing I am sure of is, that there will be many a one of them who will find that there is no place left open for them, and they will be forced to stand to one side and chew the cud of disappointment and bitterness, as they see themselves replaced by youngsters who would not have had a chance to show what they could do only for the revolt of the older players. Some of these men may get back again, but right here I want to say that if it was the proper thing for me to do any gambling, that I would wager all I could get that the NL will make an example out of the men just to help keep down the idea of another revolt in future years among the players.[5]

The NL will wait until it has its consolidation scheme completed and then there will be a bomb fired among the men that will about complete the career of several of them so far as their ball playing is concerned. The old men who will be taken back will also find they will have to be satisfied with smaller salaries than they have had for several years. This is where the young players will come to the front.

Part 8: November 22, 1890—Ella Black

Many of the ones who became famous last season were working for medium prices, and even with an increase for next year their figures would not be equal to what was paid to the old-time stars. They [sic] latter will now have to be content with what they can get, for they will find it will be several years before fancy salaries come into vogue again. Although they have won the fight, it has been a very costly victory to the NL people, and it will take a few seasons' playing to big crowds for them to make up their losses of the past twelve months. They will economize and watch their dollars closer than ever before, while advance money will not be floating around as liberally as it did in days of yore.[6]

This, though I think every one will agree, will be a blessing in disguise to many of the players. Where the men could get a big advance they generally spent the winter in a lazy manner, and many of them did more or less dissipating. The result was that when spring came they would all be badly out of condition and would have to go in for a hard course of training, and even then it was often the case that it would be several weeks after the season opened before they were in proper shape, and maybe their poor condition had cost their club several games that would have been won if the men had been able to do the work they should have done, and these same games would have made a big difference in the club's standing at the close of the season. Now these men, when they cannot get their usual advance money will have to turn in and work during the winter and this will keep them in good condition, and they will be better able to play good ball when the season opens than they have ever been before. I have seen the effects of too much advance money right in this city when there would be a long string of defeats in the spring because the men had not taken any care of themselves during the winter.[7]

NOT A PROPHETESS.

I see your very able Cleveland correspondent, in the last issue of THE SL, is inclined to have a little amusement at my expense because of the consolidation of our local clubs, after I said there did not seem to be any chance of a move being made. I am no prophetess, or even the daughter of one, but in this case I will admit I was badly fooled, and I guess there were a good many others in the same boat as myself. At the

Appendix A

time I wrote there did seem to be but little chance of the consolidation being effected, and I never imagined that such men as the ones who composed the directory of the local PL club would recede from the stand they had taken and come down to their opponents the way they did here. It has taught me that in the future no dependence is to be placed on what a man or men may do, even if they have agreed to anything, and that they are just as fickle and liable to change of mind as we women are popularly supposed to be.[8]

PITY FOR JOHN WARD.

The downfall of the PL will have more effect on John Ward than on almost anyone else. It was the pet idea of his life and only those who were close to him can have any knowledge of how hard he worked to bring it through. Now all his labor has gone for naught. It must be hard for him to feel that after he had organized what promised to be the greatest base ball body ever known in this country, that it has been destroyed by the treachery and carelessness of men that he had worked for and placed in a position where they could be more independent than they had ever been before, yet now they throw away the benefits he had secured for them and go back to the same places they held before.[9] Unless I am greatly mistaken Ward has played his last game of ball, unless the PL should get a new lease of life and continue its career next year. I do not think Ward is a man who would return to the ranks of the NL, even if he could.[10]

WHAT WILL PITTSBURG HAVE?

How the consolidated local club will be made up is a matter that is puzzling those who are interested in the game here. As yet, the new management has not organized owing to the absence of some of the old League people in New York. Just how the offices will be divided is not known, but the most interesting point now is what players will be on the team. At present no one seems to be able to tell if ex–Buffalo players, with whom Manager Hanlon had a written agreement, will come here next year or not, and whether Martin Duke, the Western pitcher, will wear a Pittsburg uniform. Indeed, it just now looks very much as though next year's team would be largely made up from the same material that has played for several years.[11]

Part 8: November 22, 1890—Ella Black

There is now some talk of Fred Pfeffer going to play here, but as yet it is nothing but talk. I see that Anson has got his entire team signed for next season, and if that is the case and the PL passes away, it will leave nearly all the old Chicago men out in the cold.[12] This would be an excellent chance for the local management to get some good players, and it is to be hoped it will not repeat the experience of nearly all the former managements in this city, and delay so long that every one else gets in ahead of it.

I was very sorry to hear the other day of the death of Ren Mulford's little one. It is a dreadful loss for anyone to have to bear and he has the sympathy of all who know him, either personally or through his writings.[13]

ELLA BLACK.

Part 8 Notes

1. Newly elected PL President and Boston Red Stockings backer Charles Prince did appear to be one of the league's stalwarts, along with the Wagner brothers, who backed the Philadelphia Quakers. By January of 1891, however, Prince was negotiating with the AA for a franchise in Boston (Alexander, 114). Of the New York, Brooklyn, and Pittsburgh backers who were stricken with "consolidation fever" at the time of the league meetings, Arthur Irwin was quoted as saying, "Glasscock is a gentleman compared with such people," a sentiment that would not have been lost on Ella Black (*BG*, November 11, 1890, eve. ed., 1).

2. If Albert Spalding is to be believed, the answer lay in his ability to bluff the inexperienced PL backers in early October. The UA was too lopsided to take hold and the AA was about to enter its swan season as the league that catered to the lower-class audience.

3. From the reports that came out of Pittsburgh during the PL meeting, there was little time—or energy—to devote to rule changes. Of New York, Brooklyn, and Pittsburgh, the three cities rumored to be ready to consolidate, only Black's hometown formally resigned from the PL and left the meeting, despite the fact that their resignation was not accepted by the rest of the league. John Ward, Charles Prince, and Al Johnson were dispatched to New York City to confer with the NL teams about consolidation. Secretary Brunell believed that New York and Pittsburgh would stick if the NL refused to consolidate, only to appear out of the know when the PL teams started falling one by one. By Thursday, November 13, King Kelly was rumored to be holding a signed NL contract and the press was criticizing him for "always making a show of himself," and Comiskey was quoted as saying, "The trouble with the PL is that there are too many confidence men with a little money in the venture" (*BG*, November 12, 1890, eve. ed., 1; *BG*, November 13, 1890, 10; *BG*, November 13, 1890, eve. ed., 1).

4. The NL would reign supreme until Ban Johnson was successful in starting the American League in 1901. Thirteen years later, the Federal League would lead a two-year "revolt" against the National and American Leagues, only to fall to the side like the Players' and Union Leagues. From 1915 to 1953, baseball experienced a period of relative stability and became firmly established as America's national sport.

Appendix A

5. Black would have lost her bet regarding the future of the players. The overall average declined from $3,500 to $2,500, which was still well above the national wage average of $500 per year (Burk, in Di Salvatore, 411). When the AA opted out of the National Agreement in early 1891, the resulting scramble for players led to a boost in salaries for enough returning players that the owners curtailed spring training trips to make up for the increases (Alexander, 133). Although some of the Brotherhood players who joined the PL were looking for work on Opening Day in 1891, many of them found their way back onto the rosters of the teams they left in 1889. Buck Ewing rejoined the NL Giants and Comiskey returned to the Browns of the AA. After a reported offer to sign with Pittsburgh for $20,000, John Ward, the player most likely to be made "an example" of, signed to manage the Brooklyn Bridegrooms.

6. As noted above, the owners promised lean times at the end of the season, echoing the dire prophecies of Chadwick as Cato the Elder, but were forced to open their wallets in the spring of 1891.

7. While it was no doubt difficult for her *SL* readers to argue with Black's homespun reasoning in this passage, the lack of specific examples demonstrated that her reports were most effective when she named names instead of making blanket assertions. Fourteen years later, Ring Lardner supported her claims with his fiction when "You Know Me Al" featured the same scenario she described, suggesting that little had changed in the professional ball player fraternity (See Peterson, "More Than," "Born a Busher," "Do You Know Me Now?").

8. R. W. Wright, the Cleveland correspondent for *SL*, wrote that the words of Black's assertion that there was no hope for consolidation in Pittsburgh "were still quivering with life, the deal was closed and Miss Black took a big tumble in the minds of those who looked up to her as a prophetess in base ball" (November 15, 1890, 7). Of note here is how adroitly Black took the ribbing in stride before landing some teasing of her own at the end of the paragraph.

9. Ward echoed Black's take on the demise of the PL when he said it was due to "stupidity, avarice, and treachery" (Di Salvatore, 312).

10. Despite expressing ambivalence about his future in the game during his meeting with Albert Spalding in December of 1890, Ward played four more seasons in the NL, mostly as a second baseman. He led the league with 88 steals in 1891 and batted .328 in 1893 after returning to the New York Giants. In 1896, Ward asked for and received his release from the NL; thus his name was removed from the reserve list before it could be tested in court again (Di Salvatore, 365).

11. Black proved to be more of a prophetess here as several of the Burghers were re-signed for 1891 in Pittsburgh, including Jake Beckley, Fred Carroll, Jocko Fields, Pud Galvin, and Al Maul. Doggie Miller was the only member of the record-setting Alleghenys to return (Alexander, 128).

12. Fred Pfeffer, Jimmy Ryan, and Ad Gumbert returned to their old spots on the Chicago NL roster, joining a number of returning Colts: Bill Hutchinson, Walt Wilmot, Cliff Carroll, and Tommy Burns (Alexander, 126).

13. Henry Chadwick also expressed his condolences for the loss experienced by a fellow *SL* correspondent, which served as another illustration of the sense of fraternity that existed among baseball writers as early as 1890.

Appendix B

Individuals, Teams and Leagues

Unless indicated otherwise, the information given below pertains to the 1890 season

Ferdinand **Abell**—One of the three owners of Brooklyn Bridegrooms

Horatio **Alger**—Author of more than 100 books written for children; Alger's formulaic plots contributed to the "self-made man" concept

American Association (AA)—A lesser major league in the eyes of Chadwick and other National League (NL) supporters due to its 25-cent admission, beer and liquor sales, and Sunday games

Cap **Anson**—Player-manager of the Chicago Colts of the National League

Mark **Baldwin**—Pitcher with the Chicago Pirates of the Players' League (PL)

Baltimore Orioles—Baltimore entry in the AA

Ross **Barnes**—PL umpire; former three-time batting champion

Billy **Barnie**—Manager of the Baltimore Orioles in the AA

Beadle's Base Ball Guide—publication edited by Henry Chadwick

Ed **Beatin**—Pitcher for the Cleveland Spiders of the NL

Buck **Becannon**—Partner in Tim Keefe's sporting goods business

Jake **Beckley**—Played with the Pittsburgh Burghers after "wavering" and "jumping" back and forth between the NL and the PL several times

Charlie **Bennett**—Player with the Boston Beaneaters in the NL

Harry **Berthong**—Player with the 1867 Washington Nationals

Louis **Bierbauer**—Player with the Brooklyn Wonders of the PL

James **Billings**—Co-owner of the Boston Beaneaters in the NL

Boston Red Caps—Boston's National League entry in 1876–1877

Boston Reds—Boston's franchise in the Union Association (UA) of 1884

George Washington **Bradley**—Player with the "Outlaw" Cincinnati Reds of the UA in 1884

Walter Scott "Steve" **Brodie**—Player with the NL Boston Beaneaters

Brooklyn Atlantics—Amateur baseball team from the early days of baseball

Dan **Brouthers**—Player for the Boston Red Stockings in the PL

Tom **Brown**—Player with the Boston Red Stockings of the PL

Frank **Brunell**—Secretary of the Players' League

Appendix B

John T. **Brush**—President of the Indianapolis Hoosiers of the NL in 1889

Brush Classification System—Scheme devised by the National League in 1889 to reduce salaries of players by linking them to the player's personal habits

Charlie **Buffinton**—Pitcher with the Philadelphia Quakers of the PL

Tom **Burns**—Player with the Chicago Colts of the NL

Charles **Byrne**—Primary owner of the Brooklyn Bridegrooms in the NL

Warren "Hick" **Carpenter**—Player for the Cincinnati Red Stockings of the AA in the 1880s

Cliff **Carroll**—Player for the Chicago Colts of the NL

Fred **Carroll**—Player for the Pittsburgh Burghers of the PL

Bob **Caruthers**—Pitcher for the Brooklyn Bridegrooms of the NL

O. P. **Caylor**—Sportswriter, NL supporter, and co-editor of the *Sporting Times*.

George **Chauncey**—backer of the Brooklyn Wonders of the PL

Chicago Browns—Chicago's entry in the short-lived UA of 1884

John **Clarkson**—Pitcher for the Boston Beaneaters in the NL

Jack **Clements**—Player for the Philadelphia Phillies in the NL

Cleveland Spiders—NL franchise in 1890

Charles **Comiskey**—Player-manager of the Chicago Pirates in the PL

William **Conant**—Co-owner of the Boston Beaneaters of the NL

Congress Street Grounds—Home of the Boston Red Stockings of the PL

Roger **Connor**—Player with the New York Giants of the PL

Jimmy **Cooney**—Player with the Chicago Colts of the NL

Tommy **Corcoran**—Player with the Pittsburgh Burghers of the PL

Ed "Cannonball" **Crane**—Pitcher with the New York Giants of the PL

Bill **Daley**—Pitcher for the Boston Red Stockings of the PL

Abner **Dalrymple**—Player with Denver in 1890; former batting champion

Maurice **Daly**—1870s billiards champion and author of billiards books

Helen **Dauvray**—Actress, wife of John Ward, donor of Dauvray Cup

John B. **Day**—Owner of the New York Giants of the NL

Detroit Wolverines—National League team that won the Dauvray Cup in 1887

George **Dickinson**—Sportswriter for the *New York World* and PL supporter

Fred "Count" **Doe**—Pitcher for the Pittsburgh Alleghenys of the NL

Fred **Dunlap**—Player for the Pittsburgh Alleghenys of the NL

"Cyclone" Jesse **Duryea**—Player for the Cincinnati Reds of the NL

Charles **Ebbets**—Secretary for the Brooklyn Bridegrooms of the NL

Charles **Esper**—Pitcher for the Philadelphia Phillies of the NL

Buck **Ewing**—Player with the New York Giants of the PL

John **Ewing**—Pitcher with the New York Giants of the PL

Exposition Park—home of the Pittsburgh Burghers in the PL

Jay **Faatz**—Player-manager with the Buffalo Bisons of the PL

Bob **Ferguson**—Manager of the Brooklyn Atlantics in 1870

John "Jocko" **Fields**—Player with the Pittsburgh Burghers of the PL

250

Individuals, Teams and Leagues

Frank **Foreman**—Pitcher for the Cincinnati Reds of the NL

Dave **Foutz**—Player with the Brooklyn Bridegrooms of the NL

John **Gaffney**—Players' League umpire

James "Pud" **Galvin**—Pitcher for the Pittsburgh Burghers of the PL

Charlie **Ganzel**—Player with the Boston Beaneaters in the NL

Charlie **Getzien**—Pitcher for the Boston Beaneaters in the NL

John "Pebbly Jack" **Glasscock**—Player with the New York Giants of the NL

Kid **Gleason**—Pitcher for the Philadelphia Phillies in the NL

Wendell **Goodwin**—backer of the Brooklyn Wonders of the PL

George **Gore**—Player with the New York Giants of the PL

Frank **Grant**—Player with the Harrisburg Ponies of the Eastern Interstate League

Mike **Griffin**—Player with the Philadelphia Quakers of the PL

Ad **Gumbert**—Pitcher for the Boston Red Stockings of the PL

Will **Gumbert**—Pitcher for the Pittsburgh Alleghenys of the NL

Ned **Hanlon**—Manager of the Pittsburgh Burghers of the PL

Lew **Hardie**—Player with the Boston Beaneaters in the NL

William H. **Harris**—New York City sportswriter and *Sporting Life* correspondent

William I. **Harris**—New York City sportswriter who opposed the PL

Julian B. **Hart**—Secretary of the Boston PL club

Gil **Hatfield**—Player with the New York PL Giants, and briefly the Boston Red Stockings

John **Hatfield**—Player with the New York Mutuals of the National Association in 1872

Guy **Hecker**—Player-Manager for the Pittsburgh Alleghenys

George "Old Wax Figger" **Hemming**—Pitcher for the Cleveland Infants and Brooklyn Wonders of the PL

Walter **Hewitt**—President of the Washington Nationals of the AA

Paul **Hines**—Player for the Pittsburgh Alleghenys of the NL

William "Billy" **Holbert**—PL umpire

De Wolf **Hopper**—Comic actor; made "Casey at the Bat" famous

Joe **Hornung**—Player with the New York Giants of the NL

Michael "Mickey" **Hughes**—Pitcher for the Brooklyn Bridegrooms of the NL and the Philadelphia Athletics of the AA

William **Hulbert**—Former owner of the Chicago White Stockings and President of the NL

Bill **Hutchinson**—Pitcher with the Chicago Colts of the NL

Ed **Hutchinson**—Player with the Chicago Colts of the NL

Indianapolis Hoosiers—NL franchise owned by John T. Brush; dissolved before the 1890 season

Arthur **Irwin**—Player with the Boston Red Stockings in the PL

Dick **Johnston**—Player with the Boston Red Stockings of the PL

Edward **Keating**—Player released by the McKeesport, PA, team in April 1890

Tim **Keefe**—Player with the New York Giants of the PL

John W. **Kelly**—Composer of the 1889 song "Slide, Kelly, Slide"

Mike "King" **Kelly**—Player with the Boston Red Stockings in the PL

James **Kennedy**—Manager of the Brooklyn Gladiators of the AA

251

Appendix B

William **Kenny**—Sportswriter with the *Boston Globe*; covered the NL

Matt **Kilroy**—Player for the Boston Red Stockings in the PL

"Silver" **King**—Pitched for the Chicago Pirates of the PL

Tom **Kinslow**—Player for the Brooklyn Wonders of the PL

Bob **Larner**—Washington correspondent for *SL* and NL supporter

Arlie **Latham**—Player with the Chicago Pirates of the PL and the Cincinnati Reds of the NL

Bob **Leadley**—Manager of the Cleveland Spiders of the NL

Edward F. **Linton**—backer of the Brooklyn Wonders of the PL

Tom **Loftus**—Manager of the Cincinnati Reds of the NL

Edward "Pop" **Lytle**—Player for the Pittsburgh Alleghenys of the NL

Connie **Mack**—Player with the Buffalo Bisons of the PL

Michael "Kid" **Madden**—Pitcher for the Boston Red Stockings of the PL

John **Mandigo**—Sportswriter for the *New York Sun*

Marion **Manola**—Burlesque actress who tried to break her contract

Al **Maul**—Pitcher with the Pittsburgh Burghers of the PL

Colonel Edwin A. **McAlpin**—backer of the New York Giants of the PL

George **McCallin**—backer of the Pittsburgh Burghers of the PL

Tommy **McCarthy**—Player for the St. Louis Browns of the AA

Colonel **McCaull**—Owner of a comic acting company

Jessie **McDermott**—alleged lover of John M. Ward; changed her name to Maxine Elliot and became a well known actress and theater owner

Sandy **McDermott**—National League umpire

Joe **McDonough**—New York correspondent for *SL*; supporter of the PL

Bill **McGunnigle**—Manager of the Brooklyn Bridegrooms of the NL

Lewis **Meacham**—Sports editor of the *Chicago Tribune* in the 1870s

Middletown **Mansfields**—Connecticut entry in the National Association (NA) in 1872

George "Doggie" **Miller**—Player with the Pittsburgh Alleghenys of the NL

Mills Commission—Blue ribbon panel assembled by Albert Spalding in 1905 to determine the origins of baseball

Ed "Cannonball" **Morris**—Pitcher with the Pittsburgh Burghers of the PL

Jacob **Morse**—Sportswriter for the *Boston Herald*

Ren **Mulford**—Cincinnati correspondent for *SL* and sportswriter for the *Cincinnati Post*

Tony **Mullane**—Player for the Cincinnati Reds of the NL

Morgan **Murphy**—Played for the Boston Red Stockings of the PL

Al **Myers**—Played for the Philadelphia Phillies of the NL

Billy **Nash**—Played for the Boston Red Stockings in the PL

National Police Gazette—Weekly newspaper covering crime and sports

Nestor—Nickname given to Henry Chadwick by *SL* editor Francis Richter, figure from Homer's *Iliad*

Hugh **Nichol**—Pitcher for the Cincinnati Reds of the NL

Kid **Nichols**—Pitcher with the Boston Beaneaters in the NL

Individuals, Teams and Leagues

William A. **Nimick**—President of the Pittsburgh Alleghenys of the NL

Hank **O'Day**—Pitcher for the New York Giants of the PL

Jim **O'Rourke**—Played for the New York Giants in the PL

Dave **Orr**—Player with the Brooklyn Wonders of the PL

Fred **Osborne**—Pitcher for the Pittsburgh Alleghenys of the NL

Harry **Palmer**—*Chicago Tribune* sportswriter, NL supporter, *Sporting Times* co-editor

Fred **Pfeffer**—Player for the Chicago Pirates of the PL

Philadelphia Athletics—NA team from 1873–1874

Philadelphia Keystones—Philadelphia's entry in the UA of 1884

Philadelphia Quakers—Philadelphia's PL entry

Philadelphia White Stockings—NA team in 1875

"Whoa Bill"/"Silver Bill" **Phillips**—Pitcher for the Pittsburgh Alleghenys of the NL

Horace **Phillips**—Former manager of the Pittsburgh Alleghenys

John **Pickett**—Player for the Philadelphia Quakers of the PL

Pittsburgh Alleghenys—NL franchise in Pittsburgh

Pittsburgh Burghers—PL franchise in Pittsburgh

Charles **Prince**—Backer of the Boston Red Stockings of the PL

Joe **Pritchard**—St. Louis correspondent for *SL*

Providence Grays—Early NL Team

Joe **Quinn**—Player for the Boston Red Stockings of the PL

Charles "Old Hoss" **Radbourn**—Pitcher for the Boston Red Stockings of the PL

Al **Reach**—Owner of the Philadelphia Phillies of the NL and Reach's sporting goods

Recreation Park—home of the Pittsburgh Alleghenys in the NL

John **Reilly**—Player with the Cincinnati Reds of the NL

Bill **Rhines**—Pitcher with the Cincinnati Reds of the NL

Francis **Richter**—Editor of *Sporting Life*

Ed **Rife**—Editor of the *Ohio State Journal*

Colonel John I. **Rogers**—Part owner of the Philadelphia Phillies in the NL

Jimmy **Ryan**—Player for the Chicago Pirates of the PL

St. Louis Browns—St. Louis AA franchise owned and operated by Chris Von der Ahe

St. Louis Maroons—St. Louis entry in the UA in 1884

Harry **Schafer**—Player with the Boston Red Stockings of the 1870s

Gus **Schmelz**—Manager of the Cleveland Spiders of the NL

Frederick "Crazy" **Schmit**—Player with the Pittsburgh Alleghenys of the NL

Pop **Schriver**—Player for the Philadelphia Phillies of the NL

Frank **Selee**—Manager of the Boston Beaneaters in the NL

Billy **Shindle**—Player for the Philadelphia Quakers of the PL

Charles "Pop" **Smith**—Player for the Boston Beaneaters of the NL

Charles "Pop" **Snyder**—Player for the Cleveland Infants of the PL

Arthur **Soden**—Co-owner of the Boston Beaneaters in the NL

South End Grounds—Home of the Boston Beaneaters in the NL

Appendix B

Sporting News—Sporting weekly published in St. Louis by the Spink Brothers

Sporting Times—Sporting weekly purchased by Albert Spalding in 1889

George **Stackhouse**—Sportswriter for the *New York Tribune*

Harry **Staley**—Pitcher for the Pittsburgh Burghers of the PL

Ed **Stevens**—Sportswriter for the *Boston Herald* and *SL* correspondent

Harry **Stovey**—Player for the Boston Red Stockings in the PL

John L. **Sullivan**—Champion boxer and vaudeville star

Marty **Sullivan**—Player for the Boston Beaneaters of the NL

E. B. **Talcott**—Director of the New York Giants of the PL

John **Tener**—Player and Secretary for the Pittsburgh Alleghenys in the NL

Alfred **Tennyson**—19th century Poet Laureate of England

Adonis **Terry**—Pitcher for the Brooklyn Bridegrooms of the NL

Sam **Thompson**—Player for the Philadelphia Phillies of the NL

Frederick W. **Truax**—Player for the Pittsburgh Alleghenys of the NL

Tommy **Tucker**—Player for the Boston Beaneaters of the NL

Larry **Twitchell**—Player for the Cleveland Infants and Buffalo Bisons of the PL

Union Association (UA)—A professional baseball league that operated outside of the National Agreement in 1884

Cornelius **Van Cott**—Backer of the New York Giants of the PL

George **Van Haltren**—Pitcher with the Brooklyn Wonders of the PL

William "Peek-A-Boo" **Veach**—Player with the Cleveland Spiders and Pittsburgh Alleghenys of the NL

Lee **Viau**—Pitcher for the Cincinnati Reds of the NL

Jake **Virtue**—Player for the Cleveland Spiders of the NL

Al **Visner**—Player for the Pittsburgh Burghers of the PL

Chris **Von der Ahe**—Owner of the St. Louis Browns of the AA

George and J. Earle **Wagner**—Backers of the Philadelphia Quakers in the PL

John Montgomery **Ward**—Leader of the PL and Brotherhood union, player-manager of Ward's Wonders

Mickey **Welch**—Pitcher for the New York Giants of the NL

Gus **Weyhing**—Pitcher with the Brooklyn Wonders of the PL

Jim **White**—Player with the Buffalo Bisons in the PL

Ezekiel Stone **Wigging**—Canadian educator and theorist known as the "Ottawa Prophet"

Clarence **Williams**—Player with the Harrisburg Ponies of the Eastern Interstate League

Jimmy **Williams**—Manager of the St. Louis Browns in the AA for most of the 1884 Season

Edward "Ned" **Williamson**—Player for the Chicago Pirates of the PL

Wilmington Quicksteps—Wilmington, Delaware, entry in the UA of 1884

Walt **Wilmot**—Player for the Chicago Colts of the NL

Sam **Wise**—Player for the Buffalo Bisons of the PL

George **Wright**—former player with a number of teams, including the original Cincinnati Red Stockings, and the younger brother of Harry Wright

Harry **Wright**—Manager of the Philadelphia Phillies

R. W. **Wright**—Cleveland correspondent for *SL*

Nicholas "Nick" **Young**—President of the NL

Young Ladies of the Diamond—Pittsburgh fan club

Chapter Notes

Introduction

1. Story, 21; Wiebe, xiii, 17; Trachtenberg, 15, 122; Lears, 37; Ohmann, 55–56, 135.

2. Story, 22–4; Thorn, "1791 and All That," 122; Adelman, 58; Rossi, 19; Riess, 160; Levine, 24; W. Anderson, "Does the Cheering," 357; Orodenker, 41. See Gelzheiser, ch 4 and 5.

3. Story, 22–24; Guttman, 59; Riess, 160.

4. Oriard, 91, 115; Dicken-Garcia, 156, 162; A. Richter, 9.; Ohmann, 73; Story, 21. See Gelzheiser, ch 6.

5. Di Salvatore, 375, 377, 380; Roessner, "Hero Crafting," 39; Spalding, 47; Mack, 41.

6. Spalding, 269–70, 280, 288, 291; W. Anderson, "Does the Cheering," 361–363.

7. Spalding, 269–70, 291; F. Richter, *Richter's History*, 299; Martin, 17–18.

8. F. Richter, 121–2; Di Salvatore, 217–8; Spalding, 291; Roessner, "The Impact."

9. See Betts, Chapters 2 and 4; Garrison and Sabljak, 224–29; Hall et al., 17; Campbell, 21.

10. Betts, 40; Story, 22–24.

11. Mott, 478–80; B. Anderson, 6, 35; Seymour and Mills, 350; Reidenbaugh, 19.

12. Thorn, et al., *Total Baseball*, 612; Dicken-Garcia, 52–3; F. Richter, 299; Schudson, 41; Roessner, "Impact."

13. Dicken-Garcia, 139, 189, 202, 224, 229; Anderson, "Creating," 14; Rowe, 37–38.

14. Hall, 20–21.

15. Bakhtin, 272; Hall et al., 16–17, 21, 23–24.

16. F. Richter, 121–2; Spalding, 291; Dicken-Garcia, 162; A. Richter, 9; *SL*, March 5, 1890, 3; Roessner, "The 'Ladies,'" 137; Ardell, 192.

17. Rowe, 4.

Prelude

1. *Boston Globe* (*BG*), December 14, 1890, 6; Alexander, 112–3.

2. *BG*, December 14, 1890, 6; Lowenfish, 36–7; Bevis, web.

3. *Sporting Life* (*SL*), November 15, 1890, 12; Alexander, 112–3; *SL*, November 29, 1890, 4. If Murnane had struck out at Engel's Home Plate, he might have found Ward at the New York Athletic Club at the corner of 6th Avenue and 55th Street—even though his former teammate hadn't qualified as an amateur athlete for almost 13 years.

4. *SL*, November 15, 1890, 12.

5. Peterson, "Of Ourselves," 15; Alexander, 12.

6. Ward, *How To*, 13; Ward, "Is the Player," 315; Alexander, 13–14; Lowenfish, 32; Lamster, 253. For an extended discussion of the lead-up to the Brotherhood War, see Pearson.

7. *SL*, May 31, 1890, 7; Di Salvatore, 322.

8. *BG*, December 14, 1890, 6; *SL*, March 19, 1890, 6. The anecdote of the German sailor is not mentioned in either Di Salvatore's biography or Lamster's history of Spalding's world tour.

9. *SL*, November 15, 1890, 12; White, 163.

10. *SL*, February 12, 1890, 4; Smythe, 1–2; Anon., "The New York Athletic Club," 410; Schudson, 69.

256

Notes—Chapter 1

11. *BG*, December 14, 1890, 6; Alexander, 108; *BG*, November 9, 1890, 3; *BG*, November 11, 1890, 8.
12. *BG*, December 14, 1890, 6; Roessner, "The Impact"; Seymour and Mills, 350.
13. *BG*, December 14, 1890, 6.
14. *BG*, December 14, 1890, 6. Murnane incorrectly had Spalding resigning from the New York club, but it was the Chicago White Stockings that the future magnate quit in 1878 after serving as the captain of the team for just one game (McMahon, web). What's more, the rest of the text made it clear that the NL magnate was speaking, not Ward.
15. *BG*, December 14, 1890, 6; *SL*, April 19, 9.
16. *BG*, December 14, 1890, 6; Di Salvatore, 323.
17. *SL*, November 15, 1890, 12; *BG*, December 14, 1890, 6.; Alexander, 112–5. Demonstrating the reach of Spalding's influence, Murnane reported how the NL magnate gave audiences to the Wagner Brothers of Philadelphia, who had remained loyal to the PL cause until that point and were likely seeking Spalding's support for returning an AA franchise to their home city.

Chapter 1

1. Roessner, "The Impact"; Alexander, 61; Lowenfish, 36.
2. Schiff, 31, 40; Davies, 48; *SL*, February 12, 1890, 3. For a discussion of the competition between baseball and cricket in 1850s New York City, see Seymour and Mills, 14–15.
3. Davies, 48; Schiff, 59, 61, 145, 148, 158; Levine, 24–5; Hardy, 344.
4. *SL*, February 19, 1890, 3; Schudson, 69; Dicken-Garcia, 232–3.
5. Schiff, 145–6; W. Anderson, "Does the Cheering," 361–63; Levey, quoted in Dicken-Garcia, 163; Davies, 48; A. Richter, 4.
6. *SL*, February 12, 1890, 3; *New York Times*, October 21, 1889, 3; Lowenfish, 42.
7. Lewis, Chapter 3; Di Salvatore, 47, 182; Seymour and Mills 229; editorial reprinted in *SL*, February 12, 4.

8. *SL*, March 26, 1890, 6; Dicken-Garcia, 232–3.
9. *SL*, April 2, 1890, 6; Schiff, 154.
10. Dicken-Garcia, 55, 201; Schudson, 66, 202.
11. *SL*, April 2, 1890, 6; Schiff, 48.
12. *SL*, April 2, 1890, 5.
13. *SL*, April 2, 1890, 5.
14. *SL*, April 12, 1890, 11.
15. *SL*, March 5, 1890, 3; Welter, 44; A. Richter, 9.
16. Welter, 44; Kroeger, 34; A. Richter, 137. With regard to the other two virtues, piety and purity, Black's *SL* reports offer little or no clue.
17. *SL*, March 5, 1890, 3; Schudson, 5.
18. *SL*, March 12, 1890, 5.
19. *SL*, March 12, 1890, 5; Dicken-Garcia, 189; Welter, 44; A. Richter, 137.
20. *SL*, March 12, 1890, 5; *SL*, April 2, 1890, 6.
21. *SL*, March 12, 1890, 5; Lamster, 258; Dicken-Garcia, 163.
22. *SL*, March 19, 1890, 6; Kroeger, 72; Boorstin, 57; *SL*, September 6, 1890, 5.
23. Schudson, 69, 89; *SL*, March 19, 1890, 6.
24. *SL*, March 19, 1890, 6; Stevens, 69; Lamster, 266.
25. Stevens, 180–1; Di Salvatore, 332. Jessie McDermott went on to divorce her husband, change her name to Maxine Elliott, become a New York stage actress, own her own theater, and even star in a few silent movies.
26. *SL*, March 19, 1890, 6; Schudson, 71.
27. *SL*, March 19, 1890, 6; Kroeger, 45; *SL*, April 2, 6.
28. *SL*, March 26, 1890, 3; *SL*, April 2, 1890, 6.
29. *SL*, April 2, 1890, 6; Tiemann, 51.
30. *SL*, April 2, 1890, 6.; *SL*, March 26, 1890, 3; Thorn et al., *Total Baseball*, 106.
31. *SL*, April 5, 1890, 11; *SL*, April 12, 7; *SL*, April 5, 1890, 5.
32. Bevis, web.
33. Schudson, 65, 70–1, 74; *SL*, April 2, 1890, 5.
34. *SL*, April 2, 1890, 5; Dicken-Garcia, 232–3.
35. Trachtenberg, 214; Dana, quoted in

Park, 285; Orodenker, 11; *SL*, April 2, 1890, 5. If anyone was keeping score at home, the five Hall of Famers were Mike Kelly (1945), Sam Thompson (1974), Dan Brouthers (1945), Jim O'Rourke (1945), and George Wright (1953).
36. Dicken-Garcia, 91; Schudson, 49; Rossi, 32.
37. *BG*, April 4, 1890, 4; Schudson, 70–71. In addition to expanding the number of pages, *SL* changed publication days from Wednesdays to Saturdays with the April 5 issue.
38. *BG*, April 4, 1890, 4.
39. *BG*, April 4, 1890, 4.
40. *BG*, April 4, 1890, 4.
41. *BG*, April 4, 1890, 4; Godkin, 200.
42. *BG*, April 4, 1890, 4.
43. *BG*, April 7, 1890, 5.
44. *SL*, April 19, 1890, 9.

Chapter 2

1. Dicken-Garcia, 189.
2. Nichols, 668.
3. Boorstin, 37.
4. Schudson, 71.
5. *BG*, April 28, 1890, 8.
6. *BG*, April 28, 1890, 5.
7. *BG*, April 27, 1890, 5.
8. *BG*, April 27, 1890, 5.
9. *BG*, April 27, 1890, 5.
10. *SL*, April 26, 1890, 6.
11. *SL*, April 26, 1890, 6.
12. *SL*, April 26, 1890, 6.
13. *SL*, April 26, 1890, 10.
14. *SL*, April 26, 1890, 10.
15. *SL*, April 26, 1890, 10; Roessner, "The 'Ladies,'" 137.
16. *SL*, April 26, 1890, 10.
17. *SL*, April 26, 1890, 10.
18. *SL*, April 26, 1890, 10.
19. *BG*, May 5, 1990, 5; *BG*, April 20, 1990, 3; *SL*, May 3, 1890, 3.
20. *BG*, May 5, 1990, 5; *SL*, May 3, 1890, 3.
21. *SL*, May 3, 1890, 3, *BG*, May 5, 1890, 5.
22. *SL*, May 3, 1890, 3.
23. *SL*, May 3, 1890, 3.
24. *SL*, May 3, 1890, 10; *SL*, May 3, 1890, 3.
25. *SL*, May 3, 1890, 10.
26. *BG*, May 5, 1890, 5; *SL*, May 3, 1890, 3.
27. *BG*, May 5, 1890, 5.
28. *BG*, May 12, 1890, 2; *SL* May 10, 1890, 8.
29. *SL*, May 10, 1890, 12; *BG*, May 12, 1890, 2.
30. *SL*, May 10, 1890, 12.
31. *SL*, May 10, 1890, 12.
32. *SL*, May 10, 1890, 12.
33. Seymour and Mills, 237; *SL*, May 10, 1890, 10.
34. Schudson, 79; Dicken-Garcia, 202; *SL*, May 10, 1890, 10.
35. Schudson, 71; *SL*, May 10, 1890, 10.
36. *BG*, May 18, 1890, 4; *BG*, May 19, 1890, 5; *SL*, May 17, 1890, 8.
37. Schudson, 89; *BG*, May 19, 1890, 5.
38. Schudson, 71; *BG*, May 19, 1890, 5.
39. *BG*, May 19, 1890, 5.
40. *SL*, May 17, 1890, 8.
41. *SL*, May 17, 1890, 8; Ohmann, 24.
42. Schudson, 70; Dicken-Garcia, 162; *SL*, May 17, 1890, 6.
43. *BG*, May 26, 1890, 5; *SL*, May 24, 1890, 5.
44. *BG*, May 25, 1890, 13; *SL*, May 24, 1890, 9.
45. *SL*, May 24, 1890, 10; *BG*, May 25, 1890, 13.
46. *BG*, May 25, 1890, 13; *SL*, May 24, 1890, 10; *SL*, May 24, 1890, 9.
47. *BG*, June 2, 1890, 5.
48. *SL*, May 31, 1890, 5, 6; *BG*, June 2, 1890, 5.
49. Davies, 48; *SL*, May 31, 1890, 8, 11.
50. *SL*, May 31, 1890, 5; Dicken-Garcia, 189.
51. *SL*, May 31, 1890, 5.
52. *SL*, May 31, 1890, 5.
53. *SL*, May 31, 1890, 5, 11.

Chapter 3

1. *BG*, June 2, 1890, 5; *SL*, June 7, 1890, 9; *BG*, July 28, 1890, 5.
2. Schudson, 80; Dicken-Garcia, 5.
3. Dicken-Garcia, 91; Schudson, 71.
4. Dicken-Garcia, 189, 202, 232, 238.

5. *BG*, June 9, 1890, 5; *SL*, June 7, 1890, 9.
6. *BG*, June 9, 1890, 5; *SL*, June 7, 1890, 9.
7. *SL*, June 7, 1890, 9; *SL*, May 31, 1890, 5.
8. *SL*, June 7, 1890, 11; *BG*, June 2, 1890, 5.
9. *SL*, June 7, 1890, 11.
10. *SL*, June 7, 1890, 11.
11. *SL*, June 7, 1890, 9.
12. *SL*, June 7, 1890, 9.
13. *SL*, June 7, 1890, 9.
14. *BG*, June 16, 1890, 3; *SL*, June 14, 1890, 5.
15. *SL*, June 14, 1890, 6; *BG*, June 9, 1890, 5.
16. *BG*, June 9, 1890, 5; *SL*, June 14, 6.
17. *SL*, June 14, 1890, 5.
18. *SL*, June 14, 1890, 5.
19. *SL*, June 14, 1890, 9.
20. *SL*, June 14, 1890, 9.
21. *SL*, June 14, 1890, 5, 6, 9; W. Anderson, "Creating," 14.
22. *BG*, June 23, 1890, 3; Stevens, 115; Nichols, 668.
23. *BG*, June 23, 1890, 3; *SL*, June 21, 1890, 8, 11.
24. *SL*, June 21, 1890, 8.
25. *SL*, June 21, 1890, 8.
26. A. Richter, 137; Scott, 85–6; *SL*, June 21, 1890, 8.
27. *SL*, June 21, 1890, 8, 11.
28. *SL*, June 28, 1890, 6.
29. *SL*, June 28, 1890, 8.
30. *SL*, June 28, 1890, 9; *BG*, June 30, 1890, 5.
31. *SL*, June 28, 1890, 5; Dicken-Garcia, 232, 238.
32. *BG*, July 7, 1890, 5; *SL*, July 5, 1890, 5, 11; Alexander, 77.
33. *SL*, July 5, 1890, 5.
34. *SL*, July 5, 1890, 5.
35. *SL*, July 5, 1890, 5; Alexander, 63.
36. *BG*, July 7, 1890, 5; Holtzman, 1.
37. *BG*, July 14, 1890, 5; *SL*, July 12, 1890, 5.
38. *SL*, July 12, 1890, 9; Schudson, 57.
39. *SL*, July 12, 1890, 5.
40. *SL*, July 12, 1890, 15.
41. *SL*, July 12, 1890, 5, 15.
42. *BG*, July 21, 1890, 5; *SL*, July 19, 1890, 5.
43. *SL*, July 19, 1890, 9.
44. *SL*, July 19, 1890, 9; *New York Times*, August 2, 1889, 8.
45. *SL*, July 19, 1890, 9.
46. *SL*, July 19, 1890, 7.
47. *SL*, July 19, 1890, 7.
48. *BG*, July 28, 1890, 5; *BG*, July 3, 1890, 5.
49. Davies, 58; *SL*, July 26, 1890, 8; Lamb, 36–38.
50. *SL*, July 26, 1890, 5.
51. *SL*, July 26, 1890, 8.
52. *SL*, July 26, 1890, 8.
53. *BG*, August 4, 1890, 5.
54. *SL*, August 2, 1890, 6, 8; *BG*, August 11, 1890, 5.
55. *SL*, August 2, 1890, 9; *BG*, August 11, 1890, 5.
56. *SL*, August 2, 1890, 6, 8, 9; Pietrusza.
57. *SL*, August 2, 1890, 8; Benswanger.
58. *SL*, August 2, 1890, 6, 8.
59. Rowe, 37–38.

Chapter 4

1. *SL*, August 2, 1890, 6, 10; *BG*, August 4, 1890, 5.
2. *SL*, August 9, 1890, 1.
3. *BG*, August 11, 1890, 5; *SL*, August 9, 8, 11.
4. *BG*, August 11, 1890, 5.
5. *SL*, August 9, 1890, 8.
6. *SL*, August 9, 1890, 9, 11.
7. *BG*, August 18, 1890, 3; *SL*, August 16, 1890, 6.
8. *SL*, August 16, 1890, 6.
9. *SL*, August 16, 1890, 6.
10. Orodenker, 33; *BG*, August 19, 1890, 5; Fleitz, 97.
11. *BG*, August 19, 1890, 5.
12. *SL*, August 16, 1890, 9.
13. *BG*, August 25, 1890, 5; *SL*, August 23, 1890, 5.
14. *SL*, August 23, 1890, 9; *BG*, August 24, 1890, 4.
15. *SL*, August 23, 1890, 8.
16. *SL*, August 23, 1890, 8.
17. *SL*, August 23, 1890, 9.

18. *SL*, August 23, 1890, 8, 9.
19. *SL*, August 30, 1890, 8, 9; Roessner, "The 'Ladies,'" 139–40.
20. *BG*, September 1, 1890, 5.
21. *SL*, August 30, 1890, 9.
22. *SL*, August 30, 1890, 9.
23. *SL*, September 6, 1890, 1–2.
24. *BG*, September 7, 1890, 3.
25. *SL*, September 6, 1890, 8; Davies, 48.
26. *BG*, September 8, 1890, 3; *SL*, September 6, 1890, 5.
27. *BG*, September 8, 1890, 3; *SL*, September 6, 1890, 5.
28. *SL*, September 13, 1890, 5.
29. *BG*, September 15, 1890, 5.
30. *SL*, September 13, 1890, 8; *BG*, September 15, 1890, 5.
31. *SL*, September 13, 1890, 10.
32. *BG*, September 21, 1890, 4.
33. *SL*, September 20, 1890, 10; Seymour and Mills, 126–7.
34. *BG*, September 21, 1890, 4; *BG*, September 22, 1890, 5; Alexander, 17.
35. *SL*, September 20, 1890, 7.
36. *SL*, September 20, 1890, 7.
37. *BG*, September 29, 1890, 5.
38. *BG*, September 29, 1890, 5.
39. *SL*, September 27, 1890, 13.
40. *SL*, September 27, 1890, 10.
41. *SL*, September 27, 1890, 8.
42. *BG*, October 5, 1890, 4.
43. *BG*, October 5, 1890, 4; *BG*, October 6, 1890, 3.
44. *SL*, October 4, 1890, 3.
45. *SL*, October 4, 1890, 3.
46. *SL*, October 4, 1890, 8.
47. *SL*, October 4, 1890, 8.
48. *SL*, October 4, 1890, 8; Davies, 58.
49. *SL*, October 4, 1890, 9.
50. *BG*, October 6, 1890, 5; *SL*, October 4, 1890, 9.
51. *SL*, October 4, 1890, 9.

Chapter 5

1. *BG*, October 5, 1890, 4; *SL*, October 4, 1890, 1; *BG*, October 13, 1890, 7; *BG*, October 18, 1890, 7.
2. *SL*, October 11, 1890, 4.
3. *BG*, October 12, 1890, 4.
4. *BG*, October 18, 1890, 7.
5. *SL*, October 11, 1890, 5; *SL*, October 18, 1890, 7; *SL*, October 25, 1890, 7.
6. *SL*, October 18, 1890, 7; *SL*, October 25, 1890, 7; Stevens, 137; Di Salvatore, 312–3.
7. *SL*, October 18, 1890, 7.
8. *SL*, November 1, 1890, 7; *SL*, November 15, 1890, 5.
9. *SL*, November 8, 1890, 6; *SL*, November 1, 1890, 5.
10. *SL*, November 1, 1890, 5.
11. Alexander, 106–08.
12. Alexander, 106–7; Lowenfish, 48; Di Salvatore, 314; Spalding, 288.
13. *SL*, October 11, 1890, 5.
14. *SL*, October 11, 1890, 6.
15. *SL*, October 18, 1890, 8.
16. *BG*, October 18, 1890, 7.
17. *SL*, October 18, 1890, 7; Di Salvatore, 316; Alexander, 101.
18. *SL*, October 25, 1890, 7; *SL*, November 1, 1890, 7.
19. *SL*, October 25, 1890, 7.
20. *BG*, October 26, 1890, 2.
21. *BG*, October 26, 1890, 2.
22. *SL*, November 1, 1890, 5.
23. *SL*, November 1, 1890, 7.
24. *BG*, November 9, 1890, 3.
25. *BG*, November 9, 1890, 3.
26. *BG*, November 12, 1890, 2; Dicken-Garcia, 228; Schudson, 69.
27. *SL*, November 15, 1890, 5; *SL*, November 22, 1890, 5.
28. *BG*, November 13, 1890, 10; *BG*, November 14, 1890, 10.
29. *BG*, November 13, 1890, 1, evening edition.
30. *SL*, November 15, 1890, 7.
31. *SL*, October 11, 1890, 5; *SL*, October 25, 1890, 7; November 15, 1890, 5; *SL*, November 22, 1890, 5.
32. *SL*, October 11, 1890, 5
33. *BG*, October 11, 1890, 7.
34. Schudson, 70, 74; *BG*, October 12, 1890, 4.
35. *BG*, October 12, 1890, 4.
36. *BG*, October 13, 1890, 4.
37. Dicken-Garcia, 189, 224.
38. *SL*, October 18, 1890, 7; *SL*, November 1, 1890, 7; *SL*, November 22, 1890, 5; Alexander, 193; W. Anderson, "Creating," 14.

39. *SL*, November 8, 1890, 5.
40. *SL*, November 8, 1890, 5.
41. *SL*, October 11, 1890, 5; *SL*, November 15, 1890, 5.
42. *SL*, October 11, 1890, 6; *SL*, October 18, 1890, 8.
43. *SL*, October 11, 1890, 6.
44. *SL*, November 1, 1890, 5.
45. *SL*, November 22, 1890, 7.
46. *SL*, November 22, 1890, 7
47. Sowell, 228.

Conclusion

1. Alexander, 193; Seymour and Mills, 261.
2. Schudson, 60.
3. Campbell, 5.
4. Whannel, 181; Hall, *Culture, Media, Language*, 27.

Works Cited

Adelman, Melvin. "The Early Years of Baseball, 1845–60." *The New American Sport History: Recent Approaches and Perspectives*. Ed. S. W. Pope. Urbana: University of Illinois Press, 1997. 58–87.

Akin, William. "Steve Brodie." http://sabr.org/bioproj/person/cffef117. Retrieved 2013-4-18.

Alexander, Charles. *Turbulent Seasons: Baseball in 1890–1891*. Dallas: Southern Methodist Press, 2011.

Anderson, Benedict. *Imagined Communities: Reflections on the Origin and Spread of Nationalism*. London: Verso, 1991.

Anderson, William. "Creating the National Pastime: The Antecedents of MLB Public Relations." *Media History Monographs* 4.2 http://facstaff.elon.edu/dcopeland/mhm/mhmjour4-2.htm Retrieved 2013-5-1.

_____. "Does the Cheerleading Ever Stop? Major League Baseball and Sports Journalism." *Journalism & Mass Communication Quarterly* 78.2 (Summer 2001): 355–382.

Anonymous. "The New York Athletic Club." *Outing* 4.6 (September 1884): 403–15.

Ardell, Jean Hastings. *Breaking into Baseball: Women and the National Pastime*. Carbondale: Southern Illinois University Press, 2005.

Bakhtin, Mikhail. *The Dialogic Imagination: Four Essays*. Trans. Caryl Emerson and Michael Holquist. Austin: University of Texas Press, 1981.

Ball, David. "John Reilly." http://sabr.org/bioproj/person/df50ad73. Retrieved 2013-4-27.

The Baseball Encyclopedia, 10th Ed. New York: Macmillan, 1996.

Benswanger, William E. "Professional Baseball in Pittsburgh." *Western Pennsylvania Historical Magazine* 30.1–2 (March–June) 1997, http://upress.pitt.edu/htmlSourceFiles/pdfs/9780822959700exr.pdf. Retrieved 2014-6-3.

Betts, John Richards. *America's Sporting Heritage: 1850–1950*. Reading, MA: Addison-Wesley, 1974.

Bevis, Charlie. http://sabr.org/bioproj/person/b2017f67. Retrieved 2015-2-12.

Boorstin, Daniel. *The Image: A Guide to Pseudo-Events in America*. New York: Vintage, 1961.

Campbell, W. Joseph. *The Year That Defined American Journalism*. New York & London: Routledge Taylor & Francis, 2006.

Davies, Richard O. *Sports in American Life: A History*. Malden, MA: Blackwell, 2007.

Dicken-Garcia, Hazel. *Journalistic Standards in Nineteenth-Century America*. Madison: University of Wisconsin Press, 1989.

Di Salvatore, Brian. *John M. Ward: A Clever Baseballist*. Jefferson, NC: McFarland, 2000.

Eastern Park, Brooklyn. http://www.covehurst.net/ddyte/brooklyn/eastern_park.html. Retrieved 2014-6-7.

Fleitz, David L. *Ghosts in the Gallery at

Works Cited

Cooperstown. Jefferson, NC: McFarland, 2004.

Garrison, Bruce, and Mark Sabljak. *Sports Reporting*. Ames: Iowa State University Press, 1985.

Gelzheiser, Robert P. *Labor and Capital in 19th Century Baseball*. Jefferson, NC: McFarland, 2006.

Godkin, E. L. "Newspapers Here and Abroad." *North American Review* 150 (Feb. 1890): 197–204.

Gorn, Elliott, and Michael Oriard. "Taking Sports Seriously." *Chronicle of Higher Education* (March 24, 1995): A52.

Guttmann, Allen. *A Whole New Ball Game: An Interpretation of American Sports*. Chapel Hill: The University of North Carolina Press, 1988.

Hall, Stuart. *Culture, Media, Language: Working Papers in Cultural Studies, 1972–79*. London: Hutchinson, 1980.

———. Introduction. *Paper Voices: The Popular Press and Social Change 1935–1965*. By A. C. H. Smith. London: Chatto & Windus, 1975. 11–24.

Hardy, Stephen H. "The Sports Marketplace." *The New American Sport History: Recent Approaches and Perspectives*. Ed. S. W. Pope. Urbana: University of Illinois Press, 1997. 341–65.

Holtzman, Jerome. *No Cheering in the Press Box*. New York: Holt, Rinehart and Winston, 1974.

"John Gaffney." http://sabrpedia.org/wiki/John_Gaffney_%28a4ba%29. Retrieved 2014-6-7.

Koszarek, Ed. *The Players' League: History, Clubs, Ballplayers and Statistics*. Jefferson, NC: McFarland, 2006.

Kroeger, Brooke. *Nellie Bly: Daredevil, Reporter, Feminist*. New York: Times Books, 1994.

Lamb, Chris. *Conspiracy of Silence: Sportswriters and the Long Campaign to Desegregate Baseball*. Lincoln: University of Nebraska Press, 2012.

Lamster, Mark. *Spalding's World Tour: The Epic Adventure That Took Baseball Around the Globe—And Made It America's Game*. New York: Public Affairs, 2006.

Lears, T. J. Jackson. "The Concept of Cultural Hegemony: Problems and Possibilities." *American Historical Review* 90.3 (June 1985): 567–93.

Levine, Peter. *A. G. Spalding and the Rise of Baseball*. New York: Oxford University Press, 1985.

Lewis, Ethan M. "'A Structure to Last Forever': The Players' League and Brotherhood War of 1890." http://www.ethanlewis.org/pl/ch1.html. Retrieved 2011-9-9.

Lowenfish, Lee. *The Imperfect Diamond*. Lincoln: University of Nebraska Press, 2010.

Mack, Connie. *My 66 Years in the Big Leagues: The Great Story of America's National Game*. Philadelphia: Winston, 1950.

Martin, Brian. *Baseball's Creation Myth: Adam Ford, Abner Graves and the Cooperstown Story*. Jefferson, NC: McFarland, 2013.

McKenna, Brian. "Arthur Soden." http://sabr.org/bioproj/person/a1b2e0d0. Retrieved 2013-4-18.

McMahon, Bill. "Al Spalding." http://sabr.org/bioproj/person/b99355e0. Retrieved 2014-6-4.

Miklich, Eric. "Bob Ferguson." http://www.19cbaseball.com/players-bob-ferguson.html Retrieved 2014-6-7.

Mott, Frank. *American Journalism: A History, 1690–1960*. New York: Macmillan, 1962.

Nichols, John. "The Enchanted Baseball." *Cosmopolitan* 8.4 (April 1890): 659–668.

Ohmann, Richard. *Selling Culture: Magazines, Markets, and Class at the Turn of the Century*. London: Verso, 1996.

Oriard, Michael. "In the Beginning Was the Rule." *The New American Sport History: Recent Approaches and Perspectives*. Ed. S. W. Pope. Urbana: University of Illinois Press, 1997. 88–120.

Orodenker, Richard. *The Writer's Game:*

Works Cited

Baseball Writing in America. New York: Twayne, 1996.

Park, Robert. "The Natural History of the Newspaper." *The American Journal of Sociology*, 29.3 (November 1923): 273–289.

Pearson, Daniel M. *Baseball in 1889: Players vs. Owners*. Bowling Green, OH: Bowling Green University Press, 1993.

Peterson, Scott D. "Born a Busher or How Journalists Turned Fiction Writers Made Baseball Safe for the Middle-Class Readers of the *Saturday Evening Post*." *Baseball and Social Class*. Eds. Ron Kates and Warren Tomey. Jefferson, NC: McFarland, 2012. 44–59.

_____. "Do You Know Me Now: Cultural Reflection and Resistance in Ring Lardner's *You Know Me Al*." *Nine: A Journal of Baseball History and Culture* 18.2 (Spring 2010): 38–48.

_____. "More Than 'Clever Journalists': The Cultural Contributions of Noah Brooks, Ring Lardner, and Heywood Broun to American Sport Fiction." *Critical Insights: Sports Fiction*. Eds. Michael Cocchiarale and Scott D. Emmert. Ipswich, MA: Grey House, 2013. 73–92.

_____. "Of Ourselves We Sing: Finding an American Voice Through Early Baseball Journalism." *Baseball/Literature/Culture Essays*. Eds. Ronald Kates and Warren Tomey. Jefferson, NC: McFarland, 2008. 11–21.

Pietrusza, David. "Al Pratt: Present at the Creation." http://www.davidpietrusza.com/Pratt.html. Retrieved 2014-6-4.

Preston, J.G. "The History for Baseball's Longest Throw." http://prestonjg.wordpress.com/2009/12/04/the-history-of-the-record-for-baseballs-longest-thrown-a-tale-that-involves-john-hatfield-honus-wagner-sheldon-lejeune-don-grate-rocky-colavito-and-glen-gorbous-among-others/. Retrieved 2013-4-18.

Reidenbaugh, Lowell. *The "Sporting News"' First Hundred Years, 1886–1986*. St. Louis: The Sporting News, 1986.

Richter, Amy. *Home on the Rails*. Chapel Hill: University of North Carolina Press, 2005.

Richter, Francis. *Richter's History and Records of Base Ball: The American Nation's Chief Sport*. Philadelphia: The Dando Company, 1914.

Riess, Stephen. *Touching Base: Professional Baseball and American Culture in the Progressive Era*. Urbana: University of Illinois Press, 1999.

Roessner, Amber (Shaw). "Hero Crafting in Sporting Life, an Early Baseball Journal." *American Journalism* 26.2 (Spring 2009): 39–65.

_____. "The Impact of Francis Richter Upon the Development of Baseball." http://juro.uga.edu/2003/shaw.htm. Retrieved 2014-3-24.

_____. "The 'Ladies' & The 'Tramps': The Negotiation of A 'Woman's Place' in the National Pastime in *Sporting Life*." *Journalism History* 39.3 (Fall 2013): 134–44.

Rossi, J.P. *The National Game: Baseball and American Culture*. Chicago: I. R. Dee, 2000.

Rowe, David. *Sport, Culture and the Media: The Unruly Trinity*. Philadelphia: Open University Press, 2004.

Schiff, Andrew. *"The Father of Baseball": A Biography of Henry Chadwick*. Jefferson, NC: McFarland, 2008.

Schudson, Michael. *Discovering the News*. New York: Basic Books, 1978.

Scott, Linda. *Fresh Lipstick: Redressing Fashion and Feminism*. New York: Macmillan, 2005.

Seymour, Harold, and Dorothy Seymour Mills. *Baseball: The Early Years*. 1960. New York: Oxford University Press, 1989.

Smith, Robert. *Baseball*. New York: Simon & Schuster, 1947.

Smythe, Ted Curtis. "The Reporter: 1880–1900." *Journalism History* 7.1 (Spring 1980): 1–10.

Works Cited

Sowell, Mike. "Is She or Isn't He?: Exploring the Gender Identity Controversy Over the First Female Byline in a National Sports Publication." *Journalism History* 37.4 (Winter 2012): 228-237.

Spalding, Albert G. *America's National Game: Historic Facts Concerning the Beginning, Evolution, Development, and Popularity of Base Ball*. 1911. Lincoln: University of Nebraska Press, 1992.

Spink, Alfred H. *The National Game*. St. Louis: The National Game Publishing Co., 1910.

Stevens, David. *Baseball's Radical for all Seasons: A Biography of John Montgomery Ward*. Lanham, MD: Scarecrow, 1998.

Story, Ronald. "The Creation of the Young: The Meaning of Baseball in Early American Culture" in *Baseball from Outside the Lines*. Ed. John Dreifort. Lincoln: University of Nebraska Press, 2001.

Thorn, John. "1791 and All That: Baseball and the Berkshires." *Base Ball: A Journal of the Early Game* 1.1 (Spring 2007): 119-126.

Thorn, John, Pete Palmer, and Michael Gershman, Eds. *Total Baseball*. 4th Edition. New York: Viking, 1995.

Tiemann, Robert L., and Mark Rucker, eds. *Nineteenth Century Stars*. Cleveland: Society for American Baseball Research, 1989.

Trachtenberg, Alan. *The Incorporation of America*. New York: Hill and Wang, 1982.

Ward, John M. *Base-Ball: How to Become a Player, with the Origin, History, and Explanation of the Game*. Philadelphia: Athletic Publishing Company, 1888.

——. "Is the Base Ball Player a Chattel?" *Lippincott's Magazine* 40 (August 1887): 310-19.

Welter, Barbara. "The Cult of True Woman: 1820-1860." *Locating American Studies: The Evolution of a Discipline*. Ed. Lucy Maddox. Baltimore: The Johns Hopkins University Press, 1999. 43-70.

Whannel, Garry. *Fields in Vison: Television Sports and Cultural Transformation*. London; New York, Routledge, 1992.

White, George A. "The Manhattan Athletic Club" (part 1). *Outing* 16.3 (June 1890): 163-169.

——. "The Manhattan Athletic Club" (part 2). *Outing* 16.4 (July 1890): 308-11.

Wiebe, Robert H. *The Search for Order 1877-1920*. New York: Hill and Wang, 1967.

Index

Abell, Ferdinand 151
Addison, John 174–175, 177, 179
Albemarle Hotel 15
Alexander, Charles 8
Alger, Horatio 24, 61, 96, 152
amateur baseball 95, 108, 114, 121
American Association (AA) 6, 16, 19, 31, 56, 66, 71, 104, 113, 117, 121, 141, 168, 169, 178, 181–182, 195, 225n17, 247n1, 248n5; amalgamation of with PL 130, 131, 132, 135, 138, 143, 146, 147, 158; target audience of compared to NL 22, 87, 131, 135, 158, 169, 181–182, 247n2
The American Chronicle of Sports and Pastimes 9
American culture 12, 14, 36
American journalism: development as a profession 2, 11, 13, 30, 32, 36, 41, 58, 109, 178; development of editorial voice within 27; development of human interest stories within 39, 44; development of interviewing within 33, 36; development of news concept within 11, 12; early use of correspondents 10, 11, 27; impact of nineteenth century print media within 27; Independence of writers within 11, 13, 33–34, 101, 157, 167; nineteenth century business model of 185; nineteenth century gossip style of 11, 41, 77; response to the trivial within 11, 39, 58, 89, 93, 184; "scoop" mentality within 43–44, 66, 122, 187–188, 206; sensationalism of in nineteenth century 11, 19, 51, 77, 123, 132, 142, 145, 148, 151, 167, 178, 188; use of anecdotes within 19, 43, 50, 64, 70, 76–77, 112, 207n20
American League 198, 247n4
American Victorianism 30, 35, 58, 193
America's Cup 9
America's National Game 5, 6–7
Anderson, Benedict 10
Anderson, William 30
Anson, Cap 59, 63, 85, 88, 89, 115, 128, 134, 140, 160, 180

archery 10
Ardell, Jean 38
Associated Press 133, 241n1
Atlantic League 10, 113, 121–122, 225n8
attendance 59, 62, 65, 68, 79–80, 90, 110, 115, 123–124, 128, 130, 133, 136, 231n6; in Boston 87, 120, 137, 153, 241n1, 242n5; in Brooklyn 120–121; in Chicago 75, 78–79, 84, 95, 100, 120, 136, 137; figures of 1889 compared to 1890 numbers 60–61, 80, 83–84, 86, 87–88, 94, 100, 108, 113, 116–117, 136; in New York 100, 137; in Philadelphia 120, 137; in Pittsburgh 69, 77, 84, 92, 100, 120, 159
Austen, Jane 64, 220n18

Bahktin, Mikhail 12
Baldwin, Mark 125
The Ball Players' Chronicle 9
Barnes, Ross 62
Barzun, Jacques 2
baseball: business model of 22, 30, 163, 182; drinking by players of 29, 33, 92, 134, 167, 184, 189, 207n19, 220n9, 231n1, 231n3, 239n13; fraternity of players in nineteenth century 6, 16, 17, 51, 79, 121, 158, 167, 248n7; gambling as an issue of 4, 6, 9, 29, 33, 189; hero worship of players by fans of 74, 78, 83, 127, 129, 184; importance of statistics in 28, 29, 59, 220n9; minor leagues of 10, 23; public image of in nineteenth century 6–7, 22, 71, 92, 102, 110, 131, 163, 167, 177, 178, 180, 187, 231n3, 231n5, 238n10
Baseball (Smith book) 8
Baseball Hall of Fame 142
Baseball in 1889 8
baseball writers, fraternity of 59, 61, 64, 67, 75, 93, 140, 248n13
Bastian, Charlie 207n20
Beadle's Dime Base Ball Manual 28
Beatin, Ed 220n14
Becannon, Buck 134
Beckley, Jake 45, 76–77, 206n9, 248n11

Index

Beecher, Ed 168
Berthong, Harry 184
bicycling 10
Bierbauer, Lou 168
billiards 10, 33
Billings, James 101, 225n10, 225n11
Black, Ella 10, 14, 15, 20, 193–194, 195–196, 197; awareness of other sports journalists by 85, 101–102, 106, 118, 126, 134; comparison of to Chadwick 71, 80, 124, 134, 138, 220n7, 221n19; comparison of to Murnane 48, 55, 69, 70, 81, 89, 97; contributions to journalism of 27, 43, 67, 71; coverage of baseball business by 66, 69, 80–81, 125, 171; coverage of the Young Ladies of the Diamond (YLD) 39–40, 44–46, 65–66; as example of Modern Woman 13, 28, 37, 40, 42, 47, 65, 187–190, 205n1; Opening Day coverage by 65–66, 206n5, 206n6; print treatment of John Ward by 38, 40–43; progressive efforts of 37, 38, 41, 43, 46, 77–78, 80–81, 138; reporting by 42–43, 46, 65–66, 75, 104, 111–112, 122–123, 133–134, 137, 148, 153–154, 168–169, 171; restrictions as female journalist experienced by 67, 69–70, 77–78, 86, 105, 145; special attacks made by 97–98, 99–100; use of anecdotes by 71, 77, 134; use of baseball historian role 70; use of editorial style by 40–41, 44, 46, 76, 80–81, 84, 110–111, 131–132, 138, 141, 150, 159–160, 171, 174, 175; use of interview 105, 107, 154; use of "riding the cars" method by 44, 46, 107, 206n8; use of slang 80, 138
Black Sox Scandal 198
Blue Laws 55, 66, 128, 181
Bly, Nellie *see* Cochrane, Elizabeth Jane
Boston Beaneaters (NL) 47, 55–56, 63, 74, 89, 96, 117, 124, 130, 142, 153, 225n6, 225n8
Boston Braves 6
Boston Globe 18, 27, 48, 51, 55, 72, 139, 144, 182–184
Boston Herald 72
Boston Journal 72
Boston Red Caps (NL) 47
Boston Red Stockings (NA) 17
Boston Red Stockings (PL) 21, 24, 48–56, 72, 74, 79, 83, 103, 108–109, 110, 111, 112, 118, 124, 125, 130, 137, 140, 143, 147, 148, 149, 153, 155–156, 162, 164–165, 169, 197; Fast Day game of 35, 51–53, 61, 182–183, 242n2; pennant chase of 195, 239n16
Boston Reds (UA) 16, 47
Boston Referee 16
Boston Triumvirs 87, 101, 103, 115, 118, 122, 153, 224n1

boxing 10
Bradley, George Washington 165
Brodie, Walter Scott 221n21
Brooklyn Bridegrooms (NL) 63, 71, 72, 83, 99, 115, 117, 120, 130, 136, 141, 147, 149, 157, 162, 167, 168, 173, 248n5
Brooklyn Gladiators (AA) 72, 239n14
Brooklyn Tip-Tops (Federal League) 6
Brooklyn Wonders (PL) 15, 35, 54, 72, 74, 79, 83, 97, 117, 120–121, 130, 137, 140, 143, 147, 150, 212n7, 239n16
Brotherhood of Professional Base Ball Players 1, 5–6, 8, 16, 18, 31, 35, 44, 51, 173, 176, 197; deserters from 19, 49–52, 115, 205n2
Brotherhood War 1, 3, 5–8, 11–13, 15, 18, 60, 82, 92, 166, 197–198, 206n7; ability of cities to support two teams during 80, 83, 96, 159–160, 181–182; aftermath of 23, 119–120, 123, 182, 225n17, 248n5, 248n6; amalgamation as a solution to 130–132, 135, 146, 147, 158, 163; compromise as solution to 92, 114, 117, 121, 131, 133, 135, 146, 153, 162–163, 169, 171, 173–177; conference committees of 21, 162, 169, 170–176, 231n6, 247n2; consolidation of leagues as a solution to 21, 25, 163, 167, 169, 172, 174, 176, 180; economic loses caused by 162, 172; New York consolidation negotiations of 171–173, 176–178; Pittsburgh consolidation negotiations of 171, 175–178, 190, 247n3
Brouthers, Dan 50, 62, 85, 140, 146, 164, 257n3
Brown, Tom 184
Brunell, Frank 25, 86, 90, 121, 133, 143, 150–151, 166–167, 238n9, 241n1, 247n3
Brush, John T. 69
Brush Classification System 4, 18, 23, 31, 90, 166, 219n2
Bryant, William Cullen 212n11
Buffalo Bisons 6, 75, 137, 140, 143, 221n20
Buffington, Charlie 182, 213n18
bulldozing 59, 92, 152, 189
Burkett, Jesse 154
Burns, Tom 89, 248n12
Byrne, Charles 71, 84, 90, 101, 105, 115, 121, 136, 140, 149, 151, 153, 167, 212n6, 238n9

Cahill, W.H. 108–109
Campbell, W. Joseph 9
Capitoline Grounds 75, 212n1
Carroll, Cliff 248n12
Carroll, Fred 142, 206n11, 248n11
Caruthers, Bob 238n11
Caylor, O.P. 46, 49, 51, 212n10
celebrity 33, 42; of baseball players 3, 5, 25,

268

Index

36, 41, 53, 55, 58, 59, 70, 74, 83, 112, 118, 195, 197; "undeserved" fame of 11, 118, 134, 137, 232n8
Century 81
Chadwick, Henry 4, 9, 10, 14, 15, 17, 40, 75, 114, 192–194, 195–196; awareness of other sports journalists by 35, 85, 101–102, 106, 131, 151, 154, 187, 220n10, 248n13; comparison of to Black 43, 44, 67, 98, 125, 138, 176, 180, 196, 231n2, 231n4, 232n11; comparison of to Murnane 44, 48, 51, 52, 55, 56, 89, 97, 101, 122, 156, 178, 195, 224n2; contributions to journalism of 27, 185–187; coverage of baseball business by 88, 100, 125; criticism of "noisy coaching" by 114, 121, 221n22; "millennium" argument of 108, 114, 131, 219n1; moralistic style of 21, 31, 33, 54, 71, 114, 144–145, 158, 166–167, 186, 212n12; Opening Day coverage by 63–64; print treatment of John Ward by 30–36; promotion of the NL by 29, 84–85, 239n18; scientific batting discussion by 25, 131, 155, 186–187, 220n15, 237n2; as *Spalding's Guide* editor 7, 28; use of baseball historian role 27–29, 62, 87, 151, 165, 185; use of Cato the Elder persona by 82, 88, 95–96, 102, 104, 108, 121–122, 124–125, 131, 135–136, 137–138, 141, 144–145, 219n4, 220n11, 220n12, 220n13; use of editorial voice by 13, 27, 30–31, 34–36, 63–64, 71–72, 82–83, 88, 147, 157–158, 165–167, 170, 172–173, 176, 178, 181–182; use of interview by 30–36, 121, 165–166; use of slang by 64, 144, 238n8; work as a reporter by 32, 63–64, 114
"The Charge of the Light Brigade" 122
Chicago Colts (NL) 59, 78–79, 83, 89, 130, 134, 136, 149
Chicago Pirates (PL) 78–79, 83, 88, 89, 92, 95, 99, 104, 110, 136, 140, 147, 149, 158
Chicago Tribune 29
Chicago White Stockings (NL) 16, 17, 95, 104, 140
Cincinnati Outlaw Reds (UA) 45, 165
Cincinnati Porkers (AA) 150
Cincinnati Reds (NL) 69, 83, 99, 114, 115, 130, 138, 141, 150, 158, 238n5; sale of 150, 151, 158, 170, 195, 242n7; secret signings of players of 114–115, 122–123, 187–188, 194
Clarkson, John 64, 103, 115, 119, 125, 242n8
class: "better class" of baseball audience 9, 11, 21–22, 29, 30, 37–38, 40, 45–46, 59, 61, 63–64, 70–71, 95, 97, 99, 100, 105, 114, 118, 121, 155, 167; 169, 181, 189, 205n2, 206n5, 220n15, 237n2; differences between players and owners 135; upper-class media 58
Clements, Jack 50
Cleveland Infants (PL) 143, 150
Cleveland Spiders (NL) 69, 89, 140
Cobb, Ty 5
Cochrane, Elizabeth Jane 1, 37–38, 188, 193
Comiskey, Charles 75, 95, 104, 147, 178, 180, 247n3, 248n5
Conant, William 153, 179, 225n10, 225n11
Congress Street Grounds 52–53, 62–63
Connor, Roger 62
consumer culture 3
Coogan's Bluff 58
Cooney, Jimmy 89
corporate capitalism 3, 4
The Cosmopolitan 58, 81, 104
Crane, Ed 144, 184, 239n17
cricket 10, 28, 82, 257n2
croquet 10
Cult of True Womanhood 37, 40, 42
Cunningham, Bert 137

Daily, Con 54
Daley, Bill 74, 146, 155
Dalrymple, Abner 63
Daly, Maurice 32
Dana, Charles A. 50
Daniels, Pete 207n16
Dauvray, Helen 31, 41–43, 67, 206n7, 221n19
Dauvray Cup 31, 42; 1890 series of 162, 165, 168–169, 173
Davies, Richard 8
Day, John B. 45, 111, 128, 166, 172, 177
Detective Randall 96, 100
Detroit Wolverines (NL) 140
De Wolfe Hopper's Comic Opera Bouffe 31
Dicken-Garcia, Hazel 11
Dickens, Charles 144
Dickenson, George 100, 104, 135, 175, 178, 238n9
Di Salvatore, Brian 42–43
Dixwell, "General" Arthur 53, 143, 183
Doe, Fred 137
Dombey and Son 144
Donnolly, J.F. 97, 132, 238n6
Doubleday Cooperstown hoax 7
Dow, Clarence 65, 74, 83, 86, 99, 104, 120, 133, 144, 148, 220n17
Dryden, Charles 134
Duke, Martin 168
Dunlap, Fred 69, 84, 206n15
Duryea, Jesse 139

The Early Years 8
Eastern League 137

269

Index

Ebbets Charley 136
Elias Sports Bureau 62, 124
Elmira, New York 108–109, 164
Engle's Home Plate 16, 25, 256n3
ESPN 35
Evans Charles 184
Ewing, Buck 92, 97, 104, 121, 128, 142, 154, 165–166, 177, 197, 232n7, 248n5
Ewing, John 104–105, 144, 196, 239n17
Exhibition Park 65, 66, 70, 84, 120, 171, 205n3, 207n21

Faatz, Jay 137
Federal League 6, 198, 247n4
Fields, Jocko 248n11
Forest City Club (Cleveland) 45
Foutz, Dave 238n7, 238n11
Frank Leslie's Illustrated Newspaper 9, 27, 58

Gaffney John 74, 213n21
Galvin, James "Pud" 80, 84, 125, 142, 206n5, 206n12, 248n11
Garrison, Edward 140
Gelzheiser, Richard 8
Getzien, Charlie 225n5
Gilded Age 1, 2, 33, 37
Glasscock, John 44–45, 110–111, 116, 194, 247n1
Gleason, Kid 50, 74
Godkin, E.L. 54
Goodwin, Wendell 176, 212n4
Gore, George 62
Gorn, Elliott 2
Grant, Frank 122
Grant, Ulysses 178, 196
Griffin, Mike 213n17
Gumbert, Ad 124, 147, 156, 159, 225n19, 248n12
Gumbert Will 107, 124, 159, 194

"Hail the Conquering Heroes" 184
Hall, Stuart 2, 9, 12, 14; definition of "special rhetoric" 12
Hanlon Ned 77, 99, 111, 134, 168
Harper's Weekly 9, 27, 58, 81
Harris, William H. 67, 160, 212n8
Harris, William I. 178, 212n10, 226n20
Harrisburg Ponies 122
Hart, Julian 109, 148, 241n1
Harvard baseball 49
Hatfield, Gil 143, 225n15
Hearst, Randolph 196
Hecker, Guy 46, 75, 80, 96, 98, 99, 117, 206n15
hegemony 4
Henry IV, Part Two 238n9

Hines, Paul 75, 80
Hoey, William 184
Holbert, William 213n22
homing pigeons 10
Hopper, De Wolfe 32, 184
Hornung, Joe 182, 242n4
Hughes, Michael 239n13
Hulbert, William 29–30, 121, 158
Hutchinson, Bill 89, 125, 248n12

Illinois-Iowa League 10
The Imperfect Diamond 8
Indianapolis Hoosiers (NL) 44, 45
International Association 45
Irwin, Arthur 56, 112, 116, 140, 156, 225n16, 247n1

Johnson, Al 25, 147, 148, 150, 174, 247n3
Johnson, Ban 247n4
Johnston, Dick 118
jumping (contracts, leagues) 4, 16, 19, 44

Kansas City Blues 56, 76–7
Keating, Edward 207n18
Keefe, Tim 62, 125, 134–135, 197
Kelly, John W. 112
Kelly, Mike 21–22, 35, 48–54, 59, 62, 73, 85, 92, 103, 112, 116, 118, 121, 126, 134, 146–147, 149, 156, 164–165, 169, 177, 179–180, 183–184, 194, 196, 197, 226n21, 247n3, 257n35
Kelly's Killers (AA) 150
kicking 59, 71, 80, 88, 92, 108, 114, 121, 158, 189, 221n22
Kilroy, Matt 225n14
King, Silver 74, 76, 125, 206n6
Knickerbocker Club 3
Koszarek, Ed 8, 13
Kuehne, Bill 142

labor, Brotherhood issue and 13, 18, 19, 21, 24, 25, 27, 48, 55, 183, 198; lawsuits and 30–32, 34, 76–77, 88, 143, 212n15
Lardner, Ring 248n7
Latham, Arlie 132, 151, 205n4
Levey, Augustus A. 30
Lewis, Ethan 8, 13
Linton, Edward F. 212n4
Lippincott 81
Loftus, Tom 69, 238n4
Long, Herman 64
Louisville Colonels (AA) 104, 117, 144, 150, 162, 168, 173
Lovett, Tom 238n6, 238n11
Lowenfish, Lee 8
Lucas, Henry V. 27
Lytle, Edward 134, 232n13

270

Index

Mack, Connie 6, 75, 137, 168, 172
Madden, Michael ("Kid") 213*n*20
Mandigo, John 178, 212*n*8
Manhattan Athletic Club 15–17, 20
Manola, Marion 30–31
Mathewson, Christy 5
Matthews, Bobby 207*n*22
Maul, Al 248*n*11
McAlpin, Colonel Edwin 119, 135, 164, 172, 174–175, 176–177, 180, 212*n*4, 225*n*18, 238*n*9
McCallin, George 38, 84
McCauley, Al 141
McDermott, Jessie 43, 67, 257*n*25
McDermott, Sandy 95
McEwen, Arthur 50
McGunnigle, Bill 165, 212*n*8
Meacham, Lewis 29
Middletown Mansfields (NA) 47
Miller, George 76–77, 98, 144, 159, 171, 239*n*12, 248*n*11
Mills, Dorothy Seymour 8, 10
Mills Commission 7
Morris, Ed 76, 80, 134, 231*n*5
Morse, Jacob 212*n*9
Mulford, Ren 81, 86, 139, 188, 238*n*9
Mullane, Tony 70, 81, 139
Murnane, T.H. 10, 14, 15–25, 193–194, 195–197; awareness of other sports journalists by 85, 97, 101, 116, 126, 156–157, 183, 212*n*2; comparison of to Black 43, 44, 67, 104, 169, 171, 176, 196, 231*n*2, 232*n*11; comparison of to Chadwick 62, 65, 82–83, 95, 124, 135, 158, 220*n*7; coverage of baseball business by 61–63, 72–73, 91, 125, 213*n*23; as example of Reporter 13, 28, 48–55, 137, 171–172, 174–175, 177–180; "old Jeffersonian doctrine" argument of 24, 56, 127, 171, 193, 224*n*2; Opening Day coverage by 61–63; progressive agenda of 55; promotion of Boston Red Stockings by 140, 149, 153, 155, 164–165, 182–184; promotion of PL by 47, 61, 73, 84–85, 89, 112, 150–151, 212*n*5, 225*n*13; special attacks made by 96–97, 100, 108–109, 115–116, 118–120, 122, 135, 242*n*2, 242*n*6; use of anecdote by 19, 50; use of editorial role by 55, 79–80, 224*n*3; use of interviews by 62, 89–90, 130–131, 134–135; use of slang by 54, 149
Murphy, Morgan 156
Myers, Al 50, 115

Napoleon 52, 54
Nash, Billy 50–51, 54, 103, 130, 156
National Agreement 16, 23, 24, 49, 56, 135, 152, 182, 248*n*5

National Association (NA) 4, 18, 29, 30, 47, 87, 151, 183, 224*n*3
National Association of Base Ball Players 33
National Base Ball Reporters Association 11
The National Game 8
National League (NL) 147, 168, 181, 189; alleged "comp" conspiracy of 115, 119, 122, 141, 194, 225*n*9; blacklist of players 22–23, 48–49; capitalist model of 7; conflicting schedule created by 62, 114, 207*n*21; dominance of 27; 1890 national meeting of 169, 178–180; 1890 pennant race of 83, 113, 117, 120, 124, 146, 149, 152–153, 162; labor practices of 23; target audience 22; *see also* Spalding, Albert
National League Jubilee celebration 6
New York Athletic Club 20, 256*n*3
New York Clipper 5, 16, 28
New York Giants (NL) 31, 44, 58, 83, 143, 221*n*20
New York Giants (PL) 62, 88, 99, 117, 143, 147, 150, 153, 154, 164–165, 179, 213*n*24, 221*n*20
New York State League 10
New York Sun 109
New York Times 27
New York World 135, 212*n*7
Nichol, Hugh 132, 139
Nichols, Kid 225*n*5
Nick Engle's Home Plate 25, 165–166
Nimick, William A. 70, 76, 77, 107, 171
Northwest League 10

O'Day, Hank 164
Ohio State Journal 139
O'Neill, J. Palmer 70, 77, 84, 96, 98, 99–100, 107, 119, 124, 125, 134, 142, 144–145, 148, 159, 171, 179, 194
Opening Day (1890) 61–66
Oriard, Michael 2, 5
O'Rourke, Jim 51, 257*n*35
Orr, Dave 54, 213*n*19
Osborne, Fred 131
Outing 20

Pacific Northwest League 139
Palmer, Harry 49, 51, 101, 119, 224*n*4
Paper Voices 9, 12, 14
Park, Robert 50
Paterson, NJ 146, 164, 165
Patriot's Day 52
Pearson, Daniel 8
Pfeffer, Fred 75, 89, 104, 134, 248*n*12
Philadelphia Athletics (NA) 47
Philadelphia Inquirer 146

Index

Philadelphia Phillies (NL) 49, 99, 117, 120, 132
Philadelphia Quakers (PL) 72, 74, 77, 88, 117, 120, 147
Philadelphia Sunday Times 185
Philadelphia White Stockings (NA) 47
Phillips, Bill 133-134, 232n10, 232n13
Phillips, Horace 117-118, 160, 168
Physical Culture 16, 20
Pickett, John 76-77, 212n15
Pittsburg Commercial-Gazette 31
Pittsburgh Alleghenys 39, 40, 43, 45, 65, 69, 75-77, 81, 84, 92, 96, 97-98, 99-100, 107, 111-112, 117, 124, 131-132, 133-134, 137, 141, 144, 145, 147, 148, 150, 154, 159-160, 179, 232n9
Pittsburgh Burghers 40, 65, 69, 75-76, 81, 84, 104, 112, 116, 117, 124, 137, 140, 141, 143, 148, 150, 154, 159-160, 171, 179
Players' League 59, 61, 121, 143; business model of 25, 63, 72-3, 74, 108, 131, 141, 147-148, 166-167, 172-173; capitalist backers of 21, 170-171; double umpire system of 34, 88, 143, 158, 172, 182, 220n11, 220n12, 220n13; 1891 plans for 19, 177; labor principle of 1-2, 4-5, 6-7, 11, 13, 18, 21, 23, 27, 55, 116, 138, 171, 231n3; modifications to baseball made by 34-35, 79, 82, 85, 88, 100, 124, 131, 154, 172, 186, 220n15; national meeting of 169, 179-180, 247n3; pennant race of 21, 83, 86, 113, 117, 124, 138, 140, 146-147, 149, 152-153, 155, 162, 182-184, 239n16; *see also* Ward, John M.
Polo Grounds 58, 88
Pratt, Al 125-126, 145
Prince, Charles 16, 25, 177, 180, 247n1, 247n3
Pritchard, Joe 67
professional middle class 3, 4
professional spectator sports 3; perceptions of fans 10, 11, 38
Progressive Era 1, 2
Providence Grays 16, 31, 47, 140

Quinn, Joe 126

Radbourn, Hoss 103, 125, 140, 147
Reach, Al 135, 146
Recreation Park (Pittsburgh) 45, 69, 205n3
Reed, Charlie 184
Reidenbaugh, Lowell 10
Reilly, John 237n3
reserve rule 2, 8, 18, 23, 31-32, 51, 90, 166, 198, 219n2
Rhines, Bill 139
Richard III 220n11

Richardson, Hardy 140, 146, 155-156
Richter, Amy 40
Richter, Francis 7-8, 9-11, 17, 25, 27, 30, 67, 87, 93, 107, 109, 122, 172, 220n16; attitudes toward women of 13, 66, 97, 140, 205n1, 239n14; comments on players by 144, 220n14, 225n14, 238n10, 239n13, 242n8; comments on PL by 83, 130, 137, 138, 139, 141, 146; editorial decisions by 27, 32, 37-38, 62, 85, 99, 138-139, 141, 162, 181, 185, 196, 242n2; millennial plan of 7, 11, 219n1
Rife, Ed 139
Robinson, Yank 150
Rochester Herald 68
Roessner, Amber 11
Rogers, John I. 212n10
rounders 3
Rusie, Amos 154
Ryan, Jimmy 248n12

St. Louis Browns (AA) 95, 104, 138, 148, 178
St. Louis Maroons (UA) 47
Schafer, Harry 183
Schmelz, Gus 89, 119, 238n4
Schmidt, Frederick 206n14, 220n9
Schriver, Pop 50
Second Industrial Revolution 3, 4
Selee, Frank 242n4, 242n8
Seymour, Harold 8, 10
Shakespeare, William 108, 167, 220n11, 238n9
Shindle, Billy 213n17
shooting 10
Smith, Charles 242n4
Smith, John 159
Smith, Robert 8
Snyder, Charles 242n6
Soden, Arthur 119, 122, 225n10, 242n6
South End Grounds 53, 63, 122
Sowell, Mike 38
Spalding, Albert 5, 6-7, 8, 15-25, 78, 96; on gambling in baseball 9, 87; as a leader of the NL 29, 34, 41, 47, 53, 60, 78-79, 86-88, 90, 92, 94, 100, 101, 104, 114-115, 119, 121-122, 128, 131, 133, 135-136, 137, 171, 174, 177-180, 257n17, 212n13, 220n5; as owner of Chicago White Stockings/Colts 11, 110, 142; as owner of Spalding sporting goods 18, 68, 125, 131, 134-135, 144-145, 174; as player 17, 34, 225n12, 237n1, 257n14; role of in the Brotherhood War's conclusion 151, 170; world tour of 18, 31, 42-43
Spalding's Guide 7, 28, 29
Spink, Alfred 8

272

Index

The Sporting Life 9, 59, 184; circulation of 10, 22 description of 9–12; impact of sporting weeklies 22, 29; "moral wars" waged in 30, 49, 51; national audience of 10
The Sporting News 8, 43; circulation of 10, 22; national audience of 10
The Sporting Times 41, 46, 49
sports journalism 2, 17, 33, 59, 60, 184; "cherry-picking" by writers of 100, 104, 124–125, 212n14, 220n17, 239n18; Civil War rhetoric used in 18, 28, 31, 32, 34, 48, 49, 56, 166, 187; "curiosity shop" concept 9, 11, 14, 93; development of 9, 12, 13, 81; 1890 print feuds of 32, 59, 93, 126, 129, 187, 212n3; "Gee Whiz!" school of 50; impact on baseball's public image by 102, 134, 137, 167, 170, 171, 174, 177–178, 184, 185, 189–190, 205n4, 232n8; increased coverage found in 59, 71–72, 85, 139, 185; as a male domain 37; toy department concept of 127
sports media complex 14, 85, 192, 198
Stackhouse, George 212n8
Staley, Harry 80, 168, 206n13
Staten Island Athletic Club 114
Stein, Ed 141, 232n12
Stern, Aaron 150
Stevens, David 42
Stevens, Ed 242n8
Story, Ronald 3
Stovey, Harry 50, 130, 137
Sullivan, John L. 97–98
Sullivan, Marty 144, 238n10
Sunday, Billy 69, 106, 114, 132, 142

Talcott, E.B. 86, 158, 166, 172, 175, 176–177, 238n8
Taylor, Charles 183
Tener, John 77, 80, 105, 137, 206n13
tennis 10
Tennyson, Alfred Lord 29, 122
Terry, Adonis 238n11
Texas League 10
theater 10
Thompson, Sam 50–51, 115, 257n35
Thorn, John 10
Thurman, Allan 16, 25, 180
Toledo Blue Stockings (AA) 70
town ball 3
Tremont Hotel (Boston) 52
Tremont Hotel (Chicago) 128, 149
Truax, Frederick 137
T.T.T. (Baltimore *SL* correspondent) 113, 141, 148
Tucker, Tommy 212n15
Turbulent Seasons 8

Twain, Mark 2
Twitchell, Larry 143, 239n15

Union Association (UA) 11, 18, 27, 45, 47, 78, 152, 165, 173, 247n2
University of Virginia 49

Van Cott, Cornelius 172
Van Haltren, George 54, 213n16
Vaughn, Harry 184
Veach, William 238n7
Viau, Lee 132
Virtue, Jake 238n7
Visner, Joe 206n10
Von der Ahe, Chris 138, 150, 178

Wagner, Earle 143, 247n1, 257n17
Wagner, George 143, 247n1, 257n17
Walker, Dr. Mary 77
Walker, Moses Fleetwood 70
Ward, John M. 5, 7, 9, 15–25, 47, 54, 58; depiction of in fiction 58, 103–104; as leader of the PL 35, 59, 92, 97, 120, 131, 135, 137, 143, 166, 172, 176–180, 247n3, 248n9; as leader of players' union 16, 121, 134; as player 74, 79, 248n5, 248n10; as player-manager 72, 115, 120, 130–131, 143, 147, 153, 188; treatment of in print 30–36, 38, 40–43
Washington Nationals (1867) 17, 184, 237n1
Washington Nationals (NL) 44
Washington Park 63, 84, 121
Welch, Mickey 125
Western League 10
Weyhing, Gus 125
"Where Did You Get That Flag" 183
White, George A. 20
White, Jim 63
Whitman, Walt 2
Wiggins, Ezekiel Stone 87
Wilcox, Ella Wheeler 68, 193
Williams, Clarence 122
Williamson, Ned 42–43, 207n20
Williamson, Nellie 42
Wilmington Quicksteps (UA) 207n20
Wilmot, Walt 89, 248n12
Wise, Sam 182, 226n20
Wolfe, Thomas 2
Wright, George 64, 237n1, 257n35
Wright, Harry 50–51, 88, 182
Wright, R.W. 117, 248n8

Xantha Club 125–126

Young, Cy 141
Young, Nick 242n3
Young Ladies of the Diamond (YLD) 39, 40, 44–45, 65–66, 154, 206n6, 206n17

www.ingramcontent.com/pod-product-compliance
Ingram Content Group UK Ltd.
Pitfield, Milton Keynes, MK11 3LW, UK
UKHW041930140426
5217IPUK00014B/400